The Business

PRE-INTERMEDIATE Student's Book

Karen Richardson, Marie Kavanagh and John Sydes with Paul Emmerson

MACMILLAN

The Business
PRE-INTERMEDIATE

To the student

The objective of *The* Business is to help you learn two things: how to do business in English and the language you need to do it. The new language and structures are presented in the Student's Book whilst the DVD-ROM provides language practice and extension.

Here is a summary of what you will find in each.

Student's Book

The modules

The Student's Book contains 48 modules in eight units. Each unit deals with a key sector of activity in the business world. There are six different types of module:

1 About business

These modules contain information and language for the topic area of each unit. The focus is on understanding the topic and the general sense of the texts – don't worry too much about details such as new vocabulary.

2 Vocabulary

These modules build on the important words and phrases introduced in the previous module and provide thorough practice.

3 Grammar

The first part of these modules – Test yourself – tests your knowledge of important grammatical structures. Do this before and / or after the practice activities in the second part. If necessary, refer to the Grammar and practice section at the back of the book for help.

4 Speaking

These modules develop understanding and speaking skills in typical business situations. Good and bad examples are given for comparison, and the speaking activities allow you to practise key phrases and skills in realistic situations with other people.

5 Writing

These modules provide practice for the most important types of document you will need to write at work. Model texts are examined and used as a basis to write your own.

6 Case study

The case studies provide an opportunity to apply all the language, skills and ideas you have worked on in the unit. They present authentic problem-solving situations similar to those you will meet in business.

Internet research

Every module includes an Internet research task. The Internet provides almost unlimited resources for improving your English and learning more about business. These tasks direct you to interesting background and details on topics related to each module. The tasks can be done before or after working on the module.

Other features

In addition to the eight main units, the Student's Book contains the following:

Reviews

These units can be used in three ways: to consolidate your work on the units, to catch up quickly if you have missed a lesson, and to revise before tests or exams.

Additional material

This section contains all the extra materials you need to do pair or group work activities.

Grammar and practice

The section gives a very useful summary of rules with clear examples, but also provides further practice of the essential grammar points in this level of the course.

Recordings

Full scripts of all the audio recordings are given, allowing you to study the audio dialogues in detail. However, try not to rely on reading them to understand the listenings – very often, you don't need to understand every word, just the main ideas.

Wordlist

In the modules, words which you may not know are in grey; you will find definitions in the wordlist, often with examples. Words in red are high-frequency items, which you should try to learn and use. The others, in black, are words you just need to understand.

The DVD-ROM

The DVD-ROM is designed to help you continue improving your English on your own, away from the classroom. It includes an interactive workbook which, like the Review units in the Student's Book, can be used in three ways: to improve your listening, grammar, vocabulary and pronunciation; to catch up on lessons you have missed; to revise for tests and exams.

Interactive workbook

This includes everything you would normally find in a workbook, and more; activities for vocabulary, grammar, pronunciation, writing and listening practice.

Video

Each unit includes an episode of a mini-drama illustrating the communication and people skills practised in each unit, with exercises to practise the functional language used in the video.

Business dilemmas

There are four problem-solving games to allow you to review and practise functional language from the Student's Book. Try doing these with a partner to practise discussing problems and solutions.

Tests

Four tests, one for every two units, allow you to check your progress through the DVD-ROM. If you do well on a test, you get 'promoted'; if you do well on all four tests, you become CEO!

Business documents

There is a model document for each unit, including letters, invoices, CVs, etc. Each document includes annotations explaining the structure and key phrases, and a follow-up activity tests understanding of this.

Grammar reference

You can refer to this section any time for helpful grammar rules and examples.

Class audio

This section of the DVD-ROM contains all the audio recordings from the Student's Book, together with scrollable scripts.

Downloadables

The DVD-ROM includes a set of downloadable files for use outside the DVD-ROM or away from your computer. There is a downloadable and printable PDF of the answers to the Student's Book exercises; a Word file containing the text of each Business document; scripts for all the videos and MP3 files of all the Student's Book audio that you can transfer to your MP3 player or iPod for listening on the move.

We sincerely hope you will enjoy working with *The* Business.
Good luck!

John Allison   Marie Kavanagh   John Sydes
Paul Emmerson   Karen Richardson

Contents

	About business	Vocabulary	Grammar
1 Living abroad PAGE 6	1.1 Working abroad	1.2 Living abroad	1.3 Present simple and prepositions of time
2 Dealing with customers PAGE 18	2.1 The shopping experience	2.2 Telephoning and customer care	2.3 Countable & uncountable nouns, requests and offers
Reviews 1 and 2	PAGES 30–31		
3 Operations PAGE 32	3.1 Lean manufacturing	3.2 Trends and planning	3.3 Present continuous, adverbs, present simple passive
4 Success stories PAGE 44	4.1 Business leaders and success stories	4.2 Describing yourself and being successful	4.3 Past simple, past continuous and *used to*
Reviews 3 and 4	PAGES 56–57		
5 Selling PAGE 58	5.1 Advertising	5.2 Buying and selling	5.3 Comparatives, superlatives and asking questions
6 The organization PAGE 70	6.1 Entrepreneurs	6.2 Types of companies	6.3 Reported speech
Reviews 5 and 6	PAGES 82–83		
7 The stock markets PAGE 84	7.1 Keep it in the family	7.2 Dealing with figures	7.3 *will* and *won't*, *be going to* and first conditional
8 Going global PAGE 96	8.1 Franchising	8.2 Setting up a franchise	8.3 Past simple and present perfect
Reviews 7 and 8	PAGES 108–109		

Additional material	PAGES 110–117
Grammar and practice	PAGES 118–133
Recordings	PAGES 134–147
Wordlist	PAGES 148–158
Irregular verb list	PAGE 159

Speaking	Writing	Case study
1.4 Making small talk	1.5 Formal and informal emails	1.6 Global Recruit
2.4 Telephoning – handling complaints	2.5 Dealing with an email of complaint	2.6 The Panorama conference
3.4 Presentations – signposts and stepping stones	3.5 Instructions and procedures for an exhibition stand	3.6 ScotAir
4.4 Appraisals	4.5 Profiles of business leaders	4.6 The English Academy
5.4 Negotiating	5.5 Negotiating by email	5.6 Coolhunters
6.4 Interrupting in meetings	6.5 Agendas and action minutes	6.6 Soup kitchen vs Gourmet to go
7.4 Negotiations – making offers, agreeing deadlines	7.5 Describing figures	7.6 Trading stocks
8.4 Presentations – handling questions	8.5 Reports of recommendation	8.6 Choosing a franchise

The *Wordlist* is a module-by-module glossary of all the words in grey in this coursebook.

1 Living abroad

1.1 About business Working abroad

Discussion

1 Look at the people in the photos. They all work away from home. Read the quotes below and match them with the people.

1 I work abroad but I never stay in one country for very long. I install software systems and train people how to use them. I'm in Thailand at the moment and I'll be here for another six months.
2 My university has links with engineering firms in Germany. As part of my degree I'm working for one of them in Hamburg.
3 I spend two months every year in India buying supplies for my jewellery business. At the moment I'm staying in Jodhpur.
4 I spend ten months every year working abroad. I never know where I'm going to be. It's always in places where there are medical emergencies.

Have you ever lived or worked abroad? Do you know anyone who lives or works abroad? Compare your answers with a partner.

Collocations

2 You are going to read an article about how to get a job abroad. Before you read match a word on the left with a word on the right to make a collocation.

1 career	a) process	5 degree	e) letter
2 work	b) language	6 cover	f) an application
3 foreign	c) placement	7 short	g) subject
4 application	d) ladder	8 withdraw	h) list

Reading for detail

3 Read the article and mark the sentences T (true) or F (false). Change any false sentences to make them true.

1 To have a successful career these days you need to have experience of working abroad.
2 A work placement abroad will help your application attract attention.
3 Nannette Ripmeester thinks that the Euro CV is the best kind of CV to use when looking for a job.
4 You need to check that your employers will recognise your degree subject.
5 CVs are more important than cover letters.
6 A cover letter in France may be studied by a specialist.
7 Sarah Hall withdrew her application for a job in Spain because she didn't like the questions in her interview.
8 When working abroad you should behave in a similar way to those around you.

Listening and note-taking

4 🔊 1:01–1:04 Listen to the four people from 1 talking about their work experience abroad and complete the table.

name	country	how long	likes
Kiki	India	1)	2)
Anil	Thailand	3)	meeting people
Jean Marc	4)	5)	working with children
Marika	Germany	6)	her local family

Listening for detail

5 Listen to the interviews again and answer the questions.

1 Who was in Venezuela last year?
2 Who hopes to get a good reference from their company?
3 Who found the food strange when they first arrived?
4 Who is going on holiday when their job is finished?
5 Who is staying in an expensive hotel?
6 Who has a lot of business contacts in the country where they are?

KIKI YI, 54, Hong Kong, jewellery retailer

ANIL BASU, 35, UK, software analyst

JEAN-MARC SABATIER, 32, France, doctor

MARIKA LAANET, 22, Estonia, engineering undergraduate

Internet research

Search for the keywords *working abroad* to see what jobs are on offer. Hold a class vote to choose the three most attractive jobs.

6 The Business

Discussion

6 In small groups discuss the questions.

1. Which countries would you like and not like to go and work in?
2. What problems do you think people who work abroad have?
3. Do you think working abroad is essential for a successful career? Why / Why not?

CULTURAL chameleons

IN today's competitive job market, not spending time abroad can seriously damage your chances of climbing the career ladder. It is no surprise then that more and more graduates and professionals are looking for opportunities to live and work in a foreign country.

With record numbers of workers hoping to relocate, it is no longer enough to have done a work placement abroad or to speak a foreign language. 'This is no longer something that makes you different,' says Nannette Ripmeester, director of Expertise in Labour Mobility. 'It is something employers expect.'

But even if you are a strong candidate, the application process for foreign jobs is far from straightforward. The EU has introduced the Euro CV to standardise application procedures throughout Europe, but Ripmeester believes that a culturally adapted CV is better. 'What do I mean by that? For example, in the UK, it is customary to add hobbies and interests at the bottom of the page. In Italy however, that information is not necessary.'

When you write your CV it is also a good idea to check whether a photo is necessary and whether an English-language CV should be written in American or British English. Another point to think about is whether or not employers will recognise your degree subject, especially when you have studied a subject, such as Wireless Network Systems, which doesn't necessarily translate into another language and culture.

You also need to consider the cover letter, the first thing that an employer will read. Approaches differ from country to country: get the CV right but the cover letter wrong and you destroy your chances of getting shortlisted for interview because the cover letter is the first thing that an employer will read. The

> **mirror the kind of messages you get about communication and appearance**

British usually write long letters to draw attention to relevant sections on the CV, the Italians want one or two sentences and the French expect candidates to handwrite detailed letters which may be analysed by handwriting experts.

When it comes to interviews, make sure you know about the work culture and understand the importance different countries place on language and speech. For example, the French use short sentences and hate silence, while Scandinavians have a deep respect for pauses. You may think these points are not important but by not paying attention, you are showing that you do not respect the culture of the country you wish to work in.

Making a mistake at the interview is something Sarah Hall knows all about. She is from Liverpool in the UK and has worked in Germany, Sweden and Spain.

'My advice is be aware of 'culture clash.' In Britain there is usually a maximum of two interviews. In southern Europe they will call you back for a third or fourth interview. I lost a very good job in Spain when I thought they weren't serious. I withdrew my application because they asked me to go for a fourth interview. Looking back, I now realise they were doing as they always do. I behaved wrongly.'

'It's important to show that you understand the working culture. Adapting a similar style of dress to your co-workers, eating the kind of food they eat, enjoying similar activities - these things help to win trust and respect.'

'Think of yourself as a cultural chameleon, mirror the kind of messages you get about communication and appearance. People like people who remind them of themselves, and nobody likes what they don't understand.'

1 Living abroad

1.2 Vocabulary Living abroad

Discussion
1 Look at the picture above. What everyday problems do people who live abroad have?

Reading and vocabulary
2 Read the extracts from an article on living abroad. Find the correct heading for each extract.

health ☐   opening a bank account ☐   mobile phones ☐   accommodation ☐

3 Read the texts again and use the words in the boxes to fill in the spaces.

bills   notice   contract   deposit   apartment

> **1** Perhaps the most difficult thing to organize is where you are going to live. Your employer might help you find an (1)_____ or it might even be provided for you. The best advice is to start looking before you go. Use the Internet to look for places to rent and post your own advert on bulletin boards. It is important to view anywhere though before you sign a (2)_____ and give a large (3)_____ to a landlord. You also need to check whether or not the utility (4)_____ are included and how much (5)_____ you need to give when you want to move out. Many people choose to live with a local family as a way of learning about the culture of the country they are in.

credit cards   salary   overdraft

> **2** To open a bank account in another country you will need to show your passport, proof of earnings, proof of your address and residency. It is also likely that you will be expected to show proof that your monthly (6)_____ will be paid into this account. Remember that rules regarding banks are not the same in every country. You have to pay for an (7)_____ on your account in France, and the rules on (8)_____ can differ greatly, make sure you check before you sign up!

1.2 Vocabulary

check-up   insurance scheme   national health service

3 In most countries you have to pay for medical treatment. For trips of up to three months in Europe, the European Health Insurance Card may allow you to be treated for free by the (9)_____ of the country you are in. Your employer may have an (10)_____ that you can join or you might want to take out your own insurance policy. This will help you if you need to see a doctor while you are abroad. You may need to register with a doctor and you may also need to have a (11)_____.

top-ups   landline   contract   number

4 In many countries, the process of buying a mobile phone is straightforward: you choose the phone and the provider you want, you are then given a (12)_____. Italy is one exception, where you will need your national ID card and your tax code. When you don't know how long you are planning to live in the country, many people choose prepaid packages that allow (13)_____. This means you can cut off the service when you want without worrying about being tied into a (14)_____. These days many providers also offer wireless Internet access meaning you won't need to have a (15)_____ put into your flat or apartment.

CARMEN, from Brazil, working for a pharmaceutical company in Auckland

PETRA AND CRIS, from Germany, working as architects in Nice

MR GOODMAN from the USA, working for Athens Bank in Greece

YUKI from Japan, working for an engineering company in Copenhagen

Listening for gist

4 🔊 1:05–1:08   These people are all living abroad. Listen to four conversations. Where is each person? What is he or she trying to do?

Listening for detail

5 Listen to the conversations again and answer the questions.

Conversation 1
1 What does Carmen want to do?
2 Which documents does Carmen need to show?

Conversation 2
3 How many bedrooms are there in the apartment?
4 How much is the rent?

Conversation 3
5 Does Mr Goodman have a European Health Insurance Card?
6 How tall is Mr Goodman?

Conversation 4
7 Why doesn't Yuki want a phone with a contract?
8 How much free talking time does the phone have?

Giving advice

6 Look at the eight pieces of advice for people who are going to live abroad. For each set of four match the beginning with the correct ending.

1 You might have to pay two month's rent
2 When you move out of a flat
3 You can have an overdraft
4 You can use your bank card from home
5 You need to be registered with a doctor
6 Most employers include medical insurance
7 Using top-ups
8 You need to check that there is

a) for free with most banks.
b) your landlord will check the inventory.
c) to withdraw money from a cash point.
d) as a deposit before you move into a flat.
e) broadband access in the area where you live.
f) means you don't need to sign a contract for your mobile phone.
g) to get medical treatment.
h) as part of their employment package.

Which pieces of advice are true for your country? Which are different? What other advice and information could you give? Compare your answers with a partner.

Internet research

Search for the keywords *moving abroad advice* to read more about what you need to do when moving to another country.

The **Business**   9

1 Living abroad

Refresh your memory

Present simple
She works in London.
permanent situations
I usually get up at 7.00 am.
routines and things we do regularly

▶ Grammar reference page 118

Prepositions of time
on
weekdays
dates
special days
the weekend (US)

at
the weekend (UK)
festivals
times

in
months
seasons
parts of the day
years

dates
US English
month/date/year
02/14/2010
UK English
date/month/year
14/02/2010

▶ Grammar reference page 119

1.3 Grammar   Present simple and prepositions of time

Test yourself: Present simple

1 Read four descriptions of people's jobs. Write the correct form of the missing verbs into the text. Find the correct job for each text.

| computer programmer   architect   human resource manager   business student |

| attend   enjoy   do   spend   like |

1 _____
There are only two of us in the department, so I (1)_____ a bit of everything! I (2)_____ a lot of long meetings – many of these are related to budgets and to company policy development and I (3)_____ them. I also (4)_____ a lot of time interviewing candidates for jobs. This is one of the areas of the job I (5)_____ the most.

| work   develop   create   spend   travel |

2 _____
My company (6)_____ educational software for primary school children. Usually I (7)_____ on maths projects but we also (8)_____ Spanish language learning programs. Sometimes I (9)_____ to Spain for meetings but I (10)_____ most of the time at a desk in my office.

| buy   want   search   send   not have |

3 _____
I need to repay my student loan so I (11)_____ to find a job before the end of the year when my course finishes. Every day, I (12)_____ the Internet for suitable job vacancies and I (13) _____ the national and local newspapers to look at the job ads. I also (14) _____ my CV to companies I am interested in working for, even if they (15) _____ any vacancies at the moment.

| not have   be x 2   work   meet   not like   think |

4 _____
Normally I (16)_____ on one or two projects over a three or four-year period. My latest project is a church and I (17)_____ very excited about it. The church (18)_____ very old and it (19)_____ enough light. I need to design some more windows. Every week I (20)_____ the Bishop to talk about the project. Sometimes he (21)_____ my ideas but other times he (22)_____ they're great.

10 *The* **Business**

1.3 Grammar

Internet research

Work with a partner. Search for the keywords *festivals in Japan* or *festivals in Mexico* to read more about festivals in these countries. Tell your partner what happens on special days in these countries.

Test yourself: Prepositions of time

2 Complete the text about Elspeth from Germany using prepositions of time from the Refresh your memory box.

I came to London about six months ago. I started my job as a wine buyer at Marks & Spencer (1)_____ February. To be exact, I started (2)_____ February 14th. Before coming here, I worked at a winery in South Africa and before that, (3)_____ 2004, I was in New York State working as an au pair. No matter where I am in the world, I always phone my parents (4)_____ the weekend. I try to call them (5)_____ Sundays (6)_____ 6 o'clock (7)_____ the evening. The other thing I try to do is go home for Christmas. I do like to spend time (8)_____ Christmas with my family. If you ever get the chance, you really should go to Germany (9)_____ December. The German Christmas markets are the best in the world.

Listening for detail

3 🔊 1:09–1:15 Listen to seven descriptions of national festivals and and write the date.

1 Australia Day
2 Boxing Day (UK)
3 Groundhog Day (USA & Canada)
4 Bastille Day (France)
5 April Fool's Day
6 Showa Day (Japan)
7 Day of the Dead (Mexico)

Listen again. What does each holiday celebrate? What happens?

4 Question forms

Use the present simple to make questions for these answers.

1 _____
   From a small village in south-west France called Marsac.
2 _____
   Usually at 9am but sometimes at about 8.45.
3 _____
   Languages? English and French quite fluently and also a bit of Chinese.
4 _____
   In a small apartment near the centre of town.
5 _____
   Usually by bus, but if the weather is really good I sometimes walk.
6 _____
   I usually go on holiday in June.
7 _____
   Sometimes in the company canteen, but more often I go to the café round the corner.

Work with a partner. Take it in turns to ask and answer the questions.

5 Discussion

Work with a partner. Describe a local festival or custom either in your home town or the place where you are studying. Think about special food, clothes and typical activities that take place on this day.

1 Living abroad

1.4 Speaking — Making small talk

Discussion

1 Look at the tips for small talk below. What is small talk? Do you think the tips are useful?

Tips for small talk

TECHNIQUE ONE

Always wear a Whatzit

What's a Whatzit?
Some people have developed a clever technique that works well for social or corporate networking purposes. The technique requires no special skill on your part, only the courage to wear a *Whatzit*.
A *Whatzit* is anything unusual – a unique brooch, an interesting scarf, a strange tie, a funny hat. A *Whatzit* is any object that draws people's attention so that they walk over and ask, 'Uh, what's that?'

TECHNIQUE TWO

Whoozat?

What to do when you haven't got a Whatzit…
Like a politician, go to the host and say, 'That man / woman over there looks interesting. Who is he / she?' Then ask for an introduction.
-or-
Find out about the stranger's job, interests or hobbies. The host might say, 'Oh, that's Joe Smith. I'm not sure what his job is, but I know he loves to ski.' Aha, you've just been given the icebreaker you need. Now walk over to Joe Smith and say, 'Hi, you're Joe Smith, aren't you? Susan was just telling me what a great skier you are. Where do you ski?'

Reading for detail

2 Read the article below about small talk to find:
1. three topics that you can make small talk about
2. two topics that you can't make small talk about
3. two tips for managing small talk.

What is small talk?

Your company sends you to an important international conference in the USA. While you are travelling from the hotel to the conference centre you meet somebody who works for the Spanish division of your company for the first time. The conversation that you have will probably be what we call small talk.

What do people make small talk about?

There are certain safe topics that people usually make small talk about. The weather is probably the number one thing. Sometimes even friends and family members discuss the weather when they meet or start a conversation. Sports news is a common topic, especially if a local team is doing extremely well or badly. If there is something that you and the other speaker have in common, that may also be acceptable to talk about. For example, if the bus is extremely full and there are no seats available you might talk about reasons why.

There are also some subjects that are not considered acceptable when making small talk. Personal information such as salaries or divorce are not talked about between people who do not know each other well. Negative comments about another person not involved in the conversation are also not acceptable: when you do not know a person well you cannot be sure who their friends are. It is also not wise to continue talking about an issue that the other person does not seem comfortable with or interested in. Lastly, avoid one word answers, and ask questions to show that you want to keep the conversation going.

Listening for gist

3 🔊 **1:16–1:18** Listen to three conversations where people are making small talk. For each conversation decide:

1 where the people are
2 what small talk topics they talk about
3 how many questions the speakers ask to keep the conversation going.

Listening for detail

4 Listen to the conversations again and write the questions that the speakers use.

Conversation 1
1 _____ _____ _____ good weather?
2 _____ _____ _____ go?
3 _____ _____ _____ enjoy it?

Conversation 2
4 _____ _____ _____ _____ visit there?
5 _____ _____ _____ stay?
6 _____ _____ _____ the Continental?

Conversation 3
7 _____ _____ _____ _____ _____ for work or on holiday?
8 _____ _____ you do?
9 _____ _____ _____ your job?
10 _____ _____ _____ _____ visit India?

Making small talk

5 Work with a partner. Choose one of the topics below to make small talk about. Student A should prepare some things to say about one of the topics, Student B should prepare a list of questions to keep the conversation going.

1 Your last weekend
2 Your job/studies
3 Your journey to class today
4 What you're doing after class
5 The last time you went to a restaurant
6 The weather today

Beginning and ending small talk

6 Put the words in the correct order to make some useful phrases for beginning and ending small talk.

1 but Sorry have to go I now.
2 meeting It's nice been you.
3 believe can't how busy it I is.
4 journey have you Did a good here?
5 your was How weekend?
6 Enjoy rest the of the conference.
7 to talking Nice you.
8 It's weather lovely today.

Mark each phrase *B* (for beginning a conversation) or *E* (for ending a conversation).

Can you add any more?

7 Work in small groups. You are all at an international conference and it is the break between two presentations. You don't know any of the other people in your group and so you need to make small talk. Student A turn to page 110. Student B turn to page 111. Student C turn to page 112. Student D turn to page 113.

Internet research

Search for the keywords *small talk* to find more tips. With a partner, list the three most useful tips.

1 Living abroad

1.5 Writing — Formal and informal emails

Discussion

1 Work with a partner. Discuss the questions about emails.

1 How many emails do you write in a week?
2 Who do you write emails to?
3 Have you ever written a formal email?

Reading for detail

2 Read the email below and answer the questions.

1 Who is the email from?
2 Who is the email to?
3 What three things does the writer ask the reader to do?
4 Where is Ms Lee going?

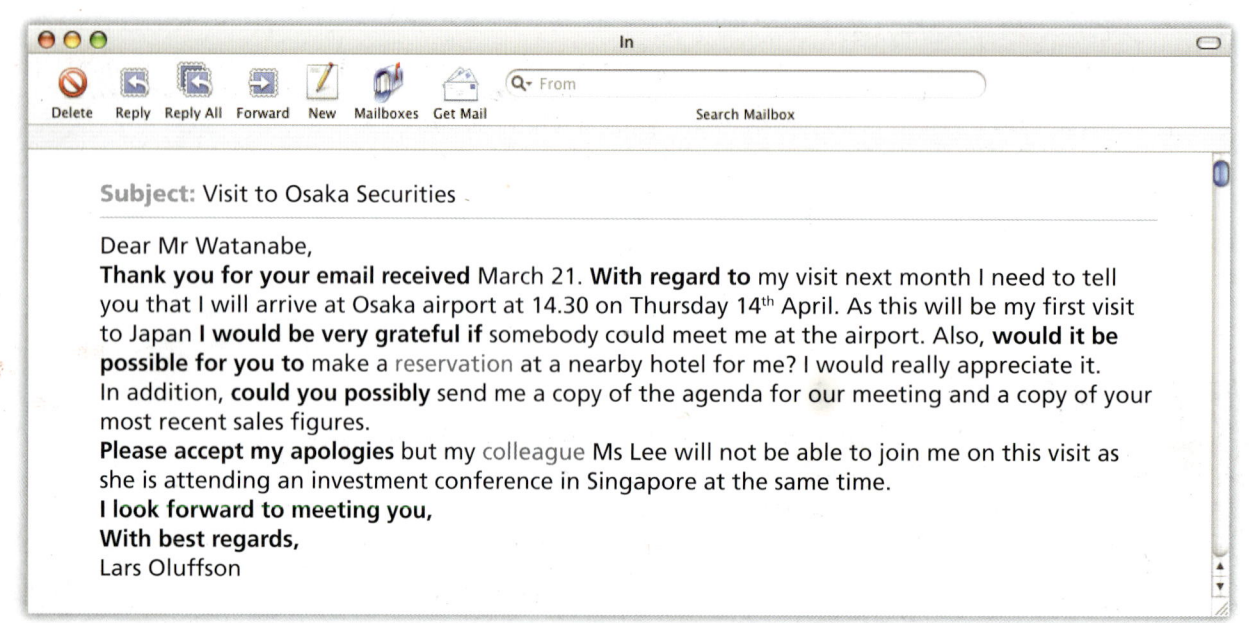

Subject: Visit to Osaka Securities

Dear Mr Watanabe,
Thank you for your email received March 21. **With regard to** my visit next month I need to tell you that I will arrive at Osaka airport at 14.30 on Thursday 14th April. As this will be my first visit to Japan **I would be very grateful if** somebody could meet me at the airport. Also, **would it be possible for you to** make a reservation at a nearby hotel for me? I would really appreciate it.
In addition, **could you possibly** send me a copy of the agenda for our meeting and a copy of your most recent sales figures.
Please accept my apologies but my colleague Ms Lee will not be able to join me on this visit as she is attending an investment conference in Singapore at the same time.
I look forward to meeting you,
With best regards,
Lars Oluffson

14 *The* Business

Informal language

3 Read another email and find informal phrases to match the phrases in **bold** in exercise 2.

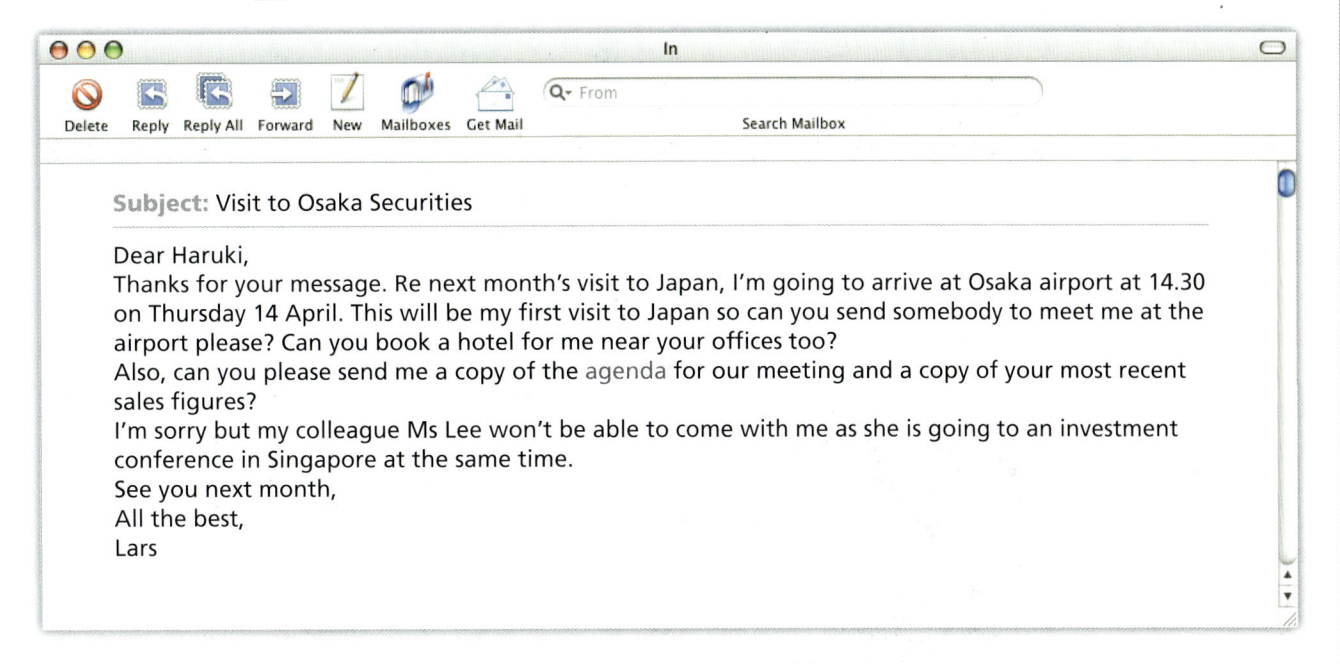

Subject: Visit to Osaka Securities

Dear Haruki,
Thanks for your message. Re next month's visit to Japan, I'm going to arrive at Osaka airport at 14.30 on Thursday 14 April. This will be my first visit to Japan so can you send somebody to meet me at the airport please? Can you book a hotel for me near your offices too?
Also, can you please send me a copy of the agenda for our meeting and a copy of your most recent sales figures?
I'm sorry but my colleague Ms Lee won't be able to come with me as she is going to an investment conference in Singapore at the same time.
See you next month,
All the best,
Lars

Formal and informal language

4 In each set of four, match a formal word on the left with an informal word on the right.

1	inform	a) come to	5	further	e) want
2	assistance	b) help	6	grateful	f) more
3	require	c) tell	7	near future	g) happy
4	attend	d) need	8	would like	h) soon

5 Read Manuela's email to Laura and write it as a formal email. Use the expressions from 2 and words from 4.

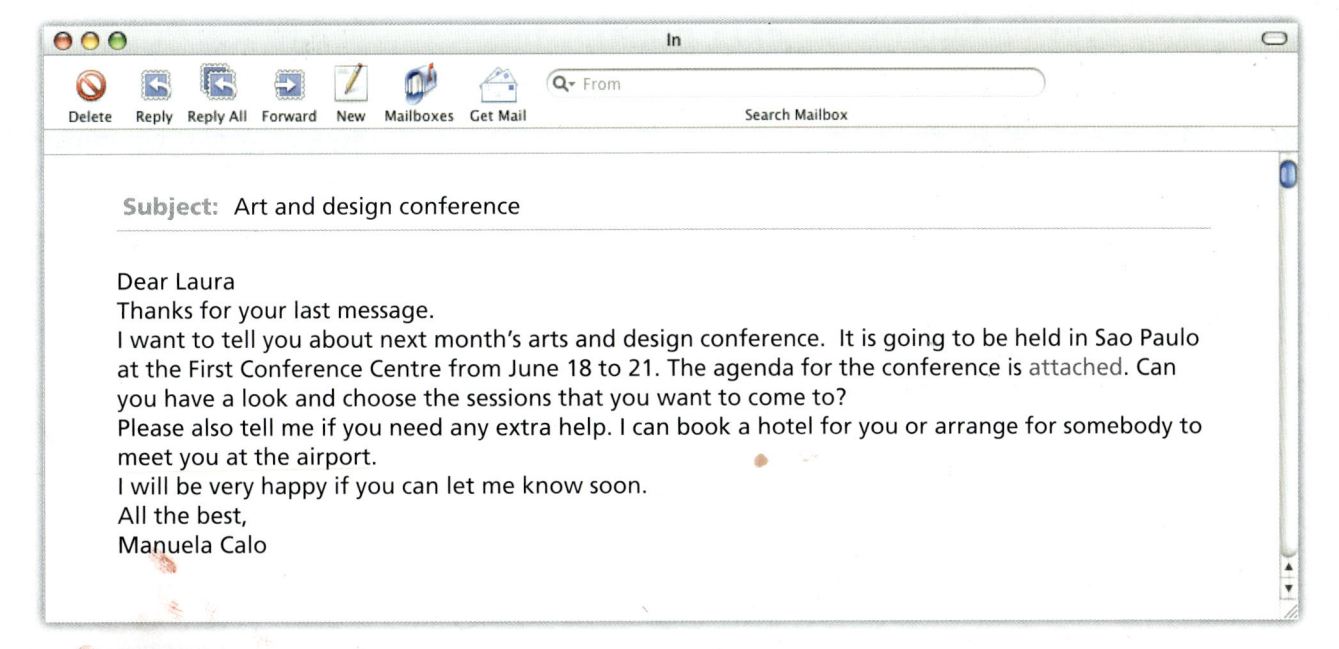

Subject: Art and design conference

Dear Laura
Thanks for your last message.
I want to tell you about next month's arts and design conference. It is going to be held in Sao Paulo at the First Conference Centre from June 18 to 21. The agenda for the conference is attached. Can you have a look and choose the sessions that you want to come to?
Please also tell me if you need any extra help. I can book a hotel for you or arrange for somebody to meet you at the airport.
I will be very happy if you can let me know soon.
All the best,
Manuela Calo

Writing

6 Write a formal reply to Manuela's email. Use the information below:

- you are going to attend the conference
- you can not stay for all three days
- the sessions you want to go to are *New design methods* and *The future of art*
- ask Manuela to make a reservation at a hotel
- ask Manuela to organize a taxi to pick you up at the airport.

Internet research
Search for the keywords *online etiquette* to read more about how to write professional sounding emails

1 Living abroad

1.6 Case study   Global Recruit

Discussion

1 Read the information below about Global Recruit. What are the advantages and disadvantages of using an organization like this to help you find a job?

Global Recruit

Looking for a job abroad?

Global Recruit may be able to help you. We work with a number of high-profile organizations all around the world and find the right candidate to fill their vacancies. Our job is to find staff who have the right skills and qualifications for these companies. We arrange interviews and give advice and support on the location and the requirements of the jobs. We can also help with visas and other legal requirements.

Reading and discussion

2 Read the two job advertisements. Which job would you prefer? Why?

Job TC / 428

CALL DUBAI, the Middle East's leading mobile phone company, has an excellent opportunity for an experienced sales advisor in their retail unit in central Dubai.

The job will involve advising customers, processing customer orders, and dealing with queries and complaints.

Applicants for this position should have a minimum of a year's sales experience within an international company, should have knowledge of mobile technology and experience of working with customers. Experience within an international company is a strong advantage, as is knowledge of English, French or Arabic.

Job WA / 926

Web Analyst in central Brazil. Brazilian MTM, Brazil's largest online clothes retailer, has an excellent opportunity for a senior web analyst.

The position includes analysing customer actions on our website, reporting on customer habits, maintaining and updating the website and managing a team of web analysts.

For the position you need to have knowledge of the following languages: ASP, PHP, Cold Fusion, Java or Net, experience of working in the clothing industry, managerial experience and a basic knowledge of Portuguese.

The job is based in our offices in Rio de Janeiro.

DVD-ROM Further interactive problem-solving on the DVD-ROM

1.6 Case study

Internet research

Search for the keywords *work in Dubai* or *work in Brazil* to read more about job opportunities in these countries. Try to find a job you would like to do and tell your partner about it.

Reading for gist

3 The four candidates below were all short-listed for one or other of the positions. Scan the information and see if you can guess which position they applied for.

NAME:	Tomas Visser
AGE:	25
QUALIFICATIONS:	Business studies degree
WORK EXPERIENCE:	(1)_____
LANGUAGES:	English, Flemish, French
HOBBIES / INTERESTS:	(2)_____
CURRENT POSITION:	Currently unemployed

NAME:	Panayota Mitropoulos
AGE:	(3)_____
QUALIFICATIONS:	Geography degree
WORK EXPERIENCE:	(4)_____
LANGUAGES:	English, French, German, Chinese
HOBBIES / INTERESTS:	(5)_____
CURRENT POSITION:	Works in family taverna

NAME:	Miroslav Kalata
AGE:	27
QUALIFICATIONS:	(6)_____
WORK EXPERIENCE:	Designs websites for boutiques
LANGUAGES:	(7)_____
HOBBIES / INTERESTS:	Computers and parties
CURRENT POSITION:	Website designer

NAME:	Francesca Di Ponti
AGE:	28
QUALIFICATIONS:	Modern languages degree from Italian university
WORK EXPERIENCE:	(8)_____
LANGUAGES:	English, Spanish, French, Portuguese
HOBBIES / INTERESTS:	(9)_____
CURRENT POSITION:	Currently unemployed

Listening for detail

4 🔊 **1:19–1:22** Listen to the four people introducing themselves and fill in the missing information on their profiles.

Discussion

5 Work with a partner. Decide who is the best candidate for each job. Give reasons for your decisions.

Listening for detail

6 🔊 **1:23** Dana is the Recruitment Manager and Heidi is an administrator at Global Recruit. Heidi is calling Dana about the references that she has for each of the candidates. Listen to the conversation and note down any problems that they find with the four candidates.

Discussion

7 Work with a partner. Discuss again who you think is the best candidate for each job. Has the information from the references changed your decisions?

The Business

2 Dealing with customers

2.1 About business   The shopping experience

Discussion

1 What can shops do to attract more customers? Think about the shops that you like to go to and discuss the questions with a partner.

1 What is your favourite shop and why?
2 How often do you go there?
3 What do you like to buy there?
4 Do you shop in department stores? Why? Why not?

Vocabulary

2 Below are some of the customer services and benefits that shops can offer their customers. Put each one into the correct column below.

customer parking   money-off vouchers   childcare   alteration services
private fitting rooms   store card   beauty salon   special offers   gift wrapping
home delivery   refunds   hairdresser's

facilities	services	financial services & benefits
customer parking		

Reading for detail

3 Scan the article about the German department store Breuninger to find answers to the questions.

1 Where does Breuninger have department stores?
2 Which departments in paragraph 2 would you go to if you wanted to find the following: soap and shampoo, coffee cups, a handbag, a yoga mat?
3 Which customer services and benefits from the lists in 2 can you find in the text? Put a tick (✓) next to them.
4 Find at least five more customer services and benefits in the text. Add them to the lists in 2.

4 Read the last paragraph about the luxury personal shopping service and answer the questions.

1 What things can customers do before they come to the store?
2 What two services can customers use whilst at the store?
3 What two services can customers use after they leave the store?
4 Do you think that Breuninger do everything possible to create a luxury shopping experience? Can you think of anything else they could do?

Listening for detail

5 1:24 Listen to Rafael Fernandez, an expert on luxury customer services in retail and complete the sentences.

1 Luxury consumers want products that are high quality and _____.
2 Sales assistants have to give luxury consumers lots of _____ _____.
3 Luxury consumers want to know the things they are buying are _____ _____ _____.
4 If luxury consumers are pleased with the service they receive they _____ _____ _____ _____ _____.

Internet research

Search for the keywords *luxury retail* to learn more about this kind of shopping.

Discussion

6 Work with a partner. You run the sports and leisurewear department in a successful department store. Your manager has told you that the department must improve its customer service and develop a luxury personal shopping service. Decide with your partner on six new services and benefits you are going to offer. Present these to the class.

BREUNINGER
The beautiful things in life

BREUNINGER is a chain of upmarket department stores in Germany, which are famous for their high standards of customer care. The company, founded in 1881 by Eduard Breuninger, now consists of a flagship store in Stuttgart and a further thirteen stores across Germany.

The stores offer gentlemen's and ladies' fashion, perfume and cosmetics, lingerie, shoes, accessories, sport and leisurewear, household goods and lifestyle products. They promise their customers a taste of 'the beautiful things in life.' The stores themselves are elegant and stylish and the goods on sale are luxury, top-of-the-range items from labels such as Burberry, Dior, Gucci and Yves Saint Laurent. Breuninger believes that it is the company's commitment to excellent customer service which makes the Breuninger shopping experience so special.

Breuninger have always had an eye for the comfort and convenience of their customers. They were the first department store in Germany to introduce lifts and escalators in the late 1940s and the first to provide customer parking a few years later. Heinz Breuninger, grandson of Eduard, brought back the idea of providing a car park for his customers from a trip to America in the 1950s. In 1959, Breuninger was the first German department store to offer a store card. This forward-thinking decision enabled the customers to pay without cash, long before it was normal to have a credit card. Today, over 700,000 customers own a Breuninger store card. Card holders are addressed by their name at the cash desks; they receive special benefits, money-off vouchers and a present on their birthday.

Today, the stores have an exceptional range of additional facilities available for their customers. The Stuttgart store features a hairdresser's, fashion shows, cosmetic workshops, a café on each floor, live entertainment in the piano bar, and a children's room – where children can play and paint while their parents shop.

Another of these facilities is the Breuninger luxury shopping service. This service offers a unique shopping experience; the opportunity to buy the most luxurious items with personal attention from specially-trained consultants. To make this shopping experience as relaxing as possible, customers send their measurements and the colours and styles they like to the store before leaving home. The consultants then use this information to choose suitable clothes. When a luxury customer arrives at the store they are guided to one of the VIP reserved parking spaces where one of the consultants meets them. At the private fitting rooms champagne or espresso are available while the customer chooses from the latest collections from famous designers. Breuninger also offer made-to-measure services, free tailoring and luxury shoppers can even take the clothes home to try them on. When all of the shopping is finished the clothes can be gift-wrapped and taken out to the car or Breuninger can deliver them to your home.

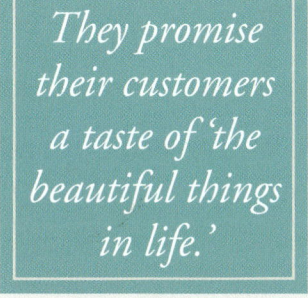

> *They promise their customers a taste of 'the beautiful things in life.'*

2 Dealing with customers

2.2 Vocabulary — Telephoning and customer care

Discussion

1 With a partner discuss the questions.

1 When was the last time you telephoned a company call centre? Why did you call – to solve a problem, make an enquiry, for another reason?
2 What was the result of the phone call? Were you happy with the service?

Reading and vocabulary

2 Read the article and complete the information about how to deal with customers on the phone. Use the words in the box to help you.

> hang up   discount   answer
> lose your temper   agree on a solution
> exchange   deal with   call back
> put through   interrupt

Customer: 'My mobile phone won't make outgoing calls.'
Helpline operator: 'Do you have the phone with you, sir?'
Customer: 'Yes, I'm using it now.'
Helpline operator: 'Well, the phone is working fine, sir. You just called me!'

The Seven Steps to Customer Satisfaction

1 **GREET THE CUSTOMER.** When you (1)_____ a call from a dissatisfied customer you need to greet them in a warm manner. Thank the customer for calling. Remember that when a customer calls to tell that something is wrong it is your opportunity to put it right.

2 **ASK WHAT THE PROBLEM IS.** You need to find out why they are calling. Simply ask what the problem is and let them explain. You may not be able to (2)_____ _____ the problem. Don't say 'I'm sorry, I can't help,' instead explain to the customer that you cannot help them and ask for their telephone number so that somebody can (3)_____ them _____. Sometimes the customer may want to wait while you (4)_____ them _____ to the correct department.

3 **LISTEN CAREFULLY.** Remember the customer may say a lot. You need to listen and try not to (5)_____. An angry customer may take a long time to explain what the problem is and so it is very important that you stay calm and that you don't (6)_____ _____ _____. It is a good idea to take notes so that you are 100% clear about all of the details. Ask questions if they are not telling you the information you need to know.

4 **DEFINE THE PROBLEM.** Once the customer has finished explaining the problem, use your notes to check you have understood the problem correctly.

5 **SUGGEST A SOLUTION.** Now that you know all of the details of the problem you can suggest a solution. Don't blame another department. Make an apology and suggest a solution. The customer may ask you to refund their money, they may ask for a (7)_____ on their next order or they might ask to (8)_____ the goods that they bought for other items. You also must be realistic. Don't promise to deliver 10,000 new parts for next week if it cannot be done. The customer will be even angrier next week when the parts don't arrive.

6 **CONFIRM THE SOLUTION.** Once you and the customer (9)_____ _____ _____ _____, confirm it so that you both understand what has been decided. Make sure that the customer knows exactly what you are going to do and when you are going to do it.

7 **END THE CONVERSATION.** Now that the customer is happy you can end the conversation. Thank the customer again for calling. It is a good idea to let the customer (10)_____ _____ first, as this gives them a final chance to add anything.

2.2 Vocabulary

Listening

3 🔊 **1:25–1:27** Listen to three telephone conversations between customer service assistants and dissatisfied customers and answer the questions.

1 Why are each of the customers calling?
2 Which of the 'seven steps' from the article opposite do the customer service assistants forget when they answer the call?

Telephone language

4 Match the beginning with the correct ending to make questions about telephoning.

1 What's the longest you've ever been put
2 Have you ever hung
3 Have you ever been put
4 Do you always ask people to confirm
5 When you call a company, how
6 Do you lose

a) on hold for?
b) through to the wrong person?
c) long should it take them to answer the phone?
d) your temper when you are talking on the phone?
e) up on somebody?
f) arrangements that you make on the phone?

Work with a partner. Take it in turns to ask and answer the questions.

Reading and discussion

5 Read the advertisements below for customer service jobs.

> A friendly, polite **telephone manner** is essential to this role, but you'll need good **listening skills** and the ability to be **reassuring**. You will be naturally **sympathetic** and be able to handle often sensitive conversations. Could you be there with the right answers?

> For this role you need an **outgoing personality** and good **interpersonal skills**. You need the confidence to speak to existing and potential customers about our services and products and the ability to **persuade**. You are always ready to take the next call.

Which do you think is for a healthcare company and which for an insurance company?

6 Match the words in **bold** in the advertisements to the definitions below.

1 to make someone agree to do something (v)
2 relationships between you and other people (two words)
3 caring and open to understanding other people's problems (adj)
4 the way you speak on the phone (two words)
5 the ability to listen (two words)
6 making someone feel less worried (adj)
7 if you have this you are friendly and enjoy talking to people (two words)

7 Work with a partner. You need to find someone for a job as a helpline operator for your school, university or workplace. They will be responsible for dealing with new customers and potential students. Decide what five essential skills and qualities they need to have and create a job advertisement. Compare your advertisement with another pair's.

Internet research
Search for the keywords *customer service* to find more information about how to deal with customers.

2 Dealing with customers

Refresh your memory

countable nouns
a computer, some computers
singular and plural form

uncountable nouns
some water, some advice
no plural form

any
Are there any computers?
There isn't any water.
questions and negatives with both kinds of nouns

some
I need some information.
Some files are missing.
positive sentences with both types of nouns

a lot (of)
He's got a lot of reports to write.
She gave me a lot of good advice.
positive sentences for both kinds of nouns

much/many
How much water is there?
How many computers are there?
much is used for questions with uncountable nouns
many is used for questions with countable nouns

▶ Grammar reference page 120

polite requests
Can or *could* are used for making polite requests. They are almost the same. However *could* is a little more polite.
Would you mind, is very polite, and is always followed by verb + *ing*.

offers
Do you want / would you like me to + verb are polite ways of offering to do something.

▶ Grammar reference page 121

2.3 Grammar Countable & uncountable nouns, requests and offers

Test yourself: countable and uncountable nouns.

1 Are these nouns countable or uncountable? Put them into the correct columns in the table below.

| company | customer | money | news | information | accommodation |
| progress | research | equipment | phone call | helpline | overtime | employee |

Countable nouns	Uncountable nouns
	progress

2 Use the words from the table above and *much / many* or *a lot* to complete the sentences.

1. Human Resources wants us to reduce our head count: how _____ _____ are there currently in this department?
2. We've spent _____ of _____ on office equipment this year.
3. I'm worried about the long hours you have been working. How _____ _____ did you do last month?
4. The director wants an update on the repair work to the building. How _____ _____ have the builders made?
5. The company is doing _____ of market _____ We want to know what that customer really thinks of the new product line.

Test yourself: Polite requests and offers

3 Complete the telephone conversation with *can* or *would you mind* and the verbs from the box.

| help   put me through   ask   calling back   give |

Receptionist: Niven and Sellars. How (1) _____ I (2) _____ you?
Carlos: Good morning. (3) _____ you (4) _____ to Marco Grella, please?
R: One moment. (5) _____ I (6) _____ who's calling?
C: My name's Carlos Torres.
R: Putting you through now, Mr Torres. Oh, Mr Grella's line's busy. (7) _____ (8) _____ in ten minutes?
C: No, that's fine. (9) _____ you (10) _____ me his direct number, please?
R: Certainly, his extension number is 357.
C: Thank you. Goodbye.
R: Goodbye.

4 Read the statements below and respond with offers and requests. Use *Do you want / Would you like me to* for offers (1–4) and *Would you mind +ing* for requests (5–6).

1. It's cold in here. (shut / window) _____
2. I think we have run out of photocopier paper. (order more) _____
3. These books are heavy! (carry for you) _____
4. I have left the report on my desk. (fetch) _____
5. We need to take a break. (make us coffee) _____
6. We are going to be late for our next meeting. (drive us station) _____

A customer survey

5 Complete the customer service dialogue using *some / any / much / many* and the verbs in brackets in an appropriate form.

A: Hello, this is Arne Schumann from Mainstream Motors. Would you mind (1)_____ (answer) (2) _____ questions about the car you bought from us last month?
B: Well, how (3)_____ time is this going to (4)_____ (take)? I'm in a bit of a hurry.
A: It won't take long, only about five minutes. There aren't very (5)_____ questions.
B: All right then.
A: First I'd like (6)_____ information about the salesman. On a scale of one to ten, how (7) _____ marks would you (8)_____ (give) him for friendliness?
B: Er, eight.
A: Good. And how (9)_____ marks for competence?
B: What do you mean by 'competence'?
A: For example, when you needed (10)_____ advice about which make or model car to buy, was he able to give it?
B: Oh, I see, yes, he was very good. He gave me (11)_____ really useful advice. I'd give him ten out of ten for competence. He certainly knew what he was talking about.
A: That's good to hear. You bought the car four weeks ago; can you tell me approximately how (12)_____ kilometres you've driven in that time?
B: Oh, not (13)_____ . The week after I bought the car, I broke my leg.
A: Oh, I am sorry to hear that. Are there (14)_____ other drivers in your household?
B: My wife can drive but she doesn't like it. She says there are too (15)_____ other drivers on the road these days.
A: And finally, are there (16)_____ questions you'd like to ask us?
B: Not at the moment.
A: Well, thank you for your time, goodbye.

Roleplay

6 Work with a partner. You are colleagues who work in the same office. You are both about to go on holiday tomorrow and you need each other's help to finish your work. Take it in turns to make requests and offers.

Student A
- You need Student B to check your accounts. There is a mistake you can't find!
- You both need to change some money. The bank closes in half an hour.
- Your passport is at Student B's house.
- You need to make a conference call to China but you can't remember how to do it.

Student B
- You need Student A to give you last month's sale figures for your report.
- You both need to check your flight departure times but Student A has no Internet connection at the moment.
- Your suitcase is broken.
- You need to write six different emails in English about the project you and Student A are working on.

Internet research
Search for the keywords *polite requests* to learn more about making them.

2 Dealing with customers

2.4 Speaking   Telephoning - handling complaints

Discussion

1 Work with a partner. What kind of complaints would you expect the following types of business to receive: an airline, an advertising agency, a bank, a mobile phone company, a computer manufacturer?

Listening for gist

2 1:28–1:31 Listen to four customers complaining. What is each customer's problem and what solution is suggested?

PAUL ROSSI | BRUNA PEREZ | MR LANGENBURG | INGRID HELLER

Listening for detail

3 Listen again and complete the expressions.

Conversation 1
1 I'm sorry _____ _____ Mr Rossi.
2 I understand Mr Rossi and _____ _____ _____ sorry.
3 Can we _____ _____ to help you with this?

Conversation 2
4 That must _____ _____ _____ .

Conversation 3
5 I'll look _____ _____ straight away.
6 What _____ _____ _____ is…

Conversation 4
7 I'm sorry _____ _____ that.
8 Let me see _____ _____ _____ do.

Dealing with problems

4 Match the problems to the correct solutions.

1 I can't access my accounts. ☐
2 You've charged me twice for my ticket. ☐
3 You've sent me a bill but I've already paid it. ☐
4 The photocopier's broken down again. It was only repaired last week. ☐
5 We've only been sent 300 parts, we ordered 400. ☐
6 The meeting room's been double-booked. ☐
7 The delivery hasn't arrived yet. ☐
8 The service in this restaurant is terrible. ☐

a) We'll credit your account.
b) We'll send somebody to fix it immediately.
c) You need to install a new version of the software.
d) Just ignore the second bill.
e) Please have a dessert on the house.
f) I'll call the driver and ask him where he is.
g) I'll check and see if another room is available.
h) We'll send 100 more to you today.

DVD-ROM Interactive pronunciation practice on the DVD-ROM

2.4 Speaking

Internet research

Visit the website howtocomplain.com to read more about things to do when you complain.

Describing and dealing with problems

5 Use the pictures to make mini dialogues with your partner.

Example:
A My son's toy robot broke as soon as he took it out of the box. He never even played with it!
B I'm sorry to hear that, sir. We'll send you a new one.

6 It is important to show interest and understanding when dealing with customers on the phone. Look at expressions 1–6 and match them with functions a) to f).

1 OK / Right / Uh-huh
2 That must have been very difficult for you.
3 I've got that.
4 I see.
5 Is that acceptable / OK?
6 Really?

a) You are listening
b) You understand
c) You are surprised
d) You sympathize with the customer
e) You have the information
f) Check that the caller agrees

Roleplay

7 Work with a partner. Think of a time when you had a serious problem with goods or services and you wanted to complain to somebody about it. Use the flow chart to have a conversation with your partner. Prepare the conversation and make notes of all that you want to complain about before you begin. Take it in turns to complain and to handle the complaint.

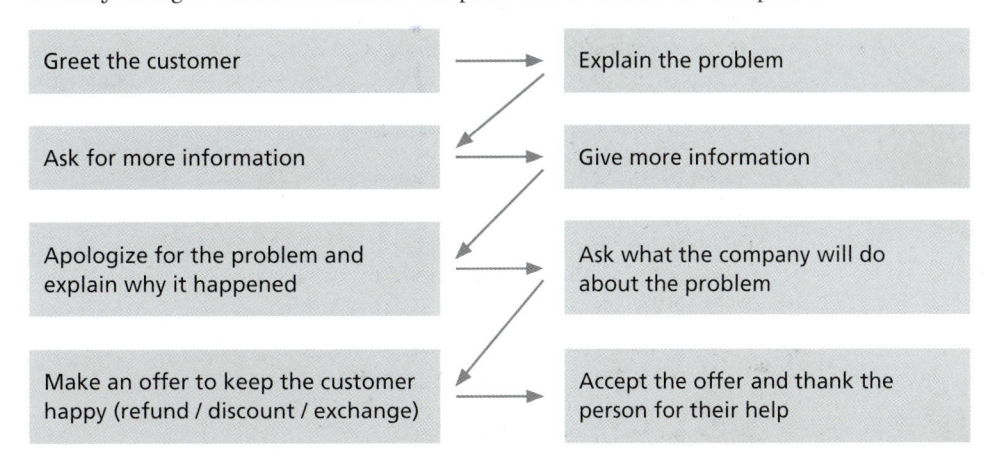

Greet the customer	→	Explain the problem
Ask for more information	→	Give more information
Apologize for the problem and explain why it happened	→	Ask what the company will do about the problem
Make an offer to keep the customer happy (refund / discount / exchange)	→	Accept the offer and thank the person for their help

The Business 25

2 Dealing with customers

2.5 Writing   Dealing with an email of complaint

Discussion

1 Work with a partner. Look at the box. What do you do when these things happen? Which do you find the most annoying when you are trying to complain?

> slow staff   rude staff   unhelpful staff   staff ignoring you
> staff not giving you an answer   being put on hold

Skim reading

2 Read an email from a dissatisfied customer and answer the questions.

1. What is the problem?
2. What action does she want?

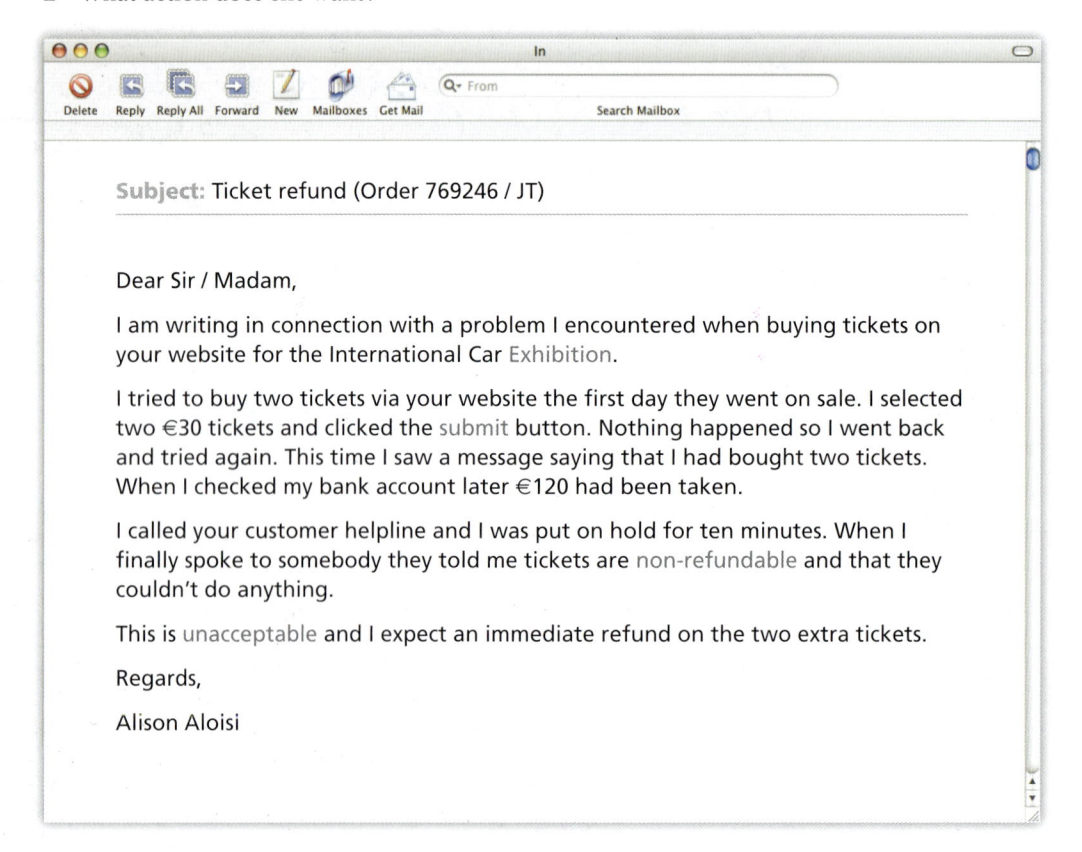

Subject: Ticket refund (Order 769246 / JT)

Dear Sir / Madam,

I am writing in connection with a problem I encountered when buying tickets on your website for the International Car Exhibition.

I tried to buy two tickets via your website the first day they went on sale. I selected two €30 tickets and clicked the submit button. Nothing happened so I went back and tried again. This time I saw a message saying that I had bought two tickets. When I checked my bank account later €120 had been taken.

I called your customer helpline and I was put on hold for ten minutes. When I finally spoke to somebody they told me tickets are non-refundable and that they couldn't do anything.

This is unacceptable and I expect an immediate refund on the two extra tickets.

Regards,

Alison Aloisi

Reading and ordering

3 Read the email that Franz Reynolds wrote in response to Alison's complaint and put it into the correct order.

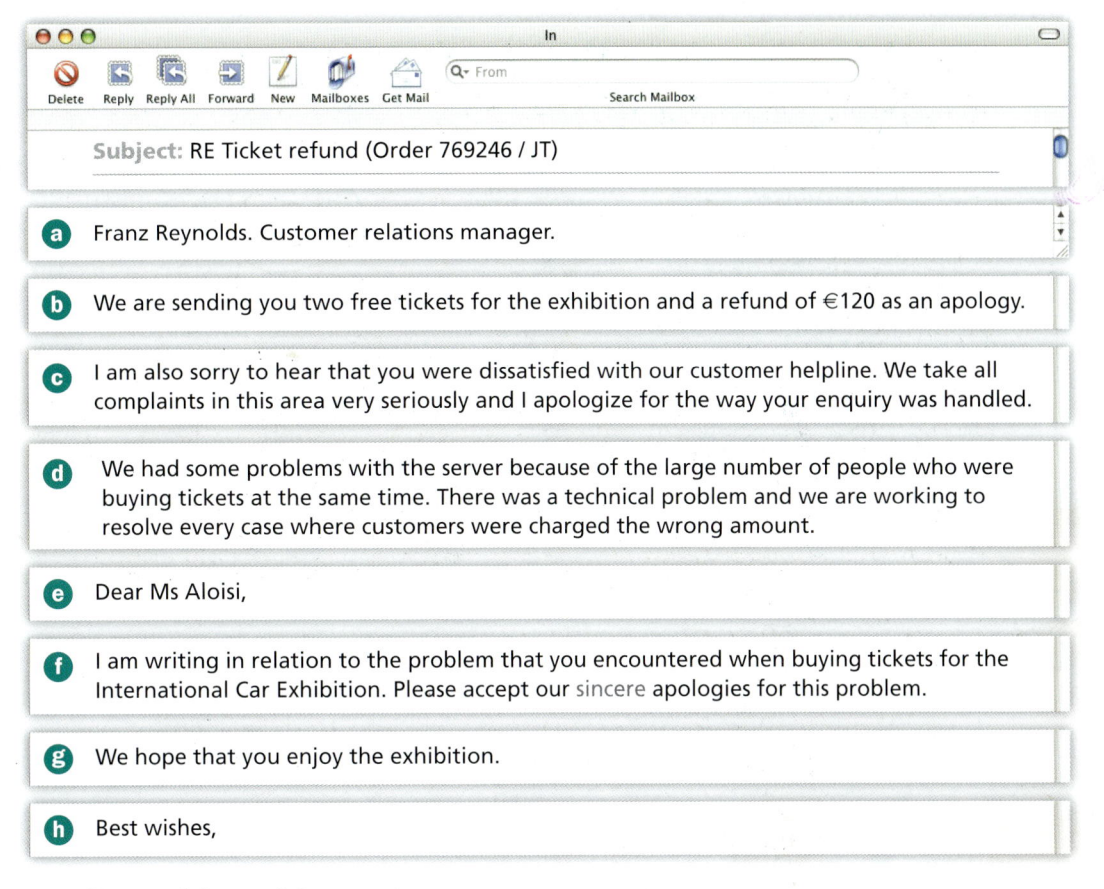

Subject: RE Ticket refund (Order 769246 / JT)

a Franz Reynolds. Customer relations manager.

b We are sending you two free tickets for the exhibition and a refund of €120 as an apology.

c I am also sorry to hear that you were dissatisfied with our customer helpline. We take all complaints in this area very seriously and I apologize for the way your enquiry was handled.

d We had some problems with the server because of the large number of people who were buying tickets at the same time. There was a technical problem and we are working to resolve every case where customers were charged the wrong amount.

e Dear Ms Aloisi,

f I am writing in relation to the problem that you encountered when buying tickets for the International Car Exhibition. Please accept our sincere apologies for this problem.

g We hope that you enjoy the exhibition.

h Best wishes,

Internet research
Search for the keywords *emails of complaint* to learn more about this subject.

Dealing with problems

4 Put the phrases in the box into the correct place in the table.

> Thank you for your email regarding…
> We will be happy to exchange the items.
> The reason for this problem was…
> I am very sorry to hear that…
> I am writing on behalf of…
> We apologize for any inconvenience that this caused.
> We have been experiencing problems with…
> We can offer you a (10%) discount (on your next order).
> We will look into this problem immediately.

Introducing	Apologizing	Explaining	Promising action
I am writing in relation to…	Please accept our sincere apologies for this problem.	There was a technical problem with…	We are sending you two free tickets.

Writing

5 You have received an email about one of the problems below. Write an email in response, explain the cause of the problem and promise action.

1. A customer ordered a computer from your online shop. The delivery arrived on time but some of the components are missing.
2. You run a private language school. A yoga group uses one of your rooms every Wednesday evening. They have received a bill even though they paid for this month two weeks ago.
3. Your company sells high quality cakes. One of your customers recently ordered a birthday cake for their 90 year old grandmother. When the cake was delivered it had 19 on it.
4. A customer tried to take €250 from one of your cash points (ATM) at a motorway service station. The machine only paid out €50 but €250 was taken from their account.

2 Dealing with customers

2.6 Case study The Panorama conference

Discussion

1 Do you ever stay in hotels? Discuss the questions with a partner.

1 Which are the best and the worst hotels that you have stayed in? Why?
2 Agree on three facilities or services which your ideal hotel could offer to its customers.

Listening for detail

2 1:32 Jan Van der Vaart organized this year's sales conference at the recently restored Panorama Hotel in Sicily. He is checking in with a number of colleagues. Listen and answer the questions.

1 How many premium class rooms did Mr Van der Vaart book?
2 What dates did he book the rooms for?
3 Are there any more rooms available?
4 What solution does the receptionist suggest?

Discussion

3 Work with a partner and discuss the questions.

1 What do you think of the solution that was suggested?
2 What other solutions could the receptionist suggest?
3 What do you think Mr Van der Vaart should do?

Reading for detail

4 Mr Van der Vaart was unhappy with his stay at the Panorama Hotel. Read his letter of complaint to the manager. What six complaints does he make?

Further interactive problem-solving on the DVD-ROM

2.6 Case study

Internet research

Search for the keywords *hotel complaints* to read more problems that guests have in hotels. Choose one complaint to read carefully. Use your own words to tell your group about it.

Discussion

5 How can the hotel respond to these complaints? Work with a partner. Decide if the complaints are reasonable.

6 You are going to read some more information about the complaints. Student A turn to page 117 and Student B turn to page 111. Look at the list of complaints again. Does the new information affect your decisions in exercise 5?

Writing

7 You are Mr Lando, the manager of the Panorama Hotel. Write a letter in response to Mr Van der Vaart's complaint. Apologize and suggest action for the complaints that you think are reasonable.

Mr Lando
Hotel Manager
Panorama Hotel
Via Umberto
Sicily

Mr Van der Vaart
Sales Manager
Electronics RDC
Kerkstraat 26
Eindhoven
Holland

February 10th 2008

Dear Mr Lando,

I am writing in relation to the marketing conference that my company held at your hotel from 5th to 8th of February this year.

When we arrived at the hotel the receptionist told us there were only eight rooms available. There were nine people from Electronics RDC attending the conference and so two of my colleagues had to share one room. This was very inconvenient.

Also, some of my colleagues complained that the hotel was too noisy for them at night. There was a lot of noise and this stopped them from sleeping. At the conference they felt tired and sleepy. Other colleagues said there was a strong smell of smoke in their rooms which was not very nice. Some of the rooms were too cold and my colleagues were not able to turn the heating up. They had to ask for extra blankets to keep warm.

The conference centre was also too far away from the hotel. In the other Panorama hotels we have used, the conference facilities were in the hotel. In yours we had to get a bus down the coast to the conference centre and this wasted a lot of time.

When we checked out of the hotel we noticed that the price on display for the premium class rooms was cheaper than the price we paid when we booked online. This is unacceptable. Electronics RDC use Panorama hotels regularly. We are Gold Class members and expect better service than this.

I expect a reply from you within ten days.

Yours sincerely,

Jan Van der Vaart

The Business

Review 1

1 Living abroad

1 Make expressions about working in a foreign country by matching each verb to a phrase a)-f) below.

1 spend ...
2 climb ...
3 draw ...
4 respect ...
5 withdraw ...
6 win ...

a) ... the career ladder
b) ... the culture of the country you wish to work in
c) ... an application for a job if you think the company isn't serious
d) ... time abroad
e) ... trust by adapting to the local culture
f) ... attention to relevant sections on your CV

2 Fill in the missing letters in these paragraphs about everyday problems when living abroad.

1 Your em___yer might help you to find an apartment, or you can use the Internet to find places to r__t. View the apartment first before you s__n a contract and give a dep__it to the land___d. Check whether the bi__s are included in the rent, and also how much n__ice you need to give when you want to m___ o__.

2 To open a bank acc___t, you will need to show proof of ear___gs, and that this salary will be paid into this account. If you spend more than you earn, you may have to pay for the over___ft on your account. You will get a credit card from your bank, but check the rules carefully before you s___ u_.

3 If you need medical tr___ment you will be treated by the national h___th service of the country where you live. Your employer might give you the chance to join an in_____ce scheme that helps to pay for private treatment.

4 When buying a mobile phone, you choose the pro__der and then pay for a monthly contract. Alternatively, you can have a prepaid pa__age that allows you to make regular t_p-u_s. These days, many providers also offer wireless internet access, so you won't need a l___ line in your apartment.

3 Fill in each gap with one of these prepositions: *about, by, for, from, into, off, on, out, with*. A preposition may be used more than once.

1 to be _____ an assignment in a foreign country
2 your apartment might be provided _____ you
3 use the Internet to look _____ places to rent
4 you can live _____ a local family to learn _____ the culture
5 to pay your monthly salary _____ an account
6 to deduct payments _____ an account
7 to pay _____ private medical treatment
8 to be treated _____ the national health service
9 you can take _____ an insurance policy
10 with a prepaid package you can cut _____ the service whenever you want

4 Complete the dialogue with present simple forms (positive/negative/question) of the main verbs in the box. Use contractions (*he is* → *he's*) where possible.

| attend | be | be | be | do | do | employ |
| enjoy | interview | want | | | | |

A: So, you ¹_____ a Human Resource Manager. How interesting! What exactly ²_____ you _____ in your job?
B: Well, I ³_____ a lot of meetings related to company policy development, and of course I ⁴_____ candidates for jobs.
A: And how big is the HR department in your company?
B: Well, we ⁵_____ many people in the HR section – only me and two others. So you can't really call it a department!
A: And your husband – what ⁶_____ he _____?
B: He ⁷_____ a computer programmer. But, I have to say, he ⁸_____ really _____ his job very much. In fact he ⁹_____ to change jobs.
A: I ¹⁰_____ sure he'll find a new job very easily, there are always jobs in the IT sector.

5 Fill in each gap with *in*, *on* or *at*.

1 _____ Monday
2 _____ the evening
3 _____ the end of the week
4 _____ the weekend (UK)
5 _____ the weekend (US)
6 _____ Christmas
7 _____ August 24th
8 _____ summer
9 _____ 11 O'clock
10 _____ January
11 _____ lunchtime
12 _____ the 1990s

6 The phrases below are used for small talk, but the words in **bold** are all in the wrong sentences. Put them back into the correct sentence.

1 **Enjoy** was your weekend?
2 I can't believe how **go** it is.
3 Did you have a good **talking** here?
4 It's **busy** weather today.
5 Sorry but I have to **lovely** now.
6 It's been nice to **journey** you.
7 Nice **meet** to you.
8 **How** the rest of the conference.

7 Match each word or phrase on the left with one on the right with a similar meaning.

1 Thank you for
2 With regard to
3 I would be grateful if you could
4 Please accept my apologies
5 I look forward to meeting you
6 With best regards
7 further
8 require

a) Can you
b) See you
c) more
d) Re
e) All the best
f) Thanks for
g) need
h) I'm sorry

Are the phrases on the right more formal or more informal?

30 *The* Business

Review 2

2 Dealing with customers

1 Fill in the missing letters in these services and benefits that shops can offer their customers:

Facilities: cu____er parking / ch___care / private f___ing rooms / beau__ sal__ / haird____er's / cosmetic wor___ops / café on each f___r / live enter____ment

Services: alter____n services / made-to-mea__re services / gift wr___ing / home del__ery

Financial services and benefits: money-off v__cher / sto__ card / special o__ers / refu__s

2 Match each item in the box to its definition below. Then translate the words into your own language.

```
convenience   escalator   fitting   flagship
household   lifestyle   made-to-measure   refund
voucher   wrapping
```

1 used in homes, or relating to homes _____
2 money that you get back if you return goods that you do not like _____
3 moving stairs that take people from one level of a building to the next _____
4 the way that someone lives, including their work, their activities and what they own _____
5 the paper or plastic that covers something that you buy _____
6 something that helps you to avoid wasting time and effort _____
7 used in the phrase '_____ room' to mean a room in a shop where you can put on clothes before buying them
8 made to a particular size (= tailor-made) _____
9 a piece of paper that you buy something with (instead of using money) _____
10 the biggest, most important, or best thing in a group (an idea that comes from the navy) _____

3 Make phrases used in customer care by matching a verb from the left to the words on the right.

1 greet   a) with the problem, if you can
2 find out   b) not to interrupt
3 let   c) why the customer is calling
4 deal   d) the customer in a warm manner
5 try   e) the customer explain the problem
6 stay   f) by thanking the customer for calling
7 take   g) the solution after you have both agreed
8 suggest   h) notes so you are clear about the details
9 confirm   i) calm and don't lose your temper
10 end   j) a solution, without blaming anyone

4 Complete the sentences from advertisements for customer service jobs using these words: *existing, handle, interpersonal, manner, outgoing, personality, potential, reassuring, skills, telephone*.

1 You'll receive a lot of calls, so you'll need a friendly, polite _____ _____
2 Customers may be worried or angry, so you'll need the ability to be _____
3 You will be naturally sympathetic, and be able to _____ sensitive conversations.
4 You will come into contact with a variety of different people so you will need an _____ _____ and good _____ _____
5 You need the confidence to speak to _____ and _____ customers about our services, and the ability to persuade.

5 Underline the correct word in each pair in *italics*.

1 How *much/many money/monies* did we make last month?
2 How *much/many employee/employees* work in their company?
3 We didn't get *much/many order/orders* at the trade fair.
4 I didn't get *much/many help/helps* from him.
5 She gave me *a lot/a lot of* useful *advice/advices*.
6 Do you have *some/any information/informations* about this project?
7 We have *some/any* equipment that *is/are* very out-of-date.
8 They didn't do *some/any research/researches* before launching the product.

6 Make requests and offers using the words below. You may have to add words, or change the form (e.g. change to –*ing* form).

1 Could / open the door / for me?
   Could you open the door for me?
2 Would / mind / open the door / for me?
   _____
3 Do / want / to open the door / for you?
   _____
4 Would you / me / open the door / for you?
   _____

7 Complete the phrases used when dealing with problems on the phone. Choose the best endings.

1 We'll credit   ... the second bill.
2 We'll send somebody   ... your account.
3 Just ignore   ... to repair it immediately.
4 I'll call the driver   ... more to you today.
5 I'll check and see if   ... and ask him where he is.
6 We'll send 100   ... another room is available.

8 Put the words into the correct order to make phrases used when dealing with problems by email.

1 I am writing to your recent problem in relation
2 Please sincere apologies our accept
3 We apologize that this has caused for any inconvenience
4 We have some technical problems been experiencing
5 We are working these problems to resolve as possible as soon
6 We will be exchange to happy the items
7 We can you offer a 10% discount your next on order
8 We will into this problem look immediately

The Business 31

3 Operations

3.1 About business — Lean manufacturing

Listening for detail

1 🔊 1:33 Listen to Andrea Livingstone giving a lecture on work organization and complete the notes below.

The organization of work in the UK

The domestic system

In this system people worked at (1) _____
The whole family made items and sold them at (2) _____
People worked part-time and production was slow

The workshop system

Very similar to domestic system
People were organized by a subcontractor – similar to a (3) _____
Families used the subcontractor's materials
(4) _____ kept all the profits

The factory system

Production moved into factories
First factory built in (5) _____ by Richard Arkwright
Production was much (6) _____ but working conditions were bad

The post-factory system

Very similar to before
(7) _____ is much more advanced
Maybe humans not needed in the future?
No – will need humans to (8) _____ and engineers to mend the machines

---

Reading for gist

2 Now read the text about a system of work organization used in Japan, and write the headings above each section.

> JIT   The result   Beyond the Japanese car industry   Lean manufacturing
> Chaos   TPS   The employees

Reading for detail

3 Read the text again and mark the sentences *T* (true) or *F* (false).

1 The Toyota Production System started 100 years ago in Japan. ☐
2 Toyota's machines are multi-purpose. They are able to produce more than one part. ☐
3 Lean manufacturing is another name for the TPS. ☐
4 Toyota's employees are involved in the production process. ☐
5 Just-in-time means that parts are ordered once a month. ☐
6 The company is important to Japanese employees. ☐
7 The TPS means that the environment the employees work in is less dangerous. ☐
8 The TPS is successful all over the world. ☐

4 Match the terms relating to TPS on the left with the definitions on the right.

1 Kaizen
2 Just-in-time
3 Lean manufacturing

a) in this process stock is only ordered when it is needed – not before.
b) a system that aims to produce more, using less. The removal of waste (waste = anything that does not add to the final product).
c) continually making small improvements which lead to greater effectiveness and higher quality.

Internet research

Search for the keywords *lean manufacturing, advantages* or *lean manufacturing, disadvantages* to find out more about the pros and cons of this system. Tell a partner what you read.

Listening for gist

5 🔊 1:34 Listen to Eric Novak, a manager, talking about when he tried to introduce TPS in his company.

1 What went wrong?
2 Why didn't it work?

32 *The* **Business**

Toyota PRODUCTION SYSTEM

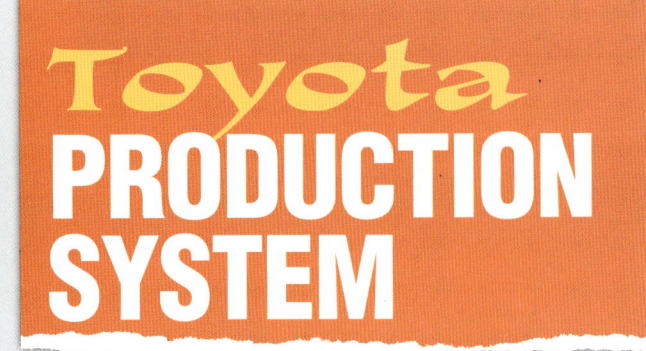

By the 1970s, car production in Europe and America was huge. Demand was high and cars were mass-produced on an enormous scale. But when demand changed, and mass production methods didn't, thousands of unsold vehicles sat outside the factories waiting to be bought. In Japan however, things were different.

The Toyota Production System (TPS) was developed in the middle of the last century by a Toyota manager named Taiichi Ohno. It created the most efficient car production system in the world. Instead of using machines that built only one specific part, Toyota designed machines that could produce many different parts. This made Toyota more flexible and able to react quickly to customers' changing needs.

By the 1990s, the term Lean Manufacturing was being used to describe TPS. Lean manufacturing combines the best elements of craftwork and mass production. It uses less labour, less machinery, less space and less time. The aim of lean manufacturing is to eliminate all defects. If something goes wrong a worker can stop the whole production line and deal with the problem immediately. If the worker didn't make this decision, production could carry on producing faulty or incorrect parts.

At Toyota, the just-in-time system makes stores or warehouses unnecessary because parts are only produced or ordered when they are needed. This means that costs are cut, and turnover is increased.

Toyota has more success with lean manufacturing than other companies because all their employees have a clear understanding of the objective and are totally committed to *kaizen*, the Japanese term for continuous improvement. Importantly, Toyota employees identify strongly with their company.

When implemented successfully, the TPS is a systematic way to satisfy customer needs and create meaningful work for every member of an organization.
The results of TPS are superior products and service quality, short lead times, low costs and a safe (physically, professionally and emotionally) working environment for the employees.

Although lean manufacturing is spreading from the car factory to other industries, manufacturers around the world who try to implement the TPS are not always successful. One of the reasons for this is that companies which have been running mass production systems sometimes find it difficult to adjust. Additionally, in the West, where employees think of themselves before the company, it is more difficult for employees to adapt to the TPS.

Listening for detail

6 Listen to the manager again and fill in the flow chart.

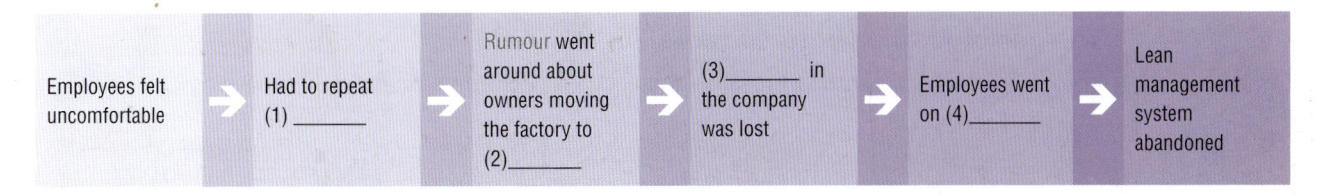

| Employees felt uncomfortable | → | Had to repeat (1) _____ | → | Rumour went around about owners moving the factory to (2) _____ | → | (3) _____ in the company was lost | → | Employees went on (4) _____ | → | Lean management system abandoned |

Discussion

7 In small groups discuss the questions about lean manufacturing.

1. What are the advantages and disadvantages of lean manufacturing?
2. Can you think of any companies that lean manufacturing would work very well/badly for?
3. What effects would lean manufacturing have on a company? Think about employees, customers, equipment, premises.

3 Operations

3.2 Vocabulary Trends and planning

Discussion

1 Work with a partner. What do you know about changes in the aviation industry? Are things improving for a) small airlines, b) large airlines, c) passengers, d) the environment and e) airline staff?

Reading for detail

2 Read a report about the recent performance of ScotAir, a large passenger airline. The words in **bold** describe different parts of the graph. Write the numbers in the correct place on the graph.

ScotAir's recent performance and trends in the passenger air travel industry

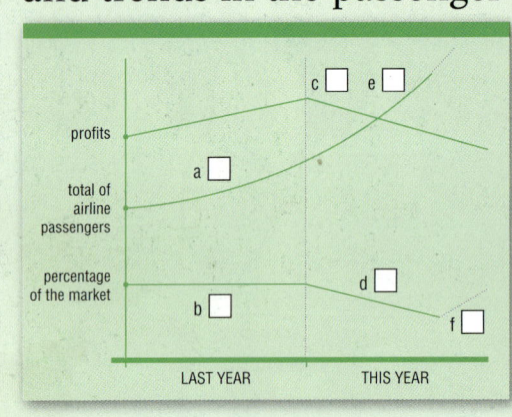

SCOTAIR

NEW LOST-COST SUBSIDIARY
Last year was a good year for the passenger aviation industry: the overall number of passengers (1) **went up**, and the trend continued into this year. We expect passenger numbers to continue to (2) **increase** for some time. However, our profits began to (3) **fall** at the beginning of the year. The reason for this was the arrival of two new low-cost competitors. The last few months have not been easy, but we hope that this difficult phase is now coming to an end. As soon as we get the green light, we plan to buy three more planes to add to our fleet. With these planes and the resources already available to us – crew, our existing planes, airport slots, etc. – we intend to set up a new low-cost subsidiary. This will be a milestone in our company's history. For many years, our percentage of the market (4) **remained steady**, but it (5) **went down** for the first time ever at the beginning of the year. However, with our new subsidiary we expect it to (6) **grow** again. We've set ourselves a deadline: to become the market leader once again by the end of next year.

Describing trends

3 Find four pairs of opposites in the box below. Then write them in the table in the correct column.

fall	decrease	go down
grow	increase	go up
rise	shrink	

↗	↘

4 What are the past simple forms of the verbs in 3?

Project planning terms

5 Match a word on the left with the correct definition on the right.

1 resources   a) a particular period of time during the development of something
2 milestone   b) a specific time or date by which you have to do something
3 green light   c) something such as money, workers, or equipment that can be used
4 deadline   to help an institution or business
5 phase   d) the official approval to go ahead with something
                    e) an event or achievement that marks an important stage in a project

Listening for gist

6 🔊 1:35 Listen to Ms Bloom, a research scientist, in a meeting with an airline company. What is the problem they discuss, and what is Ms Bloom's solution?

34 *The* Business

3.2 Vocabulary

Listening for detail – trends

7 Listen to the meeting again and fill in the missing verbs to complete these descriptions of trends.

1 The number of international airports is _____.
2 The number of people who are subjected to aircraft noise is _____.
3 As the cost of airfares _____, the demand for flights _____.
4 We are aiming to _____ noise levels by 99%.
5 While costs are _____, unfortunately our level of funding is _____.
6 This would _____ the utilization of the aircraft and at the same time _____ your overall costs.
7 That means that the local economy would _____.

Reformulation

8 In your own words, explain the benefits of the silent plane to your partner.

Listening for detail

9 1:36 The month is November. You are the council of a small island that has recently been 'discovered' by tourists. Listen to the council leader talking about the number of tourists the island has received in the last year. Draw in the lines on graph one.

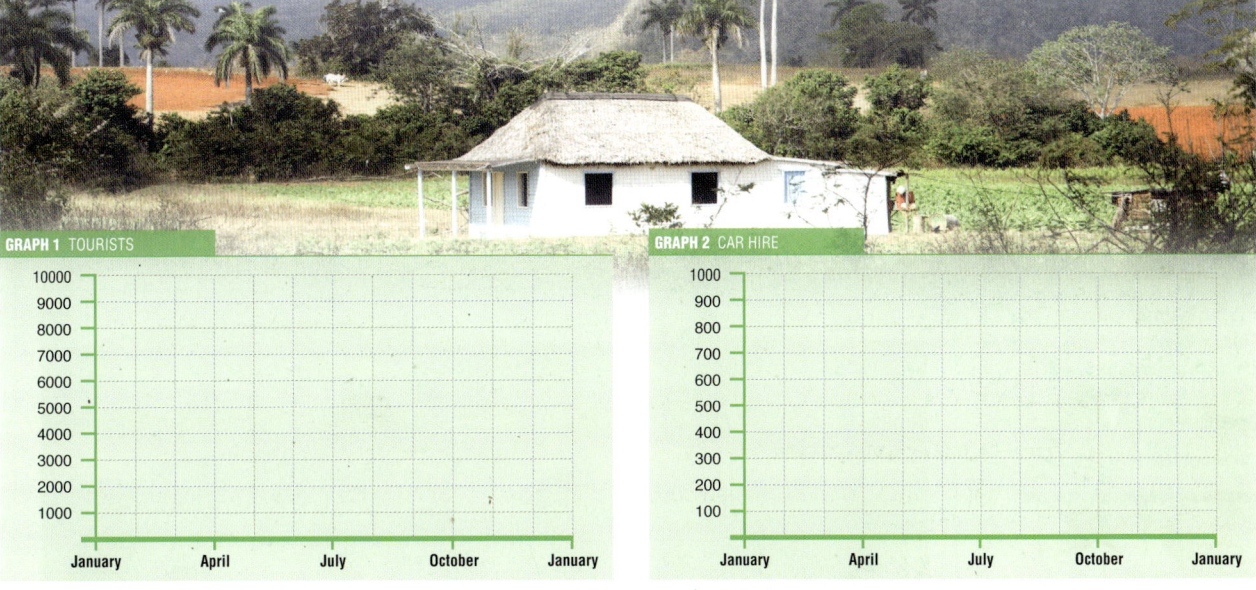

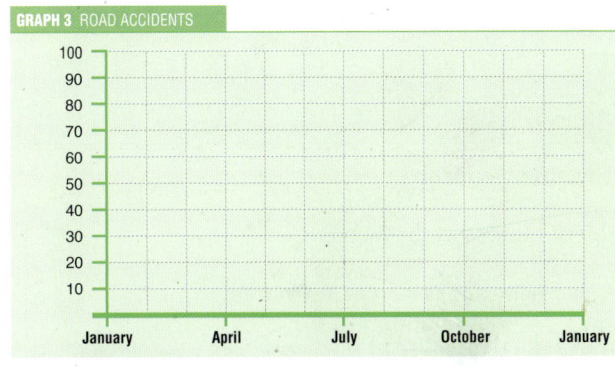

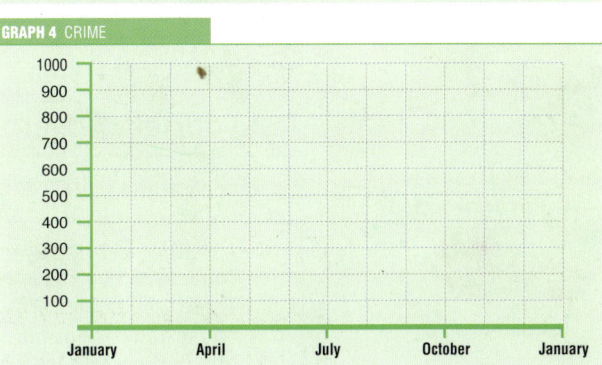

GRAPH 1 TOURISTS

GRAPH 2 CAR HIRE

GRAPH 3 ROAD ACCIDENTS

GRAPH 4 CRIME

Describing trends

10 Work in groups of three. Student A look at page 112. Student B look at page 110. Student C look at page 115. Describe your graph to your group. Listen and fill in the trends on the graph.

Discussion

11 You have $2.5 million to spend on improving the island. Work in groups of three. Student A look at page 112. Student B look at page 110. Student C look at page 115. Use the information and the graphs to make a project plan timeline. Set priorities, label the different phases, set yourselves deadlines and write a plan of action.

Internet research

Search for the keywords *silent aircraft* or *Cambridge MIT* to read about the latest developments in this project.

The **Business** 35

3 Operations

Refresh your memory

Present continuous
Sales figures are going up.
is/are + verb + ing
an action in progress and trends

▶ Grammar reference page 122

Adverbs of manner
Shares in the company rose quickly.
tell us how something happens
used to modify verbs
usually come after the main verb
To form an adverb from an adjective add *-ly* to the adjective
careful   carefully
quick   quickly
slow   slowly
When an adjective ends in *-y*, replace *-y* with *-ily*
happy   happily
angry   angrily
There are some exceptions
good   well
hard   hard

▶ Grammar reference page 123

Present simple passive
Tea is grown in India.
be + past participle
often used to describe processes

▶ Grammar reference page 123

3.3 Grammar — Present continuous, adverbs, present simple passive

Test yourself: Present continuous

1 Complete the text about the wine industry in California using the present continuous form of the verbs in brackets.

The sunny west coast state of California currently produces more than 90% of all US wine. In the past very little of this was organic, but the US wine industry (1) _____ (go) through a large and important change.

The population of California (2) _____ (grow) by half a million every year, and more people live next to farms and vineyards than ever before. Because wine growers traditionally use a lot of pesticides, people are concerned about their health. Now many wine growers want to be good neighbours and (3) _____ (change) over to organic methods.

By moving away from conventional methods, growers (4) _____ (reduce) the amount of pesticides they use. Instead of pesticides, some of them use bats and owls to keep bugs under control.

Many wine producers (5) _____ also _____ (realise) that sustainable, chemical-free farming makes good economic sense, in addition to being healthier. At first the change to an organic system increases costs by 10 to 15%. But the demand for organic wines (6) _____ (grow) every year and sales (7) _____ (go up), so the initial cost is justified. With this changing trend in production, the quality of organic wines (8) _____ (improve) all the time. This is very good news for consumers. Organic wines taste better than ever before and prices (9) _____ (fall).

And sales of organic wine (10) _____ (increase) not only in the USA, but also in such far-flung countries as Japan, France and Argentina. The future looks very bright (green!) for organic wines.

Test yourself: Adverbs

2 Complete the sentences using adverbs of manner.

1. There is a slow decrease in sales of tobacco at the moment.
   Tobacco sales are decreasing _____.
2. There was a quick growth in the organic foods market last month.
   The organic foods market grew _____ last month.
3. I think there will be a sharp rise in the share price of Hussein Solar Power Plc very soon.
   I think the price of shares in Hussein Solar Power Plc will rise _____ very soon.
4. Every day there is a slight improvement in our production process.
   Our production process is improving _____ every day.
5. Our sales in Japan are very good at the moment.
   Our products are selling very _____ in Japan at the moment.
6. There is a steady fall at the moment in the amount of waste produced by our factory.
   The amount of waste we produce is falling _____.

3.3 Grammar

Internet research

Search for the keywords *Wala* or *"Dr Hauschka"* to find out more about the company and their unique production processes.

Test yourself: Present simple passive

3 Underline two present simple passive forms in the sentences below about Dr Hauschka skincare products.

Dr Hauschka skincare products are manufactured by Wala, a world leader in the production of natural medicines and related products. Wala are very careful to make sure that only organic, natural ingredients are used in the process.

4 Complete the description below of the process for manufacturing Dr Hauschka's Rose Cream. Use the present simple passive form of the verbs in the box.

sell   store   involve   distribute   make   grow   send

1. Around 150 people _____ in the production of Dr Hauschka's Rose Cream.
2. The plants _____ under strict organic conditions in the company's own pesticide-free garden.
3. They _____ for a year under special conditions before they _____ to the laboratory.
4. All Dr Hauschka products _____ by hand, not by machines.
5. The rose cream _____ all over the world and _____ in over 40 countries.

Describing a trend

5 Work with a partner. Describe the trend shown in each diagram below. Look back at exercise 2 on page 34.

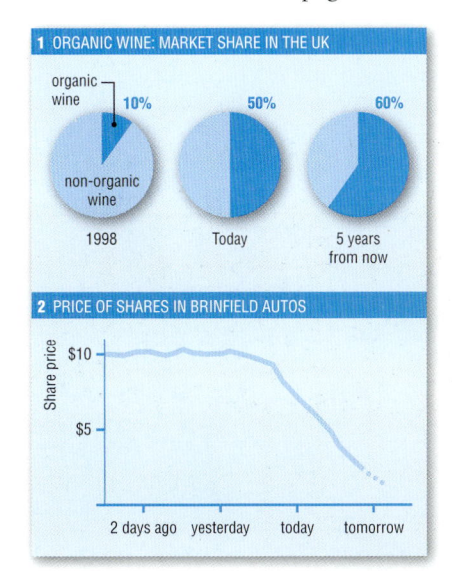

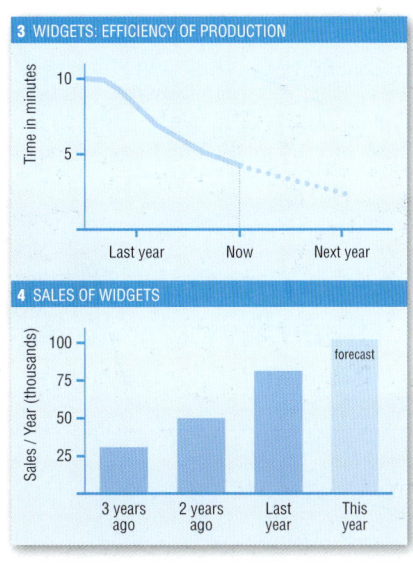

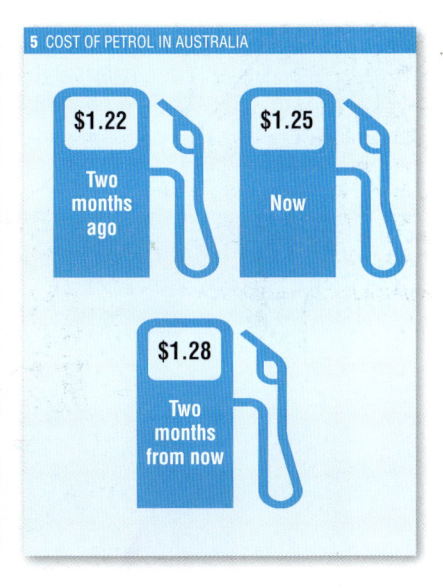

1 ORGANIC WINE: MARKET SHARE IN THE UK
2 PRICE OF SHARES IN BRINFIELD AUTOS
3 WIDGETS: EFFICIENCY OF PRODUCTION
4 SALES OF WIDGETS
5 COST OF PETROL IN AUSTRALIA

Describing a process

6 Work with a partner. Use the present simple passive to describe the process shown in the pictures below. Take it in turns to describe each step. Use the verbs in the box.

cut   transport   make   sell

the **chairs**

The Business   37

3 Operations

3.4 Speaking   Presentations – signposts and stepping stones

Discussion

1 Work with a partner and discuss the questions about presentations.
1 Why do people give presentations?
2 Have you ever given a presentation?
3 When you give a presentation what are the most important things to remember?

Signposting language

2 Put the words in the illustration below in the correct order to make some useful presentation language.

Listening

3 🔊 1:37 Now listen and check your answers to 2.

Listening for detail

4 🔊 1:38 Listen to a short presentation given by Sonia Padron Perez from DMC Wood. Answer the questions below.

1 What is Sonia's job?
2 When was the biggest fall in sales figures?
3 Why did the sales increase in September?
4 What is the name of the new model that Sonia introduces?

5 Listen to the presentation again. Match the phrases 1–6 to a)–f).

1	I'd like to start by	a) we'll look at how this has affected our share prices.
2	First of all	b) our share prices: the next slide shows us …
3	After that	c) giving you a short overview of today's presentation.
4	Moving on to	d) showing you how we aim to reach this target.
5	Let's go back and look at	e) we're going to look at the sales figures for the last two years.
6	I'd like to finish by	f) the first slide again.

Internet research

Search for the keywords *bad presentations* to find out what **not** to do when you are giving a presentation

Speech bubble: I'd / to / start / like / by

Sign: of / First / all

Sign: on / Moving / to

DVD-ROM Interactive pronunciation practice on the DVD-ROM

3.4 Speaking

Giving a presentation

6 Work in small groups. Use the phrases from 5 and the information on the presentation note cards below to prepare a short presentation.

Wine production in California

- Currently produces more than 90% of the wine in the US
- Only a small percentage is organic
- This is changing / new trend
- Organic wine is more expensive / price per bottle is falling as sales increase
- Sales of organic wine increasing by 20% a year
- Health & wealth are influencing sales
- Good news, the future looks green

Sales trends for natural cosmetics in Europe

- Natural cosmetic sales in Europe are increasing at a fast rate
- The sales figures are doubling every 2-3 years
- Better distribution / higher customer demand
- Natural ingredients / quality / fewer skin problems
- Premium brands like Aveda and Dr Hauschka are becoming very popular
- Sold in pharmacies, supermarkets and health food shops
- Online sales increasing
- The market share is highest in Germany and Austria / 4% of total cosmetic sales

The silent plane

- Number of international airports increasing
- Passenger numbers / noise / pollution increasing
- Aiming to decrease noise by 99%
- Engines above the wings / noise will go up, not down
- Single wing / more fuel-efficient
- Could fly at night / increase the amount of flights in each 24 hour period
- Expensive / need funding
- Plane should be flying by 2020

7 Work in small groups.

You work in the marketing department for the companies that make one of the products above. You are going to give a presentation to a number of people who are interested in investing in your products.

Prepare a three-minute presentation to give to the rest your class. Use the note cards from 6 and the phrases from 5 to help you.

Your class will decide which company they want to invest in.

> you / coming / for / Thank

look / Let's / back / and / go / at

like / finish / to / I'd / by

questions? / there / Are / any

3 Operations

3.5 Writing | Instructions and procedures for an exhibition stand

Discussion

1 Work with a partner. Read the text below and answer the questions.
1 Would you like to go to this exhibition? Why? Why not?
2 Why do you think companies attend exhibitions and conventions like this?

THE INTERNATIONAL Comic Convention, is an annual comic book exhibition. It is a fabulous four-day event (Thursday to Sunday) held during the summer in Seattle, at the Seattle Convention Center. Originally it showcased comic books but the exhibition has expanded over the years and it now includes seminars, workshops with comic book professionals, film previews, the chance to talk to representatives of comic book and video game companies. In addition to this there are evening events such as awards ceremonies and fantastic costume contests.

Like most exhibitions and conventions, the International Comic Convention features a large amount of floor space for exhibitors. These include media companies as well as comic-book dealers and collectors. The convention is one of the largest of its kind in the United States. When it started in 1972 there were only 115 attendees. In 2007 more than 115,000 people visited the convention – and it is still growing.

Describing a stand

2 Look at the illustration of the exhibition stand and fill in the labels using the information below.

| comfortable chairs | groups of tables and chairs | video screens | display racks |
| a raised floor | reception area | banners | counter | pavement sign |

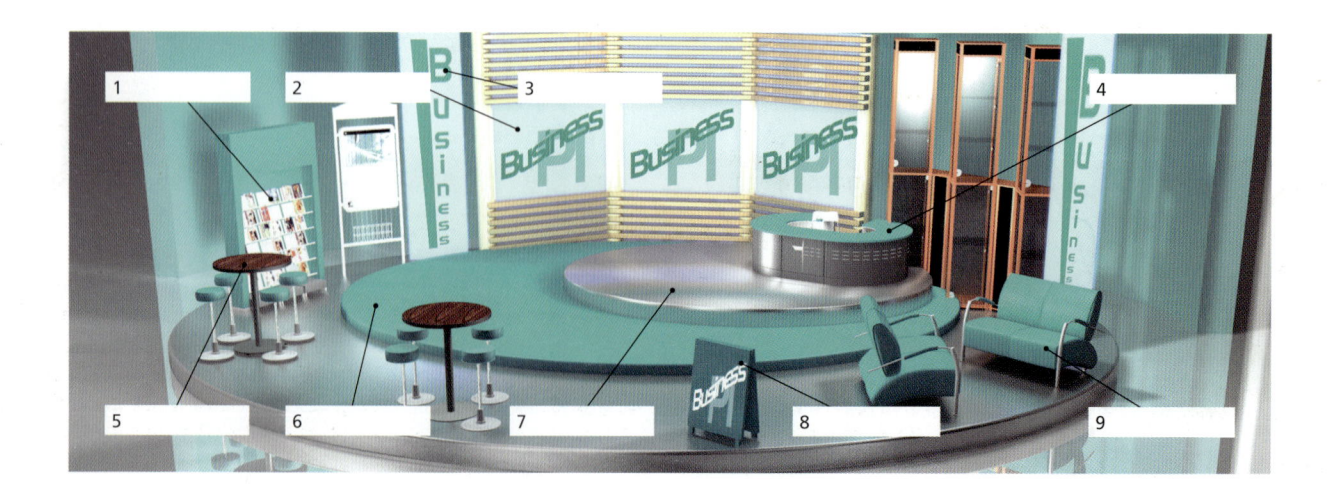

3.5 Writing

Discussion

3 You work for Coded Comics, a company that makes comics for children who are younger than 10. You received this email from your boss about the International Comic Convention. With a partner discuss the questions that Mr Gomez asks in the email.

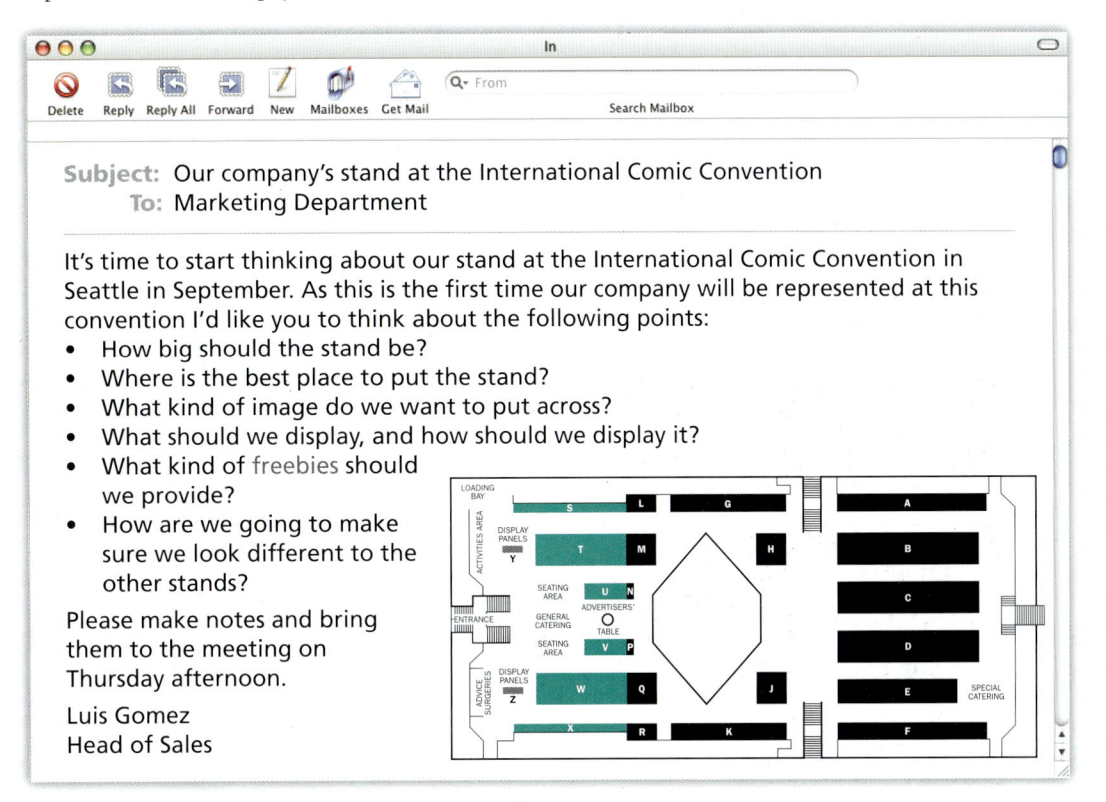

Subject: Our company's stand at the International Comic Convention
To: Marketing Department

It's time to start thinking about our stand at the International Comic Convention in Seattle in September. As this is the first time our company will be represented at this convention I'd like you to think about the following points:
- How big should the stand be?
- Where is the best place to put the stand?
- What kind of image do we want to put across?
- What should we display, and how should we display it?
- What kind of freebies should we provide?
- How are we going to make sure we look different to the other stands?

Please make notes and bring them to the meeting on Thursday afternoon.

Luis Gomez
Head of Sales

Sequencing and imperatives

4 Read the instructions for planning a stand at a convention. Use the words in the box to fill in the spaces.

| Don't forget | Then | Secondly | After that | Make sure | Firstly | Finally |

There are many things to think about when planning your stand at a convention or trade fair. Here are some ideas to get you started.

- 1) _____, decide on the budget for the stand.
- 2) _____, choose the size and the location of the stand.
- 3) _____, design the stand (shelving scheme, display area).
- 4) _____ _____ you book stand space with the exhibition organizers.
- 5) _____ _____ to think about your colour scheme, graphic panels, and audio-visual equipment.
- 6) _____ _____, organize the logistics of the delivery (stand, publicity, products).
- 7) _____, set up the stand.

Speaking

5 In pairs, decide how you want your stand for the exhibition to look. Use the advice in exercise 4 to give you some ideas.

Writing

6 You are the head of the Marketing Department at Coded Comics. Write an email to your marketing team about your stand requirements for the International Comic Convention exhibition. You need to tell your team about the exhibition, include information about what the team need to do, and in which order they should do it. Don't forget to include approximate figures and sizes. Remember that this is the first time you have had a stand at the exhibition so your instructions need to be very clear.

Internet research

Search for the keywords *"comic book convention"*. What information can you find for exhibitors?

3 Operations

3.6 Case study ScotAir

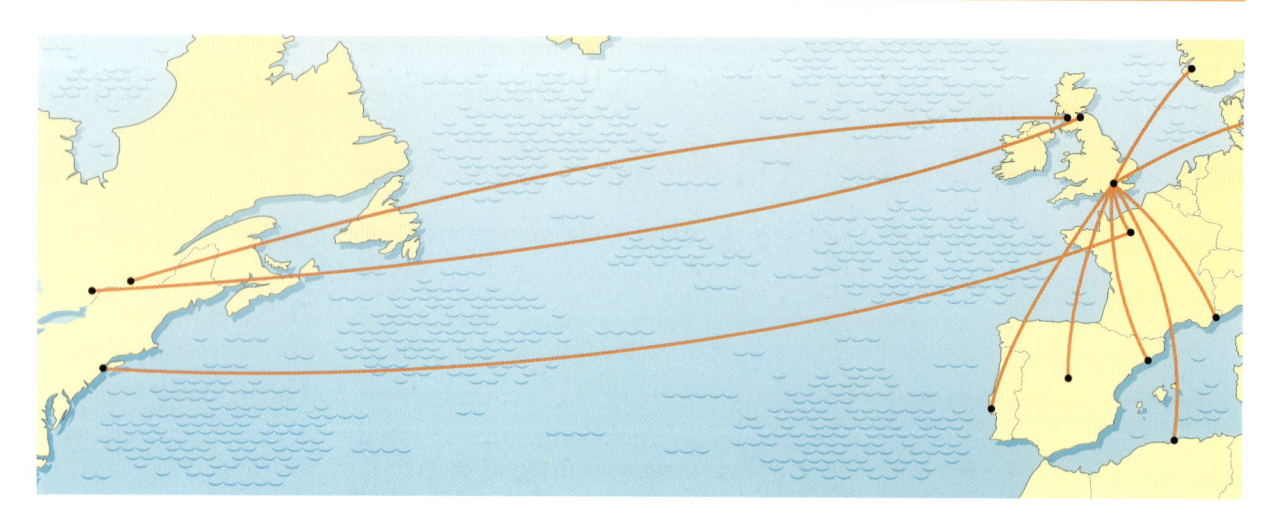

Discussion

1 How important are these things for you when you fly?

Rate the following as: *A* (very important), *B* (important) or *C* (not important).

free in-flight food ☐	wide seats ☐	seat allocation ☐
free headphones ☐	seatback TV ☐	friendly cabin crew ☐
carbon footprint of flight ☐	fast check-in ☐	free in-flight drinks ☐
a lot of legroom ☐	free newspapers or magazines ☐	a clean and tidy plane ☐

Compare your answers with a partner.

Reading for gist

2 Read the article about changes in passenger air travel over the last 70 years. What two trends does the article describe?

The changing face of air travel

When Pan Am began the first passenger service across the Atlantic from New York to France in 1939, a one-way ticket cost $375. That's about $4,000 in today's money. These days a ticket on the same route can cost you as little as $250.

In the past, if you wanted to fly commercially you had to book a seat on traditional, or national, airlines such as British Airways, Lufthansa or Air France. There were strict rules and the airlines were often accused of 'price-fixing'.

In the 1950s only the rich could afford the £70 return fare from England to Nice. It doesn't sound much, but that's equivalent to about £1,500 today. Now this has all changed. Today, easyJet will fly you to Nice for less than £15 each way.

New budget airlines are appearing all the time, and most national airlines now have their own budget subsidiary. Fares are cheap, food and drinks are not included, there is no seat allocation and the planes are often second-hand. However, it seems that most passengers will put up with a bit of discomfort in order to fly cheaply. But what about the effects budget airlines have on their employees and the environment?

42 *The* Business

DVD-ROM Further interactive problem-solving on the DVD-ROM

3.6 Case study

Listening and note-taking

3 🎧 **1:39–1:44** Listen and complete the notes on what these people say about the budget airline EvanAir.

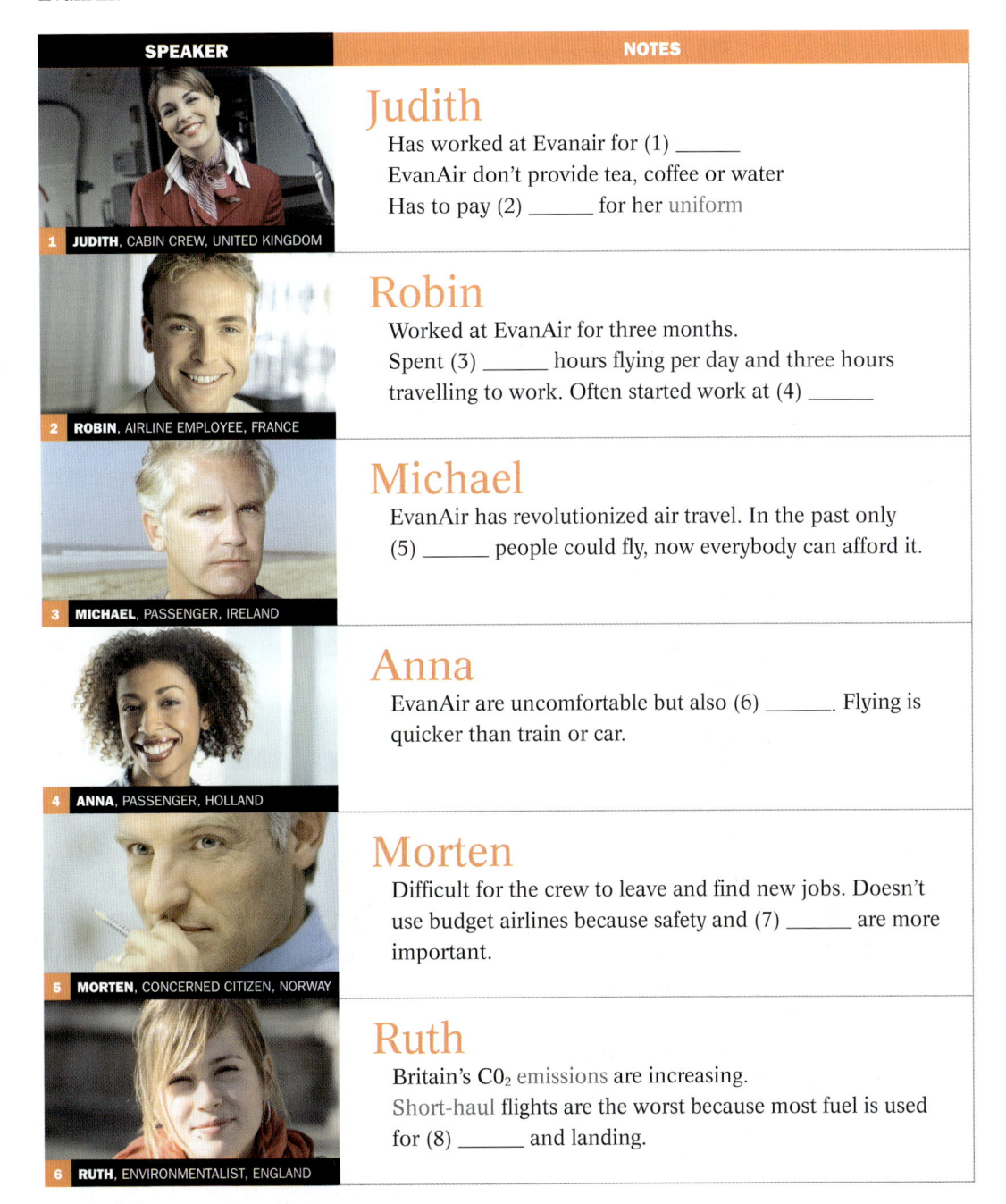

SPEAKER	NOTES
1 JUDITH, CABIN CREW, UNITED KINGDOM	**Judith** Has worked at Evanair for (1) _____ EvanAir don't provide tea, coffee or water Has to pay (2) _____ for her uniform
2 ROBIN, AIRLINE EMPLOYEE, FRANCE	**Robin** Worked at EvanAir for three months. Spent (3) _____ hours flying per day and three hours travelling to work. Often started work at (4) _____
3 MICHAEL, PASSENGER, IRELAND	**Michael** EvanAir has revolutionized air travel. In the past only (5) _____ people could fly, now everybody can afford it.
4 ANNA, PASSENGER, HOLLAND	**Anna** EvanAir are uncomfortable but also (6) _____. Flying is quicker than train or car.
5 MORTEN, CONCERNED CITIZEN, NORWAY	**Morten** Difficult for the crew to leave and find new jobs. Doesn't use budget airlines because safety and (7) _____ are more important.
6 RUTH, ENVIRONMENTALIST, ENGLAND	**Ruth** Britain's CO_2 emissions are increasing. Short-haul flights are the worst because most fuel is used for (8) _____ and landing.

Discussion

SCOTAIR

Internet research
Use an online carbon calculator to find out what your carbon footprint was on your last flight.
You can find out, for example, that a return flight from Stuttgart, Germany to London Heathrow will use 0.19 tonnes of CO_2 per passenger.

4 Work in two groups. You are the managing directors at ScotAir, a traditional airline with a long history. ScotAir is in trouble. It is losing a lot of passengers to its low cost competitors. Share prices are falling and the stockholders are demanding that something be done, quickly!

Group A
You think ScotAir needs to start a new budget subsidiary. Think of reasons why a budget subsidiary would be a good idea, consider the staff, passengers, the environment. Prepare to present your ideas to the rest of the class.

Group B
You don't think ScotAir needs to start a new budget subsidiary. Think of reasons why a budget subsidiary would be a bad idea, consider the staff, passengers, the environment. Prepare to present your ideas to the rest of the class.

The Business

4 Success stories

4.1 About business Business leaders and success stories

Discussion

1 When you start up a business the following are all important. With a partner put them in order from the most to the least important.

> financial backing   a sense of adventure   a business background   luck   ambition
> a good marketing strategy   good contacts   original ideas   hard work & dedication

Listening and note-taking

2 1:45 Listen to a podcast about the cosmetics producer, Estée Lauder and fill in the profile.

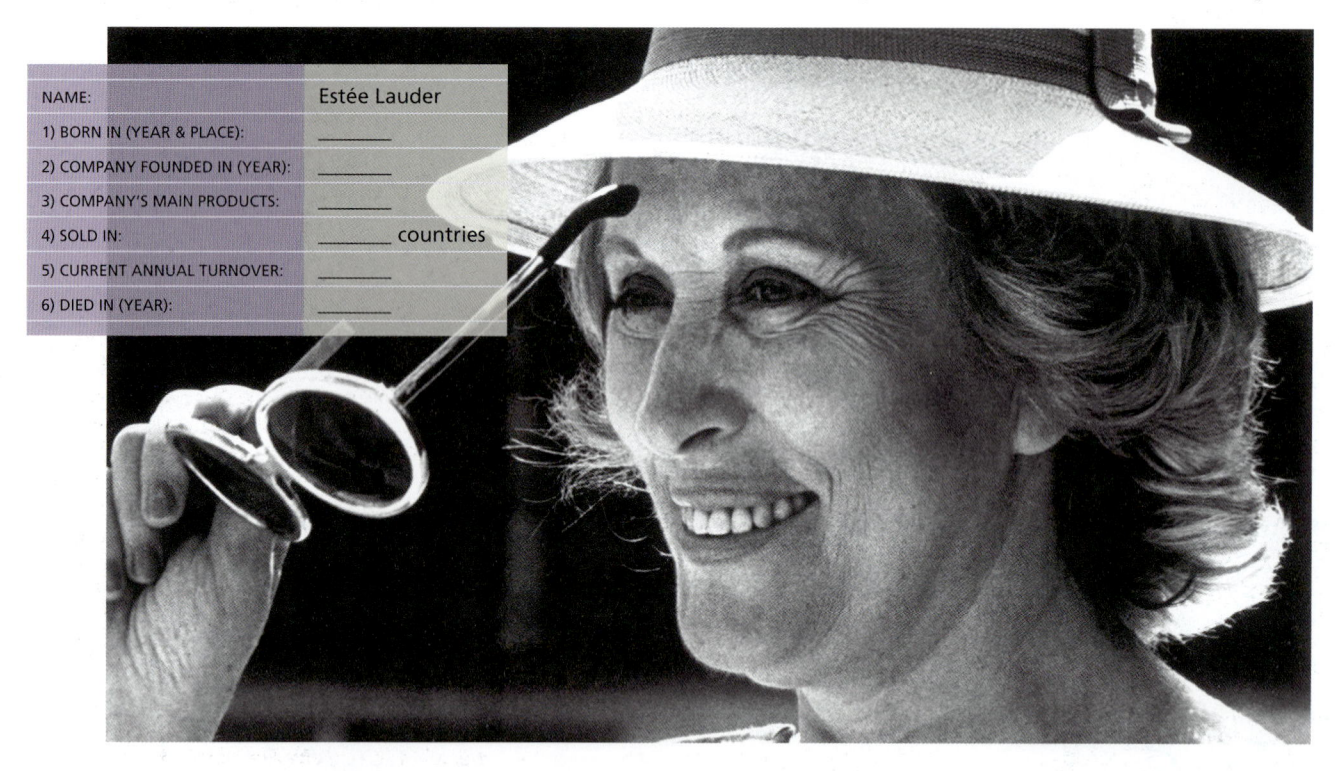

NAME:	Estée Lauder
1) BORN IN (YEAR & PLACE):	_____
2) COMPANY FOUNDED IN (YEAR):	_____
3) COMPANY'S MAIN PRODUCTS:	_____
4) SOLD IN:	_____ countries
5) CURRENT ANNUAL TURNOVER:	_____
6) DIED IN (YEAR):	_____

Listening for detail

3 Listen again and mark the sentences *T* (true) or *F* (false). If they are false, correct them.

1. Estée was born Josephine Esther Mentzer. ☐
2. Estée's parents were Bulgarian immigrants. ☐
3. The first Estée Lauder counter was opened at Saks' on Fifth Avenue in 1938. ☐
4. The company started to sell beauty products for men in the 1960s. ☐
5. The Estée Lauder Company consists of many well-known names. ☐
6. The company went public at the end of the twentieth century. ☐

Vocabulary

4 The following words are all used in the article about Estée Lauder. Match a word on the left to the correct definition on the right.

1. to spill
2. fragrance
3. to demand
4. stylish
5. makeover
6. to pioneer
7. sample
8. technique
9. revolutionary
10. unsurpassed

a) beautiful and well-designed
b) a nice smell
c) changing a person's appearance so that they look better
d) to accidentally pour a liquid out of its container
e) to say that you want something very strongly
f) better than everything else of its kind
g) completely new and different
h) a method of doing something
i) a small amount of a product given to people for free
j) to be one of the first people to do something

Internet research

Search for the keywords *"habits of business success"* to find out other tips for enjoying business success.

44 *The* Business

4.1 About business

Reading for detail

5 With a partner, read the article and make a list of what you think the six secrets of Estée Lauder's success are.

Compare your answers with another group. Did you find the same six things?

THE SWEET *smell of success*

ESTÉE LAUDER knew how to make a sale. Once when she was refused a counter at the Galleries Lafayette in Paris, she 'accidentally' spilt one of her fragrances in the crowded store. The scent wafted through the crowd of shoppers who immediately demanded to know what the lovely fragrance was and where they could buy it. Very soon after, Estée Lauder got her counter and her products went on sale in the Galleries Lafayette.

a culture of quality, style and unsurpassed customer service

Estée Lauder attributed her success to her sales technique. 'If I believe in something, I sell it, and I sell it hard', she said. She was a brilliant saleswoman and she personally visited the staff on her counters to offer them sales tips. Her approach was very hands-on. She always believed that in order to make a sale, you must touch the customer. Even today the company's motto is 'Bringing the best to everyone we touch'.

Estée knew about the importance of image. She wanted to give her products a sophisticated look and personally chose the blue colour of the bottles which she believed would look stylish in every bathroom. She believed in secrecy and didn't reveal much about her life or the ingredients used in her products. She wanted her customers to believe that they were buying not only 'beauty in a jar' but also the solution to looking and feeling eternally young. She said that 'In order to sell a cream, you sold a dream'. She put a lot of time and effort into building up that dream image.

When she began her business, she didn't have a marketing budget, but she believed that if you put the product into the customer's hands, its quality would speak for itself. She started by giving free demonstrations and makeovers using her own products anywhere she could: in hotels, beauty salons, subway stations and even on the street. Most importantly, she pioneered the idea of a 'gift with purchase'. No one had ever heard of this before, free creams, free lipsticks! She began by giving away free samples and then moved on to giving away extra products with a purchase. These days many companies use this marketing technique, but fifty years ago the idea was revolutionary.

With the combination of hard work, dedication, ambition, and belief in herself and her products, Estée created a culture of quality, style and unsurpassed customer service. This turned her company into the global cosmetics leader it is today. As she famously said, 'I never dreamed about success. I worked for it'. ■

6 Match a quotation from the text with the correct explanation on the right.

1 'Beauty in a jar'
2 'In order to sell a cream, you sell a dream'
3 'Bringing the best to everyone we touch'

a) This stresses the personal approach. It makes customers feel that they are each important to the company, but also that they are getting the best quality available.
b) The idea that you can buy beauty.
c) The key thing is not the cream itself, but encouraging women to fantasize and want a certain lifestyle, so that there is then a market for the cream.

Discussion

7 With a partner, look back at the article and your answers to 5 and answer the questions.

1 Which of Estée's secrets of success do you consider to be the most important?
2 Which of these secrets are still good business practice today?
3 Do you think there is still a market for new cosmetics companies? In which way would they need to be different?

The **Business** 45

4 Success stories

4.2 Vocabulary Describing yourself and being successful

Adjectives

1 These adjectives can be used to describe people's personality and their behaviour. Put them into the correct place in the table below. Use a dictionary if necessary.

hard-working   unhelpful   generous   hands-on   dishonest
disorganized   ambitious   uncooperative   stressed

positive	negative
calm	
	mean
honest	
	lazy
helpful	
	lacking in drive
organized	
	hands-off
cooperative	

2 Use the adjectives above to complete the sentences.
1 I never get angry. I'm a very _____ person.
2 Junita can't find the files she needs. She's so _____.
3 I don't really trust him. He seems to be a bit _____.
4 Robert is working his way up the career ladder. He's very _____.
5 Angela is a very _____ person. She gives 15% of her salary to charities.
6 Craig just won't lift a finger. He's a very _____ man.
7 Dieter never leaves the office until his day's work is finished. His colleagues all say he's the most _____ man in the company.
8 Pat won't do anything for other people. She's the most _____ woman I know.
9 Olaf likes his employees to make their own decisions. His style of management is very _____.
10 Sandra has three small children and a full-time job. She's quite _____, although she doesn't show it.

4.2 Vocabulary

Listening

3 1:46 Listen to Alan at a job interview. The interviewer asks him to describe himself. Which four adjectives does Alan use?

4 Now listen again and write the reasons that Alan gives.

Word building

5 Fill in the table with the correct form of the words.

Noun	Adjective
adventure	adventurous
1)	ambitious
2)	decisive
3)	financial
flexibility	4)
luck	lucky
5)	organized
6)	pioneering
success	7)
8)	stressful

Internet research
Search for the keywords *unusual interview questions* to find out about some strange questions that employers ask. Discuss with a partner how you could answer them.

6 Read the text about how to be a successful business owner. Fill in the spaces using the correct word from the table above.

7 Habits of Highly Successful Business Owners

Do you spend every minute at work? Is your business not making the progress that you want it to? Is your desk always in a mess? Maybe the bank gave you all the (1) _____ help that you needed but your business is still not as successful as it could be. Read our seven habits of successful business owners to find out how to make your business a success.

1 Highly successful business owners are great role models. They lead their business from the front and are very hands-on. They know that to be successful they need to show their employees that they have a sense of (2) _____ and are not afraid to take a risk.

2 Highly successful business owners invest time and money in their team and themselves. They develop their people and hold regular training sessions so that everybody who works for them is as well-informed as they can be.

3 Highly successful business owners know how to manage their time and have systems which enable them to work effectively at all times. They are always 3) _____ so that they don't waste their time.

4 Highly successful business owners are fit and healthy. They understand that a healthy mind and body improves their productivity and general well-being. They realize that by keeping themselves fit and they can cope with the (4) _____ of running a business.

5 Highly successful business owners have (5) _____ ideas. Their businesses offer new ways of doing things that other people don't think of. This makes their businesses stand out from the crowd.

6 Highly successful business owners look after their clients. They know that without clients there would be no business. They dedicate a lot of time to making sure that their clients receive the best service that they can.

7 Highly successful business owners are not afraid to make (6) _____ and take action. They don't waste time thinking about what to do, they just do it! They also have (7) _____, they know what they want their business to achieve and how they are going to achieve it.

Discussion

7 Work with a partner. Discuss the questions below.
1 Which of the seven habits do you think is the most important for a successful business?
2 Think of two more habits of successful business owners.
3 What sort of worker / student are you?
4 How would your colleagues describe you?

4 Success stories

4.3 Grammar — Past simple, past continuous and *used to*

Test yourself: Past simple and past continuous

1 Which timeline shows the past simple and which timeline shows the past continuous?

Write the example sentences from the 'Refresh your memory' box next to the correct timeline.

a 1970 — 1980 — 1990 — 2000 — NOW

b 1970 — 1980 — 1990 — 2000 — NOW

2 Complete the text about the Grameen Bank using the correct form of the verbs in brackets: past simple or past continuous.

The Grameen Bank

Professor Muhammad Yunus founded the bank in 1977 while he was working at the University of Chittagong. Along with his students he (1) _____ (launch) a research project into poverty in rural villages in Bangladesh. While he (2) _____ (work) on the research project Professor Yunus (3) _____ (discover) that many of the villagers (4) _____ (live) below the poverty line.

Professor Yunus (5) _____ (meet) some women who made bamboo furniture while he (6) _____ (visit) a village called Jobra. The women told him that in order to buy the materials they needed, they borrowed money from lenders who charged a huge amount of interest. Professor Yunus (7) _____ (lend) $27 of his own money to a group of 42 poor villagers so that they could escape the vicious circle of poverty. What made this scheme different, was that unlike other money lenders he (8) _____ (not ask) for any security or collateral and only charged a small amount of interest.

The project was very successful and (9) _____ (change) the lives of millions of women in Bangladesh. With the help of a small loan, and they (10) _____ (be) able to buy enough food and they could send all their children to school. Today the bank has lent more than $6 billion dollars to more than 7 million borrowers. In 2006, Professor Yunus (11) _____ (receive) the Nobel Peace Prize for his work.

Test yourself: *used to*

3 Complete the sentences with the correct form of *used to*.

1. I _____ (smoke), but I gave up last summer.
2. He _____ (call) me every day, but he hasn't called this week at all!
3. They _____ (live) in the same town as me, but they recently moved to the south of France.
4. She _____ (like) her job, but now that she has a new boss, she loves going to work.
5. I _____ (do) much exercise, but now I go jogging regularly.
6. I _____ (be) good with money, but these days it goes so quickly!

Refresh your memory

Past simple
Muhammad Yunnus founded Grameen Bank in 1977.
completed action

Past continuous
He was working at the University of Chittagong in the 1970s.
was/were + verb + ing
background situations

Past continuous vs. past simple
He was working at the university when he founded the bank.
during a background situation, a specific action happened

▶ Grammar reference page 124

Used to
Prof Yunnus used to teach at the University of Chittagong.
He didn't use to be a banker.
past habits or states, not true now

▶ Grammar reference page 125

4.3 Grammar

Internet research

Search for the keywords *drawbacks Grameen bank* and make a list of the advantages and disadvantages of the Grameen credit system.

Listening for detail

4 🔊 1:47 Listen to Amina explain how the Grameen Bank changed her life.

Match the beginning with the correct ending to make sentences about Amina.

1. Amina and her neighbours used to work for others,
2. She used to live below the poverty line,
3. Amina used to work for nothing,
4. Amina's daughters didn't use to go to school,
5. Women in Bangladesh used to have many children,
6. Amina and her neighbours used to pay all their earnings back to the money lenders,
7. Sufiya used to beg in the street,

a) now she is able to support her family.
b) now all her children go to school regularly.
c) now they run their own cooperative.
d) now she makes a small profit each month.
e) now they invest their profits back into their business and even save money at the bank.
f) now she sells toys and other small items.
g) now they believe that it's not necessary for their children to support them when they're old.

Speaking

5 With a partner, take it in turns to talk about something you used to do but don't do now, and, something you didn't use to do, but do now.

Writing

6 Write five sentences about yourself using the past simple and the past continuous.

Write about something you did during a certain period of your life. Write one false sentence and four true sentences.

Example: I met my boyfriend while I was studying in Berlin.
I was living with my parents when I bought my first car.

Read your sentences to your partner, can they guess which one is false?

Roleplay

TV&RADIO

THE TRAINEE

The eight week competition is almost over! There are now only two contestants left, six have left the competition and tonight is the final episode of this popular reality TV show. Last week the contestants had to present a business plan for a new pasta company in Italy and the week before they were selling coffee on the streets of London. Who will show the best business skills this week? What task will be set for them? Most importantly, who will win the contract with Tomas Flint, the leading entrepreneur?

7 Last night you were the winner of *The Trainee* and you won the prize of a £750,000 contract with the successful entrepreneur, Tomas Flint. Today all of the newspapers and magazines want to talk to you.

Student A is the winner of the reality show and Student B is a journalist from a national newspaper. Before you meet, prepare information so that you can talk about:

- what job you used to do before the show
- what you were doing before you took part in the show
- how you won a place on the show
- what the most difficult thing you had to do was
- what task you completed last night
- why you think you won the prize.

4 Success stories

4.4 Speaking   Appraisals

Listening for detail

1 🔊 **1:48** Galina is working as an intern in a large company in Hong Kong. Her six-month appraisal is next week, and she's reading through the preparation questions with her friend Suki. Listen and answer these questions.

1. What are Galina's strengths?
2. Does Suki agree or disagree?
3. What are Galina's weaknesses?
4. Does Suki agree or disagree?

Agreeing and disagreeing

2 Decide whether Galina and Suki used sentences 1–7 to agree or disagree. Write *A* (agree) or *D* (disagree) next to each.

1. Well no, not completely. ☐
2. That's right. You certainly are! ☐
3. I'm not sure. You probably are, but … ☐
4. Oh, definitely! ☐
5. Absolutely. You sure are! ☐
6. I can't agree with that. That's just not true. ☐
7. That sounds about right. ☐

3 Work with a partner. Answer the questions.

1. Which phrases can be used to strongly agree with somebody?
2. Which phrases can be used for mild agreement?
3. Which phrases can be used to strongly disagree with somebody?
4. Which phrases can be used for mild disagreement?

Disagreeing diplomatically

4 When you disagree in English, it's better to do so in a diplomatic way. Read the phrases below and circle the diplomatic (polite) ways to disagree.

> You're wrong.   I'm sorry, but I can't agree with you.   I agree with you up to a point …
> That's rubbish!   Absolutely not!   I don't really see it that way.   The problem is that …
> No way!   I'm afraid I don't completely agree with you.   Well, maybe, but I …
> Of course not!   What are you talking about?

50 *The* Business

DVD-ROM Interactive pronunciation practice on the DVD-ROM

4.4 Speaking

5 Use the table below to make dialogues using polite or diplomatic structures.

1	We should hire Tom. He has all the relevant qualifications.	→ I'm sorry but I can't quite agree with you.	a) think we need to tell a manager, it's only March!
2	The staff really need a new canteen, the one we have is too small and the food they serve is terrible.	→ I agree with you up to a point.	b) there is no money in this year's budget for that.
3	If they close this office it will give us all a fantastic opportunity to move with the company.	→ I don't really see it that way.	c) on all the points you mentioned.
4	I really think that we need to create a new position in our marketing team.	→ The problem is that	d) I think we'll all lose our jobs.
5	Have you read my email about the working conditions?	→ I'm afraid I don't completely agree with you	e) He is well-qualified but he has absolutely no experience.
6	Jane took the money from the company to pay for the Christmas party; we don't need to tell anyone we saw her doing it.	→ Well, maybe but I	f) The food isn't great but there are lots of shops nearby where staff can buy food for lunch.

With a partner, try to continue the dialogues.

Listening for detail

6 🎵 1:49 Listen to Galina talking to her manager. They are in the middle of her appraisal.

Which of these questions does the manager ask? Tick the ones you hear.

1. What do you consider to be your particular strengths? ☐
2. What elements of your job do you find most difficult? ☐
3. How do you get on with your colleagues? ☐
4. Do you agree? ☐
5. Do you have any weaknesses you'd like to work on? ☐
6. Are there any skills you would like to improve? ☐
7. What elements of your job do you most enjoy? ☐
8. What do you like and dislike about working for this company? ☐
9. How can we help you? ☐

7 Listen again. Which of the phrases in the box below does Galina use to reply to her manager?

I do think that I'm … ☐	I think I'm good at … ☐	My strengths are … ☐
People say that I'm … ☐	I'd say that I'm … ☐	The thing I hate most is … ☐
I would like to … ☐	My weaknesses are … ☐	My colleagues tell me that I'm … ☐
I often find that … ☐		

Roleplay

8 How would you answer the questions in 6 above? Make notes – they will help you to prepare for the roleplay.

Internet research
Search for the keywords *appraisal tips* to find out more about how to succeed in appraisals.

9 Work in pairs. Student A is the manager of the IT department, student B is one of the programmers. Student A turn to page 111, Student B turn to page 112.

'And your absenteeism is appalling!'

The **Business** 51

4 Success stories

4.5 Writing Profiles of business leaders

Reading for detail

1 Read the profile of Margarete Steiff, the inventor of the teddy bear, and put the events below in order.

- ☐ set up sewing workshop
- ☐ won first prize at the World Exhibition
- ☐ contracted polio
- ☐ went to school
- ☐ named a bear after a US president
- ☐ made a toy elephant

1 Biographical background

Margarete Steiff was born in 1847 in Giengen in southern Germany. Unfortunately, she contracted polio when she was a small child and as a result spent the rest of her life in a wheelchair. Although she had many operations on her legs, she never walked again. However, this didn't prevent her from having a successful business career.

2 Key moments in a career/nature of work

After leaving school, she set up a small sewing workshop in her family's home. Then, assisted by her brother she set up her own business and factory in 1877. Margarete always loved children, and so in 1880 she produced her first toy, an elephant. It was an instant commercial success. In 1902, her company produced the first 'teddy' bear with moving joints. At first, it was less popular than the elephant and sales were disappointing. However, eventually an American bought 3,000 bears at a trade fair in Leipzig. After the Steiff bear won the first prize at the World Exhibition in St Louis, everyone wanted a teddy bear. In 1904 Steiff introduced their trademark 'button in ear' and, in 1906 the teddy bear got its name: it was named after US president Theodore (Teddy) Roosevelt.

3 Charitable actions

Over the years, the Steiff Company have produced a number of limited edition charity bears. The proceeds from the sales of these bears go to support charities and good causes such as the fight against polio, and the World Wildlife Fund's (WWF) campaign to protect European brown bears.

4 Today

By 1907 1.7 million toy animals were being made a year. During her life Margarete's motto was 'Only the best is good enough for children.' Although Margarete died in 1909 at the age of 61, the Steiff Company is still going strong today. The Steiff club for teddy bear fans began in 1992 and currently has over 45,000 members. In addition to this there are Steiff galleries and teddy bear trade fairs across the world.

Linking words and phrases

2 The items in the box are useful for linking sections and putting events in order. Answer the questions below about them.

| then   currently   after (that)   furthermore   in the end |
| however   unfortunately   at the moment   in addition |

1 Which two items mean the same as *now*?
2 Which item means the same as *eventually*?
3 Which item is a more formal way of saying *but*?
4 Which two items are a more formal way of saying *also*?
5 Which two items tell you that something happened next?
6 Which item tells you that something bad happened next?

4.5 Writing

> **Internet research**
> Search for the keywords *"Pierre Omidyar blog"* to find out about his latest activities.

Structuring and ordering

3 Prepare to write a report about Pierre Omidyar, the founder of eBay, using the information below.

Read the sentences below. Mark the boxes *A*, *B*, *C* or *D* according to these subjects:

A Pierre's background and studies
B Key moments in career / nature of work
C Charitable actions
D The company today

1 _____ in 2005, Pierre gave $100 million to the university that he graduated from to launch the Omidyar-Tufts Microfinance Fund. ☐
2 _____ graduating from an American university in 1988 with a degree in computer science, he worked for Claris, a subsidiary of Apple Computer. ☐
3 _____ eBay is one of the most successful ecompanies in the world. ☐
4 _____ he was happy developing software for Claris, he left the company in 1991 and founded Ink Development Corp with three friends. ☐
5 _____, in 1998, eBay went public and _____, Pierre became a billionaire. ☐
6 _____ setting up eBay in 1995, Pierre ran an online company called Auction Shop. ☐
7 Pierre Omidyar was born in Paris in 1967, _____ his father, a doctor, moved the family to Maryland, USA while Pierre was still a child. ☐
8 _____, in 1996, Ink Development Corp, which included an internet shopping section, was sold to Microsoft. ☐

4 Write a report on Pierre Omidyar using the sentences. Put the sentences in order and into four separate paragraphs. Fill in the spaces with linking words. There may be more than one correct answer.

Writing a report

5 Use linking words and phrases to turn the notes below into a report about Zhang Yin, the world's richest self-made woman. Put the notes in the correct order.

a Shares in Nine Dragons Paper float – Hong Kong stock exchange - 2006 – keeps control of 72%
b 1976 – first job - accountant – later – move to Shenzhen – south China – paper trading company
c 1990 – move to Los Angeles – found American Chung Nam Company
d China's richest self-made person – world's richest self-made woman - 2006
e 1995 – return Hong Kong – Nine Dragons Paper set up – open first paper-making facility in Dongguan
f Today – more than 5,000 employees – company market value – 37.5 billion Yen – new huge facility close to Shanghai
g American Chung Nam successful – ship paper back – recycle in China – lots of demand - China – shortages of paper
h Born - Heilongjiang province – north east China – 1957 - eight children – eldest daughter
i Move to Hong Kong – 1985 – own paper trading company - successful - Hong Kong too small – Zhang Yin – too ambitious

The **Business** 53

4 Success stories

4.6 Case study — The English Academy

Discussion

1 Work with a partner. Think of the three most important factors of a language school from a student's point of view.

Scan reading

2 Read the text below about The English Academy in Saint-Jean-sur-Arc. Answer the questions.

1 Where in Saint-Jean-sur-Arc is The English Academy?
2 What two problems are there with computers in the school?
3 Which member of staff is not helpful?
4 Where is the new language school in Saint-Jean-sur-Arc?

Saint-Jean-sur-Arc is a large town in East Central France. It has a population of 300,000, of which 20,000 are students at the technical university. English is a compulsory element of all the courses the university offers and the demand for high quality language teaching is growing. For the last 15 years the university has sent students to a private language school called The English Academy. The school is in a very prestigious location, on one of the main streets in the centre of Saint-Jean-sur-Arc. At the moment however the classrooms and corridors look very old-fashioned and need to be repainted.

The academy has a large computer laboratory where students can surf the Internet and a big library where students can study, read newspapers and magazines and watch DVDs. The library is always full and it can be difficult to find a seat there. In addition many students complain that the Internet connection in the academy is too slow and that there are not enough computers.

In the past the English Academy was part of a franchise but a few years ago the owners decided to leave it and be independent. However, some of the teachers are reluctant to stop using the old, familiar teaching materials from the franchisor.

On the whole, the standard of teaching is very high. Most of the staff are well-qualified and their students often get good results. There are, however, some teachers who don't have the appropriate qualifications. Many students also find one of the receptionists rude and unhelpful.

Last year a new language school opened on an industrial estate on the outskirts of Saint-Jean-sur-Arc. This school doesn't have the reputation or the location of the English Academy but it offers cheaper courses. The technical university is considering using this new school because of the problems at the English Academy.

Reading for detail

3 Work with a partner. Read the text again. Make a list of the strengths and weaknesses of The English Academy.

Discussion

4 Work in small groups. Discuss what the owner of The English Academy can do to make sure the business continues to be successful.

Debate

5 Work in small groups. You think that rebranding and giving the school a new name will help the situation. You want to name the school after a great business leader. Some suggestions have already been made – see the profiles on the opposite page and the extra information on page 111. Choose one of them to name the school after and think of reasons why this person is the most appropriate.

Internet research

Search for more information about one of the business leaders by typing their name or their company's name into a search engine. Write a short report describing what they did and what their greatest achievements were.

Aristotle Onassis was born in 1906 in Smyrna, Turkey to a Greek family. His family moved as refugees to Greece in the early 1920s. From there, Aristotle moved to Argentina and worked in the family's tobacco business. In 1925 he became a joint Greek and Argentinean citizen and by 1932 he was a very successful businessman owning commercial ships, tankers and whalers. Moving from the sea to the sky, he founded Olympic Airways, the Greek national carrier, in 1957. He was married twice, firstly to married Athina Livanos, daughter of shipping magnate Stavros Livanos, and secondly to Jacquie Kennedy the widow of the murdered US president JFK. Aristotle Onassis died in 1975 at the age of 69.

Coco Chanel was born Gabrielle Bonheur Chanel in 1883 in Saumur, France. When she was six years old, her mother died and so Gabrielle grew up in an orphanage. While working as a café singer she changed her name to Coco. She opened her first shop in 1912 and was one of the first designers to introduce trousers for women. She is probably best known for her Chanel No. 5 perfume and as the creator of 'the little black dress'. She was always a hard-working woman and she was still working when she died in 1971.

Gianni Versace was born in 1946 in Calabria, Italy, and murdered outside his Miami Beach mansion in 1997. Versace spent many hours as a boy learning about making clothes in his mother's small tailor shop in southern Italy. He designed the first 'Versace' collection in 1972. From there he moved north and opened his first boutique in Milan in 1978. In 1995 he successfully expanded into the USA and his creations were worn and desired by the beautiful and famous all over the world. The year before his untimely death, the Versace Company's pre-tax profit was $112 million.

Lakshmi Mittal was born 1950 in India where he obtained a Bachelor of Commerce from St. Xavier's College, Kolkata. After leaving university he worked in his family's steel business in India. These days he is the Chairman and CEO of Mittal Steel Company. The company, which was founded in 1976, is now a global steel producer with operations in 14 countries. Mittal Steel's related activities include shipping, power generation and distribution, and mining. In 2004 Mittal Steel made profits of $22 billion. This made Lakshmi Mittal the world's third richest man and the wealthiest person in Britain, where he now lives. In 2004, he was named 'European Businessman of the year'.

Review 3

3 Operations

1 Fill in the missing letters using the clues below. The words all appeared in the text 'Toyota Production System' on page 33.

1. The amount of a product that people want is called the d_____ for the product. In business, the word is strongly associated with the opposite idea of 'supply' (the amount available).
2. Cars are mass-produced on an enormous s_____ (size, rate or level). This word is often used in the phrase 'the s… of the problem'.
3. A piece of equipment in a factory that does a particular job is called a m_____. We use the uncountable noun m_____ to refer to lots of these all together.
4. The term 'lean m_____' is used to describe a production system that uses less labour, less machinery, less space, less time and less waste.
5. A fault in the way that a product is made is called a d_____.
6. The just-in-time system makes stores or w_____s (large buildings for storing goods) unnecessary because parts are only ordered when they are needed.
7. Kaizen is the Japanese term for co_____ imp_____.
8. The results of the Toyota Production System are superior products, short l_____ t_____s (how long it takes to make something) and low costs.

2 Translate the answers you wrote in exercise 1 into your own language. Also translate these nouns from exercise 1: *supply, rate, level, waste*.

3 The phrase 'go up' can be replaced by *increase, rise* or *grow*. The phrase 'go down' can be replaced by *decrease, fall* or *shrink*. Write each of these words next to its closest definition below. Use a good English-English dictionary to help you.

1. move upwards to a higher position; increase in size, amount, quality or strength *rise*
2. become taller; increase in size, strength or importance _____
3. become larger in number or amount _____
4. go down to a lower level or amount; go quickly down onto the ground _____
5. become less _____
6. become smaller _____

4 Complete this short speech by a project manager with these words: *deadline, green light, milestone, phase, resources*.

"Okay, the planning ¹_____ of this project is now finished, and our managers have put in place all the ²_____ we need in terms of money and staff. The good news is, we've got the ³_____ to go ahead. As you all know, it's absolutely crucial that we finish the project by the ⁴_____ given, the end of June. To make sure that we do this I will be monitoring the progress of the project very carefully. I want to make sure that every ⁵_____ is reached successfully, and according to the timescale."

5 Each sentence below has two mistakes. The first is a mistake in the form of the present continuous. The second is a mistake in the form or spelling of an adverb. Correct both mistakes.

1. The production line is move quite slow today – I think there is a technical problem.
2. The advertising campaign has started and sales increasing steady.
3. I work very hardly at the moment - maybe we can meet in a week or so.
4. Yes, we're fine - everything going very good.
5. You are using this machine? It's quite complicated and you have to program it careful.

6 Complete this text by writing the correct form of the verb in brackets. Choose between present simple active (*it does*) and present simple passive (*it is done*).

I don't know why there's a problem with this machine. Every month it ¹_____ (service) by an engineer, although it's true that he ²_____ (not/send) directly by the firm who made the machine. I think he ³_____ (come) from our own technical department. Usually he ⁴_____ (spend) a full afternoon here, running checks and doing maintenance. He completes a checklist showing everything he has inspected. The list ⁵_____ (fill in) very carefully – it's a good system and I'm sure he ⁶_____ (not/miss) anything.

7 Fill in the missing letters in these phrases used in a presentation.

1. I'd like to s____ by giving you a short o_____w of today's presentation.
2. First _____, we're going to look at the sales f____s for the last two years.
3. After that, we'll look at how this has affected our s____ price.
4. M_____ to the next slide, you can see that …
5. Let's go ____ and look at the previous slide again.
6. I'd like to finish __ showing you how we aim to re___ this tar___.

8 Below you will see instructions for planning a stand at a convention. Fill in each gap with items from the box. Several answers may be possible, but one solution uses all the words in the best way.

| choose | decide | design | organize | set |
| to think about | you book | | | |

Firstly, _____ on the budget.
Secondly, _____ the size of the stand.
Then, _____ the stand (how it will look).
Make sure _____ your space with the organizers.
Don't forget _____ audio-visual equipment.
After that, _____ the logistics of the delivery.
Finally, _____ up the stand.

Review 4

4 Success stories

1 Make phrases by matching an item on the left with an item on the right. They appear in the article on page 45.

1 go
2 use sales
3 have a
4 look
5 put time
6 quality speaks
7 pioneer an
8 give
9 have belief
10 turn a company

a) hands-on approach
b) and effort into sth.
c) techniques
d) on sale
e) stylish
f) away free samples
g) into a global leader
h) in yourself
i) for itself
j) idea

2 Match a positive adjective on the left to its best negative on the right.

1 calm
2 generous
3 honest
4 hard-working
5 helpful
6 organized
7 ambitious
8 hands-on
9 cooperative

a dishonest
b disorganized
c unhelpful
d mean
e stressed
f hands-off
g lazy
h uncooperative
i lacking in drive

3 Fill in the missing letters to make adjectives. Afterwards check with the table on page 47.

1 Someone with a sense of adventure is adventu____.
2 Someone with a lot of ambition is ambit____.
3 Someone with a lot of dedication to their work is dedic____ to it.
4 Instead of saying 'the area of finance', we can say 'the finan____ area'.
5 Someone who shows flexibility has a flex____ approach.
6 Someone with a lot of luck is lu___.
7 This filing system has a good organization, it's well-organ____.
8 Someone who is a pioneer is pioneer___.
9 Someone who has a lot of success in their career is very success___.
10 A job with a lot of stress in it is a stress___ job.

4 In each sentence below put one verb into the past simple (*I worked*) and one into the past continuous (*I was working*).

1 I _____ (study) at university when I _____ (meet) my future husband.
2 I _____ (mention) the good news about your promotion while I _____ (chat) to my friends last night.

5 In each sentence below put two verbs into the past simple and two into the past continuous.

1 The flight was delayed and we _____ (have to) wait five hours at the airport. It _____ (be) awful. Some people _____ (try) to read, others _____ (sleep) on the floor.
2 I _____ (sit) at my desk and other people _____ (talk) by the water cooler. Suddenly, the fire alarm _____ (go off). At first, nobody _____ (know) what to do.

6 Complete each sentence below with one item from the left column and one from the right.

used to	do
didn't use to	don't

1 I _____ like seafood when I was young, but now I _____. It's delicious!
2 I _____ play a lot of tennis when I was at university. But I _____ any more.

7 Match the beginning with the end of each phrase to make phrases for disagreement.

1 No
2 I'm sorry but
3 I'm afraid I don't
4 Absolutely
5 I agree with you
6 I don't really see it
7 That's
8 I'm not

I can't agree with you.
completely agree with you.
not!
way!
just not true.
sure about that.
up to a point.
that way.

8 Most of the phrases in exercise 7 are polite or diplomatic. Find three that are strong and direct.

_____ _____ _____

9 Fill in the missing letters.

1 Your 'strong points' are your 'str___ths'.
2 Your 'weak points' are your 'weak____es'.

10 Match an item on the left with an item on the right.

but
currently
in addition
eventually
then

furthermore
after that
at the moment
however
in the end

11 Use an item from the right-hand column in exercise 10 to complete each sentence about Manuela. There may be several possibilities, but one solution uses each word once in the best way.

1 Manuela studied marketing at university and left in 2002. _____, she did part-time jobs for a year or two.
2 Tired of working part-time, she applied for dozens of full-time jobs. She was rejected many times. But, _____, she found something that she really liked.
3 She did that job for three years. She enjoyed it and learned a lot. _____, her luck changed and the company went bankrupt. Manuela was out of work again.
4 She decided to move from the marketing area to the sales area. There were several advantages. It was easier to find jobs – people in the sales area change jobs often. _____, it suited her personality – she was friendly and confident.
5 She still works in the sales field today. _____ she is working for a consumer goods company, and visits big stores to persuade the manager to stock more of their products. Manuela is hoping to be promoted to Regional Sales Director in the next few years.

5 Selling

5.1 About business Advertising

Discussion

1 In small groups, discuss these questions.

1 Can a product be successful without advertising?
2 What are the qualities of a good advertisement?
3 Describe an advertisement that you really like. Do the others agree?

Listening for gist

2 2:01 Listen to Tony Barkston, a college lecturer, giving a lecture to first year business students on advertising, and answer the questions.

1 Why is advertising necessary?
2 What model of advertising is the lecture about?
3 Explain what a USP is in your own words.

Listening for detail

3 Listen again and mark the sentences *T* (true) or *F* (false).

1 This is the first time Tony Barkston has talked about advertising. ☐
2 AIDA stands for attention, idea, desire, action. ☐
3 The most important part of the AIDA model is that people buy the products. ☐
4 There are a lot of good-quality products on the market. ☐
5 Products need to appear different so that consumers can recognise them. ☐
6 A USP tells consumers that a product is really different. ☐
7 A good proposition can make customers change brand. ☐

Discussion

4 How many different forms of advertising can you think of? Which forms are most effective? Why?

Scan reading

5 Scan the article about body advertising to find answers to the questions.

1 How many advertisements does the average person see in a day?
2 How much was the winning bid for when a forehead was auctioned on eBay?
3 Which type of sportsperson could be used effectively for body advertising?
4 Name three companies who have made successful use of body advertising.

Reading for detail

6 Read the article again and answer the questions.

1 Who profits from body advertising?
2 Which parts of the body are the most effective for body advertising?
3 What is one disadvantage of using sports people for body advertising?
4 Why is TV advertising not as effective as it was in the past?
5 Why might some people not like this form of advertising?
6 How did Dunkin' Donuts and Toyota use body advertising?

Collocations

7 Match a verb on the left with a noun on the right to form a collocation from the article.

1 advertise   a) a bid on eBay
2 lease   b) money
3 receive   c) products
4 earn   d) attention
5 lose   e) a body part
6 target   f) effectiveness
7 attract   g) an audience

58 *The* Business

5.1 About business

ADVERTISING SPACE

The average person not only sees over 500 advertisements every day, but is also a walking billboard for his or her favourite brands simply by wearing their clothes, carrying their handbags or driving their cars. But these people are not getting paid for this free advertising.

The idea of selling body space to advertise products is a growing trend which benefits both the wearer and the company. Potential body advertisers just choose which body part they want to lease and which company they want to advertise. They then get a temporary tattoo which they agree to wear for a certain amount of time. Foreheads and bald heads are very effective because you can always see them, even in bad weather.

The body advertising idea became popular when Andrew Fischer auctioned his forehead on eBay and received a bid of $37,378 for wearing a company logo. There are now many websites on the Internet where you can buy and sell body space.

Athletes and sports people have always earned a lot of money by wearing branded sports clothes. Now they can earn even more with body advertising. Boxers in particular offer a good wide space for advertising on their backs. The advantage of tattoo advertising is that the company name or logo is in full view all through the match and not limited to a 30 second commercial which viewers may switch off anyway. A disadvantage is that when athletes really begin to sweat, the tattoo starts to run.

In a world where people are experiencing advertising fatigue, the real challenge for marketing is to get people's attention. There are basically too many people selling too many things, and many of these things we don't really need. We see advertisements everywhere and so traditional forms of advertising are losing their effectiveness.

Innovative marketing methods such as human billboards are becoming increasingly attractive because of low cost and the ability to target your audience better. Companies now send tattoo-covered human billboards to sporting events, music festivals, beaches or popular tourist resorts to advertise their products.

Of course, some consumers may not find this type of advertising very tasteful or they might not find the body parts on show very attractive. It is also not possible in all parts of the world where there is no tradition of tattoos or showing so much skin in public is taboo.

Well-known big brands such as Toyota, Vodaphone and Dunkin' Donuts have used this method: college kids agreed to stick Dunkin' Donuts logos on their foreheads during an NCAA basketball tournament; Toyota used body art to start a word of mouth campaign for the Scion car.

Body advertising shows that it is not necessary to spend large amounts of money to fulfil advertising's prime goal, which is to attract attention and get people interested enough to buy the products.

tattoo-covered **human billboards**

Brainstorming and presentation

8 In small groups, hold a brainstorming meeting to think of an advertising campaign for a new perfume. Look at your target group below. What name do you think would attract this group? What sort of bottle and packaging would appeal to this group? And finally, think about the advertising medium. How do you want to get your target group's attention?

Group A
Your target group is men who are over 40. You are aiming your product at professional men and so they will have a good income. Think about what men in this group would be interested in and what would encourage them to buy your product.

Group B
Your target group is women who are between 50 and 60. Think about what women in this group would find appealing and what image might help your product sell.

Group C
Your target group is young people who are between 18 and 25. Your group has a limited income as most of them will be students. Think about what image people in this group would be interested in and what they would find appealing.

Present your ideas to another group, and give feedback on the ideas.

Internet research
Search for the keywords *advertising tattoo*. Find out what the rates are for different body parts.

5 Selling

5.2 Vocabulary Buying and selling

Discussion

1 Work with a partner. Decide which three of these characteristics are the most important for a good salesperson, and which are the least important. Can you add another characteristic?

- really listens to the customer / interested
- smiles all the time / friendly
- knows a lot about their products / knowledgeable
- has a smart appearance / presentable
- you feel you can trust him/her / trustworthy
- can explain the USP of the product / competent
- gives the customer time to think / patient
- good at making the customer believe in the product / persuasive
- makes small talk / chatty

2 Work with a partner and make a list of adjectives to describe a bad salesperson.

3 Work with a partner. Write a list of questions you would expect a salesperson to ask a potential customer who wants to buy a car. For example:

Do you want a used car?
How much do you want to pay?

DVD-ROM Further interactive vocabulary practice on the DVD-ROM

5.2 Vocabulary

Internet research

Search for the keywords *customer satisfaction* to find more customer collocations. Make a note of three that you think are useful to learn.

Listening for detail

4 2:02, 2:03 Listen to two different salesmen trying to sell a car to Mr Hunt and his daughter. How many of your questions were asked in the conversations? Listen again and make a note of the questions that were asked.

5 Which talk is more effective? Why?

Buying and selling

6 Listen to the conversation again and note expressions which mean:
1 it doesn't cost much to keep the car on the road.
2 prices as low as the rivals'.
3 no extra charge for borrowed money.
4 worth the price.
5 a reduction in the price.
6 current price of something.

7 Match the customers' comments on the left with the appropriate response on the right.

1 It's quite pricey.
2 I'm not sure.
3 It looks very complicated to use.
4 Is this the only model you have?
5 I saw the same model at a cheaper price in town.
6 I don't really need it.

a) I'm sure we can match that price.
b) Of course not. But you'll enjoy having it.
c) But it's a good investment for the future.
d) Take as much time as you need to think about it.
e) Let me show you how to use it.
f) No, we have the complete model range.

Role play

8 Work in pairs, Student A is a salesperson, Student B is a buyer who wants to buy a new laptop. Student A look at page 112, Student B look at page 113.

Customer collocations

9 Match the customer collocations on the left to the correct definition on the right.

1 customer incentive
2 customer satisfaction
3 customer retention
4 customer profile
5 customer loyalty

a) Description of a typical customer for this product.
b) Something which encourages a customer to buy something.
c) When many customers are happy with the product.
d) When the customer keeps buying the same product.
e) When the company tries to keep the existing customers.

Discussion

10 Work in small groups. Think of the different methods of shopping, for example online or at a market. Make a list of the advantages and disadvantages for customers of one of the methods.

The **Business** 61

5 Selling

Refresh your memory

Comparatives
Our company is smaller than theirs.
Add *–er* + *than* to adjectives with one syllable

This test is easier than the last one.
Replace *–y* with *–ier* + *than* with adjectives ending in *–y*

Superlatives
They are the smallest company on the market.
Add *the* + *-est* to adjectives with one syllable

The easiest thing to do is call the IT department.
Add *the* + *-iest* to adjectives ending with *–y*

This model is the most / least reliable on the market.
Add *the* + *most / least* to longer adjectives

There are some exceptions
good   better   the best
bad   worse   the worst
far   further the furthest

▶ Grammar reference page 126

Asking questions
Yes/no questions
Do you work in Japan?
auxiliary verb + subject + main verb

Wh- questions
Where do you work?
question word + auxiliary verb + subject + main verb
except if *who*, *what* or *which* is the subject
Who told you?
And with the verb *to be*
Where is she?

▶ Grammar reference page 127

5.3 Grammar   Comparatives, superlatives and asking questions

Test yourself: Comparatives

1 Complete the sentences by putting in the correct form of the adjectives.

1 I can assure you that this car is _____ (reliable) than your present model. You won't have a breakdown with this car.
2 This handbag is not only _____ (cheap), but _____ (attractive) than the high-priced designer versions.
3 I think you'll find that this mobile is _____ (easy) to use than the last model.
4 I can't make a _____ (reasonable) offer than that.
5 Digital cameras are _____ (simple) to operate now than a few years ago.
6 The life of this battery is _____ (long) than most of its rivals at almost half the price.
7 You'll really like these crisps. They are _____ (crunchy) and _____ (tasty) than any others on the market.
8 This no-name washing powder is _____ (good) and _____ (effective) than the branded goods.
9 I would recommend this jacket. It's _____ (stylish) than the other one and it really suits you.
10 I can't recommend this DVD player. Its test results were _____ (bad) than the others.

Test yourself: Superlatives

2 Complete these sentences by putting in the correct form of the adjectives.

1 As one of _____ (good) customers we have, I can offer you a special price.
2 This is _____ (popular) model in the store. We only have a few left so buy one now.
3 I'm sure this is _____ (comfortable) sofa you've ever sat on.
4 This watch is one of _____ (accurate) on the market.
5 We use only _____ (fresh) and _____ (high) quality ingredients for our sandwiches.
6 This is _____ (sophisticated) camera around at the moment.
7 Our mineral water is _____ (pure) on the market.
8 This is _____ (low) price I can offer.
9 That is _____ (silly) suggestion I've heard.
10 This TV gives you _____ (sharp) picture. It's worth the extra money.

Test yourself: Asking questions

3 Make questions for the answers.

1 A: *How much* _____?
   B: The laptop costs €999.
2 A: *What time* _____?
   B: The bank closes at 4pm.
3 A: *Who* _____?
   B: Frank Rider is our most successful salesperson.
4 A: *Why* _____?
   B: I use telebanking because it's so practical.
5 A: *What* _____?
   B: I think the service is very good.
6 A: *Where* _____?
   B: Women's clothing is on the first floor, Madam.
7 A: *How often* _____?
   B: I buy a new car every three or four years.
8 A: *Do* _____?
   B: Yes, I always buy the same brand.

Making comparisons

4 Read the product descriptions of GPS systems and answer the questions.

1 NewTech GPS Mapping System. This wallet-sized portable navigator has a 3.5 inch display screen and calculates your route in less than one second! State-of-the art voice recognition technology means there's no need to take your hands off the steering wheel to touch screens or press buttons. Our USP is a range of celebrity voices as a downloadable option. Includes maps of Europe, USA and Canada on the 20 GB hard disc. Bluetooth connection to mobile. $530 with a two-year guarantee.

2 GPS Route Finder. The 4 inch touch screen has full 3D colour maps. With a choice of fifteen languages to guide you through the main roads of Europe, calculating your destination in 1.5 seconds. Our special feature is speed camera detection technology so you never get another speeding ticket. Included is an integrated multi-media city guide of 28 major European cities. Total cost $499.

3 GPS Easy Navigator. Our beautifully designed hand-held receiver with a 3.8 inch screen can be operated with only three buttons. Getting around Western Europe with up-to-date maps is easy and quick, locking on to satellites to offer you turn-by-turn directions in two to three seconds. Our speciality for stressed drivers is one-touch nearest petrol and parking functions. The waterproof system comes complete with Bluetooth headsets which can be easily integrated into helmets. An unbeatable $660.

1 Which GPS navigator is the most expensive?
2 Which screen is the smallest?
3 Which system calculates your route the quickest?
4 Which system offers the fewest destinations?
5 Which system offers the most realistic pictures?
6 Which system is the most convenient for the driver to use?
7 Which system is most suited to motorbike riders?
8 Which system do you think is the best value for money?

Discussion

5 Work with a partner. Which USP (Unique Selling Proposition) or special function of the GPS systems is the most interesting for business people? Why?

Asking and answering questions

6 2:04 Esengul Badem is conducting a customer satisfaction survey outside a supermarket. Listen and answer the questions.

1 Why does the shopper use this supermarket?
2 Does the woman go shopping on her own?
3 Is she satisfied with the selection of goods?
4 Does she think the store is tidy enough?
5 Does she go shopping at any other supermarkets?
6 What does she like the most?

7 Now listen again and write the questions for the answers.

1 At least once a week.
2 Terrible! You have to walk so far to put your trolley back.
3 Yes, no problem.
4 Around €200.
5 I like to go quite early in the morning, as soon as the kids leave for school.
6 There isn't a good selection of wine. I always buy my wine somewhere else.

Discussion

8 Work with a partner. Think of something expensive you bought recently, e.g. a computer, a mobile phone, a bike. Ask each other questions. Use the ideas below.

Why he / she bought it.
Where he / she bought it.
How often he / she uses it.

How much it cost.
The best thing about it.
One thing he / she doesn't like about it.

Internet research

Search for the keywords *customer satisfaction survey*. What sorts of surveys are carried out?

5 Selling

5.4 Speaking   Negotiating

Discussion

1 Work with a partner. Look at the pictures of negotiations. What are the people negotiating about?

2 Complete the questionnaire from a business magazine about negotiating. Mark the statements *T* (true), *F* (false) or *D* (it depends). Compare your answers with a partner.

Questionnaire

1. There is always a winner and a loser in a negotiation.
2. You have to give something to get something.
3. You need an agenda.
4. Making small talk is necessary.
5. You need to prepare as much as possible.
6. You can promise anything.
7. Negotiations are the same all over the world.
8. It's a good idea to sum up agreements regularly.

Listening for gist

3 2:05–2:07 Listen to three negotiations taking place. Where are the people and what is being negotiated?

Listening for detail

4 Listen again and decide which negotiation is win-win, which is lose-lose and which is win-lose.

Internet research

Search for the keywords *win-win negotiation*. What are the principles behind it?

5 Match 1-6 with their replies a)-f). There may be several answers, but try to remember the ones from the dialogues.

1 Can't you compromise this time?
2 Can you go along with that?
3 That's my bottom line.
4 Is that your best offer?
5 Can we talk about the price again?
6 Take it or leave it.

a) I have no choice.
b) That makes two of us.
c) I can meet you half way.
d) I think it's a fair price.
e) No, I don't want to discuss this.
f) That's out of the question.

6 Listen to the three negotiations again and complete the useful expressions in the table.

1	Making proposals	What _____ Majorca? I'd like to suggest something…
2	Bargaining	I'll go to Majorca for a week _____ we go to the Alps for a week. I would only pay that price on condition that … I'll pay the 20,000 _____ _____ _____ she stays longer.
3	Accepting	_____! Let's draw up the contract. OK. It's a deal.
4	Rejecting	No way! You can't be serious. That's out _____ the _____.
5	Making concessions	I can meet you _____ _____. You have a point there.
6	Asking for agreement	Can you go _____ _____ that?
7	Clarifying	If I understand you correctly … So what you're _____ is …

Roleplay

7 With a partner, use the chart to roleplay the following negotiations.

1 The marketing company that you work for needs to save money because your competitors have increased their market share. You are going to discuss saving money through reducing catering costs.
2 The offices where you work are going to be painted. They were last painted ten years ago. You are going to discuss what colour the offices should be painted.
3 The engineering company that you work for is thinking of sponsoring a local group in order to raise consumer awareness in the area. You are going to discuss which local group to sponsor.

Student A turn to page 112.
Student B turn to page 113.

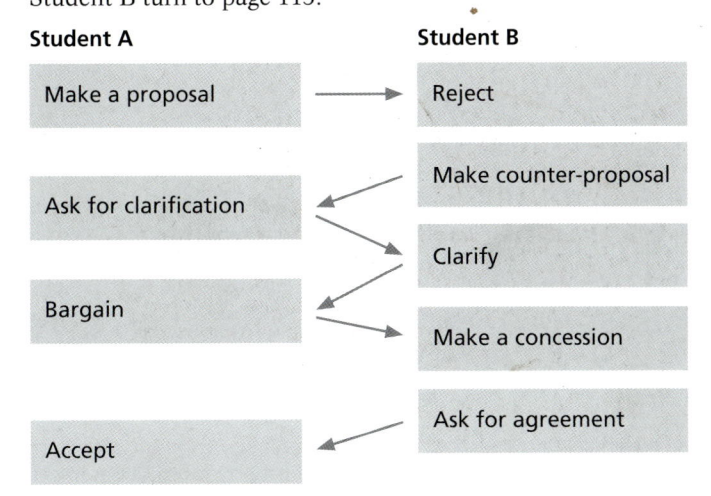

Student A → **Student B**

Make a proposal → Reject

Ask for clarification ← Make counter-proposal

← Clarify

Bargain →

← Make a concession

← Ask for agreement

Accept

5 Selling

5.5 Writing Negotiating by email

Discussion

1 In small groups discuss the questions about emails.

1 How *correct* should emails be? Is it OK to make grammar and spelling mistakes?
2 What is *email etiquette*? What are your standards? Think about emoticons, subject lines, capital letters, openings and closings.

Skim reading

2 Read the six extracts from emails below and answer the questions.

1 Which email is asking for more information? ☐
2 Which email is making a quotation? ☐
3 Which email is asking for better terms? ☐
4 Which email is accepting terms? ☐
5 Which email is refusing terms? ☐
6 Which email is placing an order? ☐

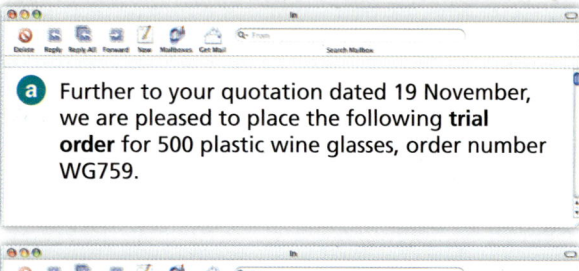

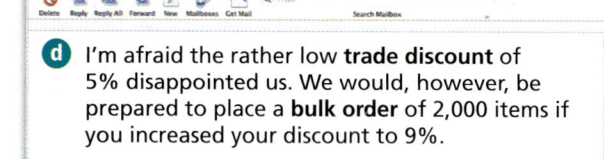

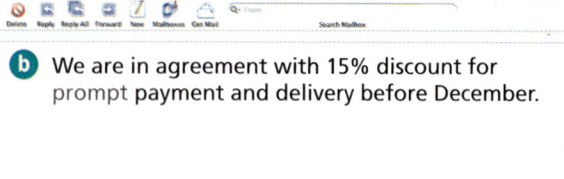

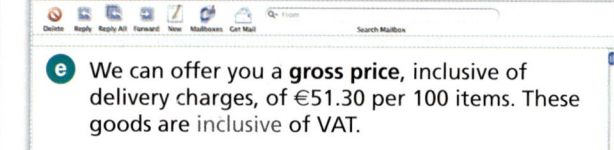

a Further to your quotation dated 19 November, we are pleased to place the following **trial order** for 500 plastic wine glasses, order number WG759.

b We are in agreement with 15% discount for **prompt** payment and delivery before December.

c We would be most interested in receiving your latest catalogue and price list, quoting your most competitive prices. Please let us know what trade discount you offer and what your **delivery lead times** are.

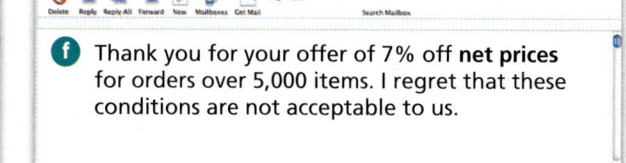

d I'm afraid the rather low **trade discount** of 5% disappointed us. We would, however, be prepared to place a **bulk order** of 2,000 items if you increased your discount to 9%.

e We can offer you a **gross price**, inclusive of delivery charges, of €51.30 per 100 items. These goods are inclusive of VAT.

f Thank you for your offer of 7% off **net prices** for orders over 5,000 items. I regret that these conditions are not acceptable to us.

5.5 Writing

Internet research

Search for the keywords *email etiquette* to find out more about this. Do you agree with the points?

Scan reading

3 Complete the sentences with the expressions in **bold** from the emails in 2.

1 The _____ is how long it takes for the goods to arrive after ordering.
2 The _____ is the total price of something without any deductions.
3 A _____ is a reduction of the selling price of a product when a manufacturer sells to a retailer.
4 A _____ is to try out products and services to see if they are satisfactory.
5 The _____ is the amount that is left after all deductions have been made.
6 A _____ is when you ask for a large number of items to be delivered at the same time.

Negotiating language

4 Match the beginning with the correct ending.

1 Further to your call,
2 I hope everything goes
3 With reference to discounts,
4 Our terms of payment are
5 Please get back to me
6 Please find attached the agenda of the meeting
7 We have submitted a
8 Transport costs are
9 We can guarantee delivery of
10 Please confirm

a) our terms are 8% discount for orders over 80,000.
b) if you need any further information.
c) according to plan.
d) I'd like to confirm the following points.
e) 3% discount for payment within 30 days.
f) that you have received this email.
g) 10,000 parts per month.
h) firm offer of €100 per item.
i) as requested.
j) free within Europe.

Placing orders

5 Complete the email from Hugh Bradshaw to Ms Noonan using the words in the box.

reply   delivery   discount   place   payment   supply   trade price

Dear Ms Noonan,

Following our telephone conversation last week, I would like to (1) _____ an order for 500 English ABC dictionaries. Your catalogue gives the (2) _____ of the ABC dictionary as €14, can you confirm that this is still the price?

Also can you send details of the terms of (3) _____ that you can offer for (4) _____ within 30 days on an order of this size?

Please note that we need (5) _____ of the dictionaries before the end of this month. We would be grateful if you could (6) _____ the items as soon as possible.

I look forward to receiving your (7) _____.

Yours sincerely,

Hugh Bradshaw.

Writing

6 Write Ms Noonan's reply. Use the information below.

- You only have 300 dictionaries in stock at the moment. Delivery of the other 200 would be in one month.
- The catalogue is out-of-date The current price is €16.
- You can offer a 7% discount for payment within seven days.

5 Selling

5.6 Case study Coolhunters

Discussion

1 In small groups discuss the questions.
1 What's trendy at the moment? Think about fashion, technology, music and cars.
2 How do you find out about new, trendy products?

Listening for detail

2 🔊 2:08 Listen to Gabriella Cortez, the managing director of the company Coolhunters talking about a new type of trendspotter. Answer the questions below.

1 What problem do marketers have today?
2 What kind of products do young people today want?
3 How do Gabriella's trendspotters find new trends?
4 What did many coolhunters list on their websites in the beginning?
5 How long does a coolhunter have to tell people about a new product?
6 What does a trendspotter do when a product becomes popular?

3 🔊 2:09 Listen to the second half of the interview with Gabriella about the adoption process and complete the pie chart with the percentages.

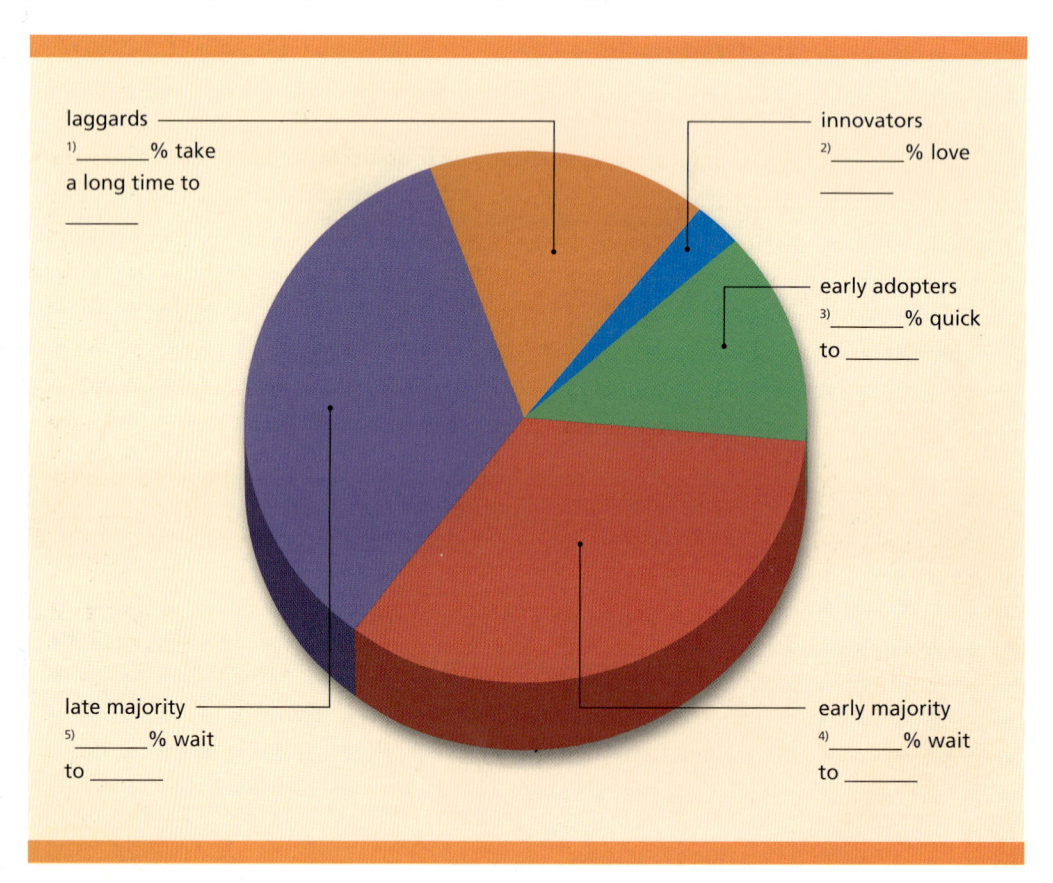

laggards
1) _____ % take a long time to _____

innovators
2) _____ % love _____

early adopters
3) _____ % quick to _____

late majority
5) _____ % wait to _____

early majority
4) _____ % wait to _____

4 Listen to the second half of the interview again and complete the notes about each group.

DVD-ROM Further interactive problem-solving on the DVD-ROM

5.6 Case study

Market segmentation

5 Marketers need market segmentation to identify the needs and wants of consumers. There are many ways of doing this: age, social class, family size, family lifecycle, and so on.

With a partner, match a name of a consumer group with a description and the correct picture.

a) full-nesters
b) DINKS (Double income, no kids)
c) bachelor
d) empty-nesters

1 This group has a very high disposable income. They are over fifty and their children have left home leaving them free to spend their money on expensive holidays and high-quality products. They have worked hard all their lives and want to pamper and enjoy themselves.
2 The young, single person with no family commitments. This group has a relatively high disposable income and they want to spend as much as possible on themselves and trying out new, innovative products.
3 This group has a high disposable income and no children and tends to mix with other couples in the same situation. They do a lot of entertaining and status symbols are very important.
4 These are couples with children. As growing children are expensive, they need to be careful with their money and they tend to have a low disposable income.

6 In small groups look at the extracts from a holiday brochure. Decide which holiday fits each consumer group.

1 Enjoy a luxurious wellness-week at the Hotel and Spa Quellenhof in the heart of Bavaria. You can relax and pamper yourself in one of our five thermal pools, sauna and Turkish bath. Our five-star restaurant offers an international cuisine. Our hotel is set among majestic mountains ideal for walking and wandering.

2 Come to EuroParc for the holiday of a lifetime! Fun for you and your children, whatever the weather outside! Ask for our latest brochure with all-inclusive rates which mean no nasty surprises when you come to pay your bill!

3 Our five-star hotels are located at top addresses all over the world. We cater for professional people with excellent taste who want to enjoy their holiday with other professional people and not with families.

4 Want to enjoy and try out an exciting range of sports with top equipment and facilities? Do you live alone, but don't want to holiday alone? Then come to exclusive Only Me Holiday Clubs and meet new, interesting young people who want to meet you.

Brainstorming and presentation

7 Work in small groups. You are going to launch a new car for one of the market groups.
- Choose one of the groups to market to.
- Brainstorm a list of features which you think are useful or necessary for your market group and add some of these to your product.

Now present your ideas to another group, and give feedback on the other groups' ideas.

Internet research

Search for the keywords *market segmentation*. Make a list of the different ways you can segment a market and some of the variables that are used.

The **Business**

6 The organization

6.1 About business — Entrepreneurs

Discussion

> 'An entrepreneur is someone who has a good idea and sees a chance to start a business with it.'
>
> **PAVARTI PATEL, START-UP CONSULTANT**

1 Work with a partner. Decide which qualities are most important for an entrepreneur to possess (1 = most important, 8 = least important).

Diplomatic ☐
Optimistic ☐
Calm ☐
Energetic ☐
Organized ☐
Willing to take a risk ☐
Determined ☐
Creative ☐

Listening for gist

2 2:10 Listen to Robin Hurd interviewing Ms Patel, a start-up consultant, about being an entrepreneur and answer the questions.

1. Can anyone be an entrepreneur?
2. What stops most people from being an entrepreneur?
3. Which countries have a lot of entrepreneurs?

Listening for detail

3 Listen to the interview with Ms Patel again and answer the questions.

Why does Ms Patel say these things are important when setting up your own business?

1. Energy
2. A social security system
3. A legal system

Scan reading

4 Scan the article about the German businesswoman Ingrid Roth to find answers to the questions.

1. What type of service does Ingrid offer?
2. Why did she set up a Ltd company?
3. Does Ingrid spend a lot of time in England because of her company?
4. How is it possible to set up a Ltd company in Germany?

Vocabulary

5 In each set of four, match an expression from the article on the left to the correct definition on the right.

1. gap in the market
2. minimum equity
3. red tape
4. modest fee

a) documents or processes that cause delays
b) a small amount of money as payment for a service
c) the lowest amount of capital allowed to start up a company
d) this product or service doesn't exist, but there is a need for it

5. Memorandum of Association
6. annual accounts
7. headquarters
8. limited liability

e) the central office of a company
f) if the company has debts, you only lose the amount of money you invested
g) a document detailing who owns the company, how much capital is invested and where it is based
h) yearly record of the trading results of your company

Internet research

Search for the key words *start up company* and find out what services are on offer to help people start up their own company.

Discussion

6 In small groups discuss the questions.

1. What could Ingrid do to expand her business?
2. Is Ingrid Roth an entrepreneur? Give reasons for your answer.

UNLIMITED LTDS IN GERMANY

INGRID ROTH was unemployed and single when she offered to organize her sister's Christmas celebrations. Her sister, Karen Regensberger happily accepted because she was married with two children and a full-time, very stressful job. Ingrid bought and wrapped all the presents, bought and cooked all the food and decorated the house. And she offered a complete service – she cleaned and tidied everything after the event. It was such a success that friends of the family wanted the same service – and not only for Christmas, for all sorts of celebrations.

Suddenly Ingrid had more work than she could cope with. There was a real gap in the market – people were too busy to organize their own festivities! She decided to set up her own company, but instead of choosing a GmbH (Gesellschaft mit beschränkter Haftung), the German legal model, she chose to register her company in England as Celebrations Ltd.

Ingrid said, 'I decided to set up a limited company and not a GmbH because it's quick, simple and cheap.' The British title Ltd is also well-known internationally just in case Ingrid would like to expand her business in the future.

Ingrid is part of a growing trend of small business owners who choose Ltds. The main advantage is that the minimum equity required is one pound, compared with a minimum of £25,000 for a GmbH. A Ltd company can be registered within 24 hours whereas a GmbH can take months and involve a lot of red tape. It is also much easier to change the company structure, such as having a new director. With a GmbH you would need to pay legal fees to change anything. Another advantage is that you don't have to do the paperwork yourself. You can pay a consultant a modest fee of £500 to register your company at Companies House, Britain's business registry office. Various documents are required, for example a Memorandum of Association which gives the details of the company. For a further £250 a year, your consultant will submit your annual accounts. Ingrid does all her business via the Internet and email. She has never been to her company's headquarters in Birmingham or met her consultant face-to-face.

Ltd companies have been growing in Germany since 2002 when the European Court of Justice allowed the use of business legal forms between countries in the European Union. There are now more than 30,000 German Ltds, these are mostly small retail or service companies like Ingrid's. One reason for this is that they are not risky and the owners' liability is only limited to the amount they invested. This means if the company runs into trouble and has debts, the owners don't lose everything.

Ingrid is not worried about going out of business; she now employs four people and works more than 12 hours a day. But, if anything happened to her company, she could start a new one within 24 hours.

> **If the company runs into trouble... the owners don't lose everything**

Discussion

7 Work with a partner. You are entrepreneurs and you have decided to start a business providing a service for young professionals who lead busy lives. Decide together where you think there is a big enough gap in the market and think about what busy people don't have time to do. Decide what kind of service you are going to provide, where your headquarters will be and how you will make sure that your business is a success. Present your ideas to the class.

6 The organization

6.2 Vocabulary Types of companies

Discussion

1 With a partner, complete the quiz about companies.

Successful companies:

		true	false	it depends
1	have to make big profits.	☐	☐	☐
2	share profits with their employees.	☐	☐	☐
3	continuously expand and diversify.	☐	☐	☐
4	offer good quality products to consumers.	☐	☐	☐
5	take over other companies.	☐	☐	☐
6	have the biggest market share.	☐	☐	☐
7	look after the environment and don't pollute it.	☐	☐	☐
8	have mission statements.	☐	☐	☐

Reading and vocabulary

2 Read and complete the company descriptions below using the words in the boxes.

1 _____

| capital | liability | accountants | share |

This is for between two and 20 people, and very often it is a group of doctors or (1) _____ who set up this type of business. Each person has an equal (2) _____ in making decisions and in whatever profit is made. The more people you have, the more (3) _____ you can put into the business. However, you are legally responsible for the other people in the business, and you all have unlimited (4) _____. So if one of you makes a mistake, you all have to pay for it.

2 _____

| investment | agreement | accounts | shareholders |

This type of company is owned by a small group of individuals, the (5) _____, who are very often the members of one family. You can only sell your shares if the owners are in (6) _____. You have limited liability so you only lose your (7) _____ if the company runs into trouble. You have a lot of paperwork to do as you have to publish your (8) _____ every year.

3 _____

| capital | fall | shares | Meeting | shareholder |

Anyone can buy (9) _____ in this company. This is a good type of company if you need to raise (10) _____ in order to to expand and diversify. You have limited liability but you can still lose money if there is a (11) _____ in the price of your shares. You have little control in the running of the company unless you are a major (12) _____ or enough other shareholders vote the same as you at the Annual General (13) _____ of shareholders.

4 _____

| debts | trading | profit | boss |

This is the easiest type of business to start. You simply need a good idea and enough money to start (14) _____. You can organize your work as you want because you are your own (15) _____, and if you make a (16) _____, you keep it for yourself. On the other hand, you have to work long hours and you have limited liability. That means if you run up (17) _____ you alone have to pay for them.

3 Read the texts again and write each company type below at the top of the correct paragraph.

Sole trader
Private limited company (Ltd)
Partnership
Public limited company (PLC)

Collocations

4 In each set of four, match a verb on the left to a word on the right to form an expression from the texts.

1 start	a) money	5 run up	e) capital
2 make	b) a company	6 publish	f) shares
3 invest	c) trading	7 buy	g) accounts
4 set up	d) a profit	8 raise	h) debts

5 With a partner mark the sentences are *T* (true) or *F* (false). You may need to read the texts above again.

1 A PLC is unlikely to have a hierarchy. ☐
2 If you are a sole trader and you go bankrupt, you may have to sell your possessions to pay your debts. ☐
3 If a sole trader becomes a partnership you have more capital to invest in the company. ☐
4 If you go bankrupt, it is better to be in a Ltd company. ☐
5 In a private limited company, shareholders can buy or sell shares as they wish. ☐
6 It is easier for a PLC to raise capital. ☐
7 You cannot lose money if you buy shares in a PLC. ☐

Discussion

6 A shareholder (AE stockholder) is someone who has shares in a company. This is different to a *stakeholder*. A stakeholder is anyone who is affected by the success or failure of a company, for example a supplier.

With a partner, label the diagram with all the different stakeholders you can think of for a pharmaceutical company.

multi-national oil company: shareholders, environmental activists, distributors, car drivers and people who live near the oil plant, suppliers, employees

pharmaceutical company:

Listening for gist

7 2:11–2:16 Listen to six different stakeholders and identify who they are, using the words in the box.

| shareholder | supplier | employee | environmental activist | customer | politician |

1 _____   4 _____
2 _____   5 _____
3 _____   6 _____

Internet research
Search for a well-known company and make a presentation about it to the group.

6 The organization

Refresh your memory

Reported speech

is → *was*
'The company is very successful.'
She said that the company was very successful.

does → *did*
'I work for an international company.'
He said that he worked for an international company.

is doing → *was doing*
'We are building a new plant.'
She said that they were building a new plant.

did → *had done*
'I joined the company three years ago.'
He said that he had joined the company three years ago.

will → *would*
'I will stay for another year.'
He added that he would stay for another year.

has done → *had done*
'The company has expanded.'
She mentioned that the company had expanded.

should and *shouldn't*
advice or recommendations
'Be punctual!'
She said that I should be punctual.
'Don't interrupt me!'
He said that I shouldn't interrupt him.

▶ Grammar reference page 128

Phrasal verbs
verb + particle (preposition or adverb)
He looked at the report.
literal meaning
I am looking forward to meeting you.
non-literal meaning
The directors closed the company down.
The directors closed down the company.
separable
We need to deal with the problem now.
non-separable

▶ Grammar reference page 129

6.3 Grammar Reported speech

Test yourself: Reported speech

1 Complete the sentences from a company tour using reported speech.

1 'The headquarters are in New York.'
2 'The company employs 65,000 people worldwide.'
3 'We made a profit of $100 million last year.'
4 'We can increase our market share by 3%.'
5 'We invest a lot of money in R&D.'
6 'The company will build a plant in India.'
7 'We have two main competitors.'
8 'No business can ignore its customers.'

1 She said
2 She said
3 She added that they
4 She continued that they
5 She explained that they
6 She mentioned
7 She said that they
8 She said

Test yourself: Phrasal verbs

2 Use the words below to make phrasal verbs to complete each sentence.

| with | for | through | up | away | into | after | up |

1 We should look _____ the environment, not pollute it.
2 Could you put me _____ to customer complaints?
3 I can't cope _____ any more work. I need a holiday.
4 If you want to be an entrepreneur, you shouldn't give _____ when you have a problem.
5 Organizations often run _____ difficulties when they try to expand too quickly.
6 I want to set _____ my own company, and be my own boss.
7 I'm looking _____ a new job.
8 The company will give _____ 10,000 copies of the new software as part of its marketing campaign.

3 Match the phrasal verbs above with a definition.

a) to transfer a call
b) to deal with
c) to take care of something
d) to stop doing something
e) to give something without receiving money
f) to found
g) to start to have problems
h) to try to find something

6.3 Grammar

Internet research

Search for the keywords *China, business and advice*. What other information can you find about doing business in China?

Listening for gist

4 🔊 **2:17** Listen to Helen Wang giving advice about doing business in China. Put the topics that she talks about in the correct order.

First meeting ☐ Names ☐ Written contracts ☐ Presents ☐
Talking about business ☐ Interrupting ☐ Business cards ☐

Listening for detail

5 Read the following extracts from Ms Wang's talk and report what she said.

1 'Shake hands with the most senior person first.'

She said that you

2 'Use the family name, not the given name.'

She added that

3 'People don't talk business straight away.'

She stressed that

4 'Sometimes people bring a present.'

She commented that

5 'A good choice of present is an expensive cognac.'

She pointed out that

6 'The Chinese prefer face-to-face meetings.'

She explained that

7 'People don't like to say *No*'.

She said that

8 'Don't interrupt people in meetings.'

She stressed that

Phrasal verbs

6 Match the beginning with the correct ending to make questions.

1 Who used to look
2 What do you do when somebody puts you
3 How do you cope
4 Who do you know that gives
5 What do you do when you run
6 What is it important to remember when you set
7 What do you look
8 What kinds of gifts do companies give

a) up as soon as they meet a problem?
b) through to the wrong department?
c) with stress at work / university?
d) after you when you were a child?
e) away in order to attract new customers?
f) up your own company?
g) for when you are when meeting a potential business partner?
h) into problems at work / university?

With a partner, take it in turns to ask and answer the questions.

6 The organization

6.4 Speaking Interrupting in meetings

Discussion

1 People often interrupt because they are not good listeners. Being a good listener is very important in any communication. Do the quiz to find if you are a good listener. The results are on page 110. Compare your score with your partner. Do you agree with the results?

Are you a good listener?

		Yes	No
1	I never finish sentences for other people.	☐	☐
2	It's no problem for me to listen to two conversations at the same time.	☐	☐
3	I focus my full attention on the other speaker.	☐	☐
4	I often interrupt other people.	☐	☐
5	I never nod, smile or frown when I am talking.	☐	☐
6	I like to ask questions.	☐	☐
7	I usually think about what I want to say while the other person is speaking.	☐	☐
8	I sometimes lose the thread of the conversation.	☐	☐
9	I like to do other things, like write emails, while people are speaking.	☐	☐
10	I repeat back what the speaker has said.	☐	☐
11	If I don't understand what someone means, I ask for clarification.	☐	☐
12	Body language is very important in any communication.	☐	☐

DVD-ROM Interactive pronunciation practice on the DVD-ROM

6.4 Speaking

Internet research

Search for the keywords *communication skills*. What are some other important points for being a good communicator?

Listening for gist

2 🔊 2:18 Listen to a meeting taking place in a company which produces radios and televisions. Lisa Spinelli, John Forbes Tom Lee and Mary Riley are meeting to decide whether or not to open a fitness centre for employees. Decide who is an expert listener, who is an average listener and who is a terrible listener.

Lisa _____
John _____
Tom _____
Mary _____

Listening for detail

3 Listen to the meeting again and mark the statements *T* (true) or *F* (false).

1 Ms Sanchez definitely wants a fitness centre.
2 This is not the first time a fitness centre has been discussed.
3 The fitness centre should be outside the company.
4 The company would need to hire more staff.
5 John thinks a fitness centre would be counterproductive.
6 There is a high illness rate only among production staff.

4 Listen to the meeting again and complete the table with phrases for dealing with interruptions.

Rejecting an interruption	Polite interruption	Impolite interruption
1 If I could just finish _____ _____.	May I interrupt here? 2 Sorry to interrupt but I'd _____ _____ _____ _____.	Let me speak for myself 3 Stop _____ _____ !
Coming back to a point	**Preventing an interruption**	**Adding an opinion**
As I was saying. 4 Could we get back to _____ _____ _____.	5 I'd like to make _____ _____ before we all start talking.	6 I've got something _____ _____ _____.

Handling interruptions

5 Match a beginning with the correct ending.

1 Please allow me to finish and
2 That's a very interesting point, which
3 Can I ask you to be brief, as
4 That's not relevant to this discussion so
5 You've said quite a lot and now
6 I don't agree with your last point

a) and I'd like the chance to explain why.
b) time is running short?
c) I'd like to come back to later.
d) then you can make your comments.
e) could we get back on track?
f) I'd like the chance to have my say.

6 Work in groups of three. Prepare a short talk for the other members of your group. Be prepared to answer any questions when they interrupt.

Student A look at page 116.

Student B look at page 114.

Student C look at page 115.

The **Business** 77

6 The organization

6.5 Writing Agendas and action minutes

Scan reading

1 Read the article on the importance of agendas for effective meetings. What information can you find on an agenda?

People hold meetings in business all the time, but not every meeting is as effective as it could be. The basis of an effective meeting is an agenda. People don't always know what the meeting is about and an agenda helps you here. An agenda tells you why you are having the meeting and gives it a clear structure. It should be circulated before the meeting so that everybody can plan and prepare. The agenda should state why the meeting is necessary, who will attend, when and where it is, and what will be discussed. Each item on the agenda is a task and should contain a verb which tells the participants what will happen. For example:
Item 2: New advertising agency
This doesn't tell us very much. It is more effective to write:
Item 2: Tony *to present* new advertising agency and costs.
    Team *to approve* new agency and costs.
After *Apologies for absence*, the agenda should start with routine items, such as *Matters arising* from the last meeting. Difficult items which need more discussion should be in the middle. Ideally, the items should be timed so that the meeting finishes on time with results. The agenda should finish with *Any other business*. These are relevant issues which need to be discussed but perhaps are too recent to be included on the original agenda. After the meeting, the minutes should be written and given to the participants. Action minutes give a short summary of what was discussed, and who will do what at which time.

2 Read the article again and mark the statements *T* (true) or *F* (false).
1 The participants get the agenda when they arrive at the meeting. ☐
2 The agenda tells you what the meeting is about. ☐
3 You don't know who is attending the meeting when you look at the agenda. ☐
4 The items on the agenda tell you what will happen in the meeting. ☐
5 The agenda should start with difficult items. ☐
6 You should make a written record of the meeting. ☐
7 Action minutes don't tell you who is responsible for which task. ☐

Agenda

Date: 4 September
Time: 3.30pm
Venue: Main conference room

1 Matters arising
2 Firat to present new quotations for building new canteen
3 Adrian to propose changes to staff newsletter
4 AOB

Internet research
Search for the keywords *effective meetings* to find out more about what you need to do to run successful meetings.

DVD-ROM Further interactive writing practice and model business documents on the DVD-ROM

6.5 Writing

Writing action minutes

3 🔊 2:19 Action minutes give a short summary of what was discussed, and who will do what at which time. Listen to the meeting and fill in the action minutes of the meeting.

Minutes of team meeting

Date: 4 September **Present:** Cristina, Firat, Lena and Adrian
Time: 3.30pm **Absent:** Birgit
Venue: Main conference room **Minute taker:** 1) _____

	Action steps	Who?	When?
Point 1 Matters arising – staff not happy about hot desking	2) _____	Lena	3) _____
Point 2 Quotations for new canteen	4) _____	5) _____	Next meeting
Point 3 Changes to staff newsletter	Write a proposal of pros and cons of a quarterly newsletter	Adrian	6) _____
Point 4 AOB – Christmas party	7) _____	8) _____	9) _____

Next Meeting: 10) _____
Venue: Main conference room

Reporting

4 Sentences 1–8 report what somebody said. Sentences a)–h) are what the person said. In each group of four match the sentences with similar meanings.

1 She disagreed with the idea.
2 She suggested discussing the issue at the following meeting.
3 He recommended the Thompson proposal.
4 She promised to finish the report by 8th of September.

5 She wondered if the Christmas party could be held in the canteen.
6 She warned that we had a problem with the atmosphere at work.
7 He pointed out how much work went into the company newsletter.
8 We approved the Thompson proposal.

a) 'Let's discuss this issue at the next meeting.'
b) 'I can have the report ready by 8th of September.'
c) 'I believe the Thompson proposal is the better one.'
d) 'I'm not in favour of that idea.'

e) 'The company newsletter needs a lot of time and energy.'
f) 'We all agree with the Thompson proposal.'
g) 'The atmosphere at work is bad and getting worse.'
h) 'Would it be possible to hold the Christmas party in the new canteen?'

5 Turn to page 113 and read the full minutes from the meeting between Cristina Firat, Lena and Adrian.

Writing

6 Work with a partner. Look at the notes taken from the follow-up meeting with Firat, Lena and Adrian and write up full minutes.

Agenda

Date: 11 September
Time: 15.30
Venue: Main conference room

1 Matters arising
2 Lena to present report on hot desking and make a proposal
3 Firat to present schedule for canteen building work
4 Adrian to make proposal for quarterly newsletter
  Team to approve
5 Lena to report on Christmas party

2 Hot desking very unpopular. Staff demotivated. Not really necessary. Problem can be solved by smaller desks for everyone. Some extra cost involved.

3 Put up temporary tent for canteen 1 November. Problem – small distance to walk in open. Clear out fittings of canteen 2–6 November. Building work 7–20 November. Open new canteen 25 November.

4 Quarterly newsletter – pros – less time-consuming. More news to report so more interesting. Less cost. Cons – not so up-to-date. Proposal – quarterly newsletter. Team approved this.

5 New canteen opens on 25 November. Enough buffer time if problems occur. Christmas party in new canteen.

The **Business** 79

6 The organization

6.6 Case study Soup kitchen vs Gourmet to go

Discussion

1 You and your partner want to start up your own business and you need money from the bank. Think of four questions the bank might ask you about your new business.

Listening for gist

2 🔊 2:20 Listen to Cristiana Vatland, a business expert, explaining what a business plan is. Add the items which are necessary for a business plan.

	Items		Questions
	Personal details	a	
1			Where is it? Is it a partnership or sole trader?
	Mission statement	b	
2			What specifically will the company do?
	Product description	c	
3			Where and how will you make the product? What equipment do you need?
	Staff	d	
4			How much money do you need to start up the business? What is your estimated profit and loss account?

80 *The* **Business**

Listening for detail

3 Listen to Cristiana again and complete the table with the questions about each item.

4 Match the expressions from the listening with the correct definition.

1 cash flow forecast
2 mission statement
3 target group
4 profit and loss account
5 return on investment

a) the people you want to sell your product to
b) accounts which show income and expenditure
c) estimate of how much money comes into the company from sales, and how much is spent
d) the money you expect to get back on the amount you invested
e) definition of why company exists

Internet research

Work with a partner. Search for the mission statements of well-known companies. What do the statements tell you about the companies?

Reading

5 Read the business plans below and answer the questions.

1 What do you think the main differences are between the two business plans?
2 Which company do you think is more likely to succeed? Why?

Gourmet TO GO

1 Owner: Tim O'Connor. Date of birth: 2.04.82. B.A. Business Administration, Diploma in Hotel and Catering. Five years' experience working as head waiter in five star hotel.
2 Gourmet to Go. Sole trader. Company offices are located on Missouri Boulevard, Little Rock, Arkansas, close to the business park.
3 Mission statement: we make high-class, gourmet dinner party food, using ingredients from all over the world to suit our customers' demands. You send your order to us and we deliver all of the food to your event.
4 Objectives: to cater for an average of 50 business functions a week at mid-morning and lunch time.
5 Product description: Our USP is that we make customised lunches for companies and corporate events. We use fresh ingredients flown in from all over the world and so can cater for any tastes or needs.
6 Production: Large kitchen of owner's own house equipped with necessary work surfaces and cooking utensils.
7 Staff: three part-time members of staff. One full-time.
8 Finance: Start-up capital – $50,000. Bank loan necessary – $100,000

SOUP KITCHEN

1 Owner: Nancy Macfadden. Date of birth: 4.09.50. Full-time mother and grandmother.
2 Soup Kitchen. Sole trader. Company located in downtown Little Rock, close to the university and central shopping area.
3 Mission statement: we aim to make healthy soups using organic only ingredients at low cost. All of the produce is locally-produced too.
4 Objective: to sell an average of 100 pots of soup throughout the day.
5 Product description: our USP is to make wholesome soups using only seasonal, local produce in an environmentally friendly way. We also use biodegradable pots so that no waste is produced.
6 Production: share kitchen facilities of Queen Hotel in Arkansas.
7 Staff: one full-time.
8 Finance: start-up capital - $2,000. Bank loan necessary - $15,000

Writing a business plan

6 Work in small groups. Brainstorm a business you would like to start in the food industry. Now write a business plan. Use the table in 2 to help you. When you have finished, present your business plan to the other groups who are all potential investors. Be prepared to answer any questions they may have.

Review 5

5 Selling

1 Use the words in the box to complete these phrases from the article on page 59.

| amounts | attention | bid | earn | goal | switch off |
| target | trend | wear | word-of-mouth | | |

1 be a growing _____
2 receive a _____ on eBay
3 _____ a lot of money
4 _____ branded sports clothes
5 _____ a commercial
6 _____ an audience
7 start a _____ campaign
8 fulfil (= reach/achieve) a _____
9 spend large _____ of money
10 attract people's _____

2 Fill in the missing letters in these words related to buying and selling.

1 A salesperson who knows a lot about their products is very knowl____able.
2 A salesperson who you can trust is trustw____y.
3 A salesperson who is good at making the customer believe in the product is pers___ive.
4 A salesperson who makes small talk is ch___y.
5 A car which doesn't cost much money to run is econ____al.
6 Prices that are as low as similar products made by rivals are comp____ive.
7 If you borrow money to buy a product, and then you pay it back over time with no extra charge, you have an int____t-free l__n.
8 If something is worth the price, then it is good v___e-f__-money.
9 If there is a reduction in the price of a product, then there is a dis____t on the product.
10 An informal expression for 'the current price' of something is the 'go___-r__e'.

3 Fill in the gaps with words from the box.

| incentive | loyalty | profile | satisfaction | retention |

1 If many customers are happy with the product, then there is a high level of customer _____.
2 If a company wants to encourage a customer to buy something, they offer an _____.
3 It is useful to have a detailed description of a typical customer: the _____ of the customer.
4 A customer _____ program is aimed at trying to keep existing customers.
5 If the customer keeps buying the same product, they show _____ to the brand.

4 Complete the dialogue using a comparative or superlative form of the adjective in brackets. Extra words like *the/than/more/less/most/least* will also be needed.

A: I need to do a round-trip from Frankfurt to Paris next week. I'm thinking of taking my car.
B: Surely the train would be ¹_____ (comfortable) your car. And maybe ²_____ (cheap) as well, when you think about the petrol.
A: The cost doesn't matter – the company is paying. The main thing is time and convenience. I need to go by ³_____ (fast) possible means of transport, and I have to travel from one meeting to the next in Paris.
B: Well then, why not fly? And use taxis for moving around the city? It will be much ⁴_____ (stressful) your car – you won't have to worry about finding the right addresses.
A: That's true. Paris is one of ⁵_____ (difficult) cities I know for driving. I want to be relaxed and able to concentrate in the meetings.
B: Okay, so the ⁶_____ (good) option might be to take the TGV train – the journey time is under four hours – and then use taxis locally. That would be ⁷_____ (stressful) option of all.
A: Yes, that's not a bad idea.

5 Complete this dialogue by writing questions. Look carefully at the answer, including the form of the verb.

A: Where ¹_____?
B: I live in Budapest.
A: How long ²_____ there?
B: I've been there for over ten years.
A: ³_____ happy there?
B: Yes I am, but I'm going to move soon.
A: Where ⁴_____ move to?
B: I'm going to move to Vienna.
A: And why ⁵_____ that decision?
B: I made that decision because there's more work in Vienna.
A: Are you sure? Who ⁶_____ that?
B: My friend told me. He works there now.

6 Match the beginning to the end of the phrase to make expressions used in negotiating.

1 Okay. It's a   suggest something.
2 That's out of the   condition that …
3 I'd like to   deal.
4 Can you go   question.
5 I'd only pay that price on   half way.
6 If I understand you   along with that?
7 I can meet you   correctly …

7 Now write the phrase number 1-7 from exercise 6 next to its use below.

Making proposals ☐   Making concessions ☐
Bargaining ☐   Asking for agreement ☐
Accepting ☐   Clarifying ☐
Rejecting ☐

8 Make collocations used in negotiating by matching an item on the left with one on the right.

1 trade   price
2 lead   of payment
3 gross   discount
4 terms   VAT
5 payment within   time
6 inclusive of   30 days

Review 6

6 The organization

1 Fill in the missing letters in these words. They all appeared in the article on page 71.

1. If an entrepreneur sees an opportunity to produce something that is not yet available, then they spot a g__ __ ___ m_____.
2. An entrepreneur starts a business by investing their own capital: this is the e___ty in the business.
3. Entrepreneurs hate r__ t___ – documents, rules or processes that cause delays.
4. Money that you pay to a lawyer is called your l___l f__s.
5. The part of a job that involves keeping records and writing reports is called the pap____rk
6. Every year a company has to show its trading results in its ann___ acc____s.
7. Another word for the 'head office' of a company is its 'headqu_____s'.
8. The amount of money that the owner of a company might lose if it goes bankrupt is their lia___ity.

2 Make collocations by matching an item on the left with an item on the right.

1	set	a)	in agreement about something
2	make	b)	of paperwork
3	put	c)	up a business
4	be	d)	into trouble when things go wrong
5	run	e)	capital into a business
6	do a lot	f)	a decision / a mistake
7	buy	g)	long hours
8	raise	h)	shares in a public company
9	lose	i)	boss
10	vote	j)	capital in order to expand
11	be your own	k)	at the AGM
12	work	l)	money if the share price falls

3 Look at the actual words spoken, then write them using reported speech.

1. "I am tired"
   She said that she _____
2. "We will open a factory in Poland next year"
   He explained that they _____
3. "We have a subsidiary in China"
   She mentioned that they _____
4. "The company is doing very well"
   He said the company _____
5. "Arrive at the meeting on time!"
   She said that I _____
6. "Don't agree to anything specific"
   He said that we _____

4 Complete each sentence with one word from the left column and one from the right.

cope	after
give	away
give	for
look	into
look	through
put	up
set	up
run	with

1. Can you _____ me _____ to customer services, please?
2. When the baby is born I will stay at home for a year or so to _____ _____ it.
3. You have so much work! How do you _____ _____ it all?
4. Keep on trying! You can do it! Don't _____ _____ now!
5. We sell a lot of goods to other companies, but we sometimes _____ _____ trouble when we don't get paid on time.
6. It's a new company. She _____ it _____ just two years ago but it's already making a profit.
7. This instruction manual is so complicated. When I _____ _____ the information I need I can never find it.
8. We have 1000 free samples to _____ _____ at the trade fair.

5 The phrases below can be used during a meeting. But the words in **bold** are in the wrong sentences. Put them back into the correct place.

1. If I could just finish what I was **running**.
2. I'd like to **get back** here.
3. Please **like** me to finish.
4. Could we **come in** to the first point?
5. Can I ask you to be **track**?
6. Time is **saying** short.
7. That's an interesting point which I'd **allow** to come back to later.
8. Can we get back on **brief**?

6 Look back at the sentences in exercise 5. Find:

1. One used to interrupt politely. ☐
2. Two used to reject an interruption and continue speaking. ☐ ☐
3. One used to block discussion of a point temporarily. ☐
4. One used to return to a previous point. ☐
5. One used when the discussion is not relevant. ☐
6. Two used when there is little time remaining for the meeting. ☐ ☐

7 Match the reporting verbs a-h with their meanings 1-8 below.

a She disagreed with ...   c She recommended ...
b He suggested that ....   d He promised that ...
e She wondered if ...   g She pointed out that
f He warned that ......   h He approved ...

1. say that you will definitely do something ☐
2. have a different opinion to someone else ☐
3. offer an idea for other people to consider ☐
4. advise that something should happen ☐
5. tell someone something they had not noticed ☐
6. think about something because you want to know more facts, or are worried ☐
7. give official permission for something ☐
8. tell people about a possible problem, so that they can avoid it ☐

7 The stock markets

7.1 About business   Keep it in the family

Discussion

1 You and your partner own a small company and need money for a project. What do you think are the pros and cons of borrowing money from:

1 family and friends
2 your bank
3 a venture capital group?

Listening and note-taking

2 2:21–2:23 John and Gunter are discussing different ways of raising large amounts of money. Listen to the conversation and make notes of the advantages and disadvantages of each way.

	Advantages	Disadvantages
Bank loan		
Venture capital		
Shares		

Internet research
Search for the keywords *Initial Public Offering* to find out more about how and why companies go public.

Vocabulary

3 You are going to read an article about the Bertelsmann group. Before you read, match a word or phrase on the left with a definition.

1 to establish
2 unlisted public company
3 requirement
4 consolidated financial reports
5 considerable
6 stake
7 IPO
8 buyback

a) something that is necessary, or that a rule says you must do
b) to start a company
c) a statement showing the assets, liabilities, income and expenses that the parent company and its subsidiaries have
d) the shares of this company cannot be bought or sold on the stock exchange
e) buying something from the person you previously sold it to
f) the part of a business you own because you have invested in it
g) the first time a company's shares are offered on the stock exchange
h) large in size

Reading for gist

4 Read the article opposite about Bertelsmann.

Find answers to the questions.

1 What kind of company is Bertelsmann?
2 What kind of company is Groupe Bruxelles Lambert?

7.1 About business

Keeping it in the family
BUT AT WHAT COST?

THE BERTELSMANN GROUP is the world's largest media company. It operates in 63 countries worldwide and employs over 78,000 workers.
In 2005 its turnover was almost €18 billion. It owns or has major holdings in companies involved in book and magazine publishing, film and music recording, online services and other multimedia activities.

Bertelsmann was established in Gütersloh, Germany in 1835 by the printer and bookseller Carl Bertelsmann. In 1887 the company passed from Carl Bertelsmann's son Heinrich to his son-in-law, Johannes Mohn. It has stayed in the hands of the Mohn family ever since.

Bertelsmann became an AG (a German public limited company) in 1971, but instead of offering shares to the public on the stock exchange, the Mohns decided to keep all the shares

Bertelsmann is now €4.5 billion poorer

themselves and to become an unlisted public company.

Why? Normally the only reason for a company to form an AG is to raise capital to finance new projects or ideas. However this also weakens the power of the original owners because the shareholders then want the company to represent their interests. Moreover a company that is listed on the stock exchange also has to meet a lot of other requirements, such as publishing its consolidated financial reports every three months. Meeting these requirements can cost a company several million euros a year.

On the other hand one considerable advantage of being an AG is that you can take over other companies without it costing you a single cent. All you need to do is to offer the owners some of your shares in return for some of theirs.

This is exactly what Bertelsmann did when they took over Groupe Bruxelles Lambert, a financial group, in 2001. They offered the owner, Albert Frère, a 25% stake in the Bertelsmann AG with an option to sell those shares on the stock exchange later.

In 2005, Frère announced that he wanted to do just that. This left the Mohn family with only two choices – they could either buy back Frère's share of Bertelsmann to keep everything in the family or let Frère do an IPO (Initial Public Offering) and risk having outside shareholders.

The Mohns decided on the buyback option. They offered Frère €4.5 billion for his share of Bertelsmann AG and Frère accepted.

As a result, the Bertelsmann Group is now €4.5 billion poorer and may have to sell its 50% stake in Sony BMG Music Entertainment, one of the world's largest and most successful music publishers, to finance the buyback.

Reading for detail

5 Work with a partner and mark these sentences *T* (true) or *F* (false).

1 Bertelsmann was established in 1835 and started producing films and records. ☐
2 When the company went public in 1971, it did not offer its shares on the stock exchange ☐
3 The company is not listed on any stock exchange. ☐
4 It can cost a company millions of euros every year to meet a stock exchange's requirements. ☐
5 The only way to take over a successful company is to offer the owners a lot of money. ☐
6 The owners of Bertelsmann paid €4.5 billion to stop the company from being listed on the stock exchange. ☐

Discussion

6 Work in small groups. Were the Mohns right to pay so much money to buy the shares back? Why? Why not?

The Business 85

7 The stock markets

7.2 Vocabulary Dealing with figures

Saying numbers

1 Can you say the following numbers?

a 5th
b 2/3
c £199,184
d 1 in 4
e 13–17 years
f 156,000,000 m^2
g 0.08
h 6,000,000 days
i 550L^3
j 7.71%

2 Complete the sentences using the numbers in 1.

1 Approximately 67%, or _____, of all start-up companies fail within the first five years.
2 In a year the chances of becoming a victim of viruses, spyware or phishing are about _____. The cost to business is estimated to be several billion dollars a year.
3 The average UK household consumes about _____ of tap water a year and can expect to receive a water bill of about £440. That works out at _____ p per litre.
4 According to research, stress is responsible for _____ lost annually in the UK.
5 The average price of a house in the UK is _____ – that's up by _____ over last year.
6 The new economic city of Hail in Saudi Arabia will have an area of _____ and house some 80,000 people.
7 The Republicans voted against increasing the minimum wage for the _____ time in less than a month.
8 The average lifespan of a car in the UK has been estimated as between _____ by the Commission for Integrated Transport.

Listening for detail

3 2:24–2:27 Listen to four economic reports and write the numbers you hear in the spaces.

❶ America

The Federal Reserve announced it would drop its key interest rate by (1)_____ to (2)_____. This is the second drop in interest rates in the last six months. Productivity grew by (3)_____ in the third quarter, compared with (4)_____ in the first six months. Employers reported (5)_____ new jobs had been created in July.

❷ Germany

Germany's job growth was stronger than expected in March. Unemployment fell by (6)_____ to 4,370,000. Its trade surplus grew again in the first quarter to (7)_____ up 0.4% over the previous quarter. The German car industry reported that a record (8)_____ vehicles were exported in the first three months.

❸ Japan

Japanese industrial production increased slightly by (9)_____ and unemployment fell by (10)_____ to 2,890,000 last year. The yen remains strong at (11)_____ yen to the dollar. Bank lending rose by 2.4% in the year to April, the fastest increase in the last (12)_____ years.

❹ The UK

Jobs in the service industry rose to (13)_____ last year while jobs in manufacturing fell by (14)_____. The National Statistical Office reported that the number of jobs paid below the national minimum wage has increased to approx. (15)_____. It also reported that (16)_____ jobs, 3.2% held by those aged (17)_____ were paid below (18)_____ an hour.

Describing trends

4 Look at the newspaper headlines below describing trends and draw an arrow to show the direction of the trend.

1. Oil prices shoot up. ↑
2. Gamebox sales up slightly after Nintendo cuts prices.
3. HOUSE PRICES REMAIN STABLE.
4. INFLATION INCREASES BY 5% IN LAST 12 MONTHS.
5. Profits in the IT industry fall dramatically.
6. Government announces massive tax increase.
7. Exchange rates between the dollar and pound fluctuate wildly.
8. UNEMPLOYMENT FIGURE UP SIGNIFICANTLY OVER LAST YEAR.
9. Intel announces slight drop in profit.
10. Share prices in travel industry stagnant.
11. Commercial TV stations announce a 20% decline in advertising revenues
12. Ministers warn of huge rise in nuclear waste.

Discussion

5 Work with a partner. Decide which headline:

a) is good news for young consumers
b) means goods and services have become more expensive
c) means there are fewer jobs
d) means that people will have less money to spend in future
e) is bad news if you have invested in companies like Adobe or Dell
f) will affect the plastics industry and make their products more expensive.

Internet research

Search for the keywords *current economic trends* to find out more about new developments in the world of business.

Adverbs and adjectives

6 Read the extracts below from economic reports. Do the underlined adverbs and adjectives in the extracts describe:

a big change? (*A*)   a sudden or fast change? (*C*)
a small change? (*B*)   a slow change? (*D*)

You may need to use more than one letter.

		Trend
1	Unemployment in Germany has fallen <u>slightly</u> over the past 12 months.	B and D
2	The overall cost for information technology shows a <u>gradual</u> decrease each year.	
3	There has been a <u>considerable</u> rise in sales of smaller, more economical cars in the last year.	
4	The share price fell <u>dramatically</u> after PGT announced it was planning to close its factory in China.	
5	The market for consumer electronics designed for 'older' people will grow <u>steadily</u> over the next few years.	
6	The company has grown <u>rapidly</u> over the last five years. Profits are expected to be up 30% on last year.	
7	The European Central Bank has said it is thinking of increasing its key lending rate <u>fractionally</u> in the autumn.	
8	Wages and salaries in the Indian IT industry have risen <u>quickly</u> in the last few years	

Discussion

7 Look at the extracts above. Are the trends *P* (positive) or *N* (negative)? Think about who they are positive or negative for.

1 _____ 2 _____ 3 _____ 4 _____ 5 _____ 6 _____ 7 _____ 8 _____

7 The stock markets

Refresh your memory

will and won't
The Japanese economy will grow next year.
It won't grow as quickly as this year.
predictions

▶ Grammar reference page 130

be going to
We're going to open a new branch in Moscow next year.
plans or intentions – things we have already decided to do

▶ Grammar reference page 130

First conditional
If you offer a discount (then) we will increase our order.
if + present simple, (then) + will
likely future events

▶ Grammar reference page 131

7.3 Grammar   *will* and *won't*, *be going to* and first conditional

Test yourself: *will* and *won't*

1 Complete the dialogues below with `'ll` (= will) or *won't* (= will not).

1 JG: Right then, Luigi, I'd like to know why you don't think we (1) _____ be able to sell our pizzas in Italy. I thought Italians liked pizzas!
   Luigi: Well, JG I think the name's wrong. JG's Spicy Pizza Grandy isn't Italian and I don't think the name (2) _____ appeal to Italian consumers.
   JG: OK, so we change the name. No problem!
   Luigi: That's a good idea, JG, but I think we (3) _____ still have a problem. Italians don't seem to like curry flavour pizzas!

2 Antonio: OK everyone, I'd like to hear your thoughts on the idea of taking over RGB. Sheila.
   Sheila: Hmm... I think it's a bit risky, Antonio. It (4) _____ be cheap. It could cost us between €2,500,000 and €3,200,000 to get a majority stake in RGB. That's a lot of money.
   Peter: Yes, Sheila, but RGB is an established company and if we can afford that, we (5) _____ have a company that has over 357,000 customers, a turnover of €28,000,000 and a really good name.
   Tom: Yes, but we (6) _____ also have to invest about another €800,000 in RGB. The management hasn't done anything for the last five years

3 Manuel: So, Jean, you think shares in the tourist industry (7) _____ fall.
   Jean: Yep, that's right Manuel, unemployment is up again and that means a lot more people (8) _____ be able to afford a holiday. Fuel prices are up so flights (9) _____ be more expensive... and these reports about more terrorist attacks (10) _____ help.
   Manuel: OK, so a lot of people (11) _____ want to travel abroad, but what about our local tourist industry?

Test yourself: *be going to*

2 We asked people on the street what they thought about these trends. What have they decided to do? Complete the sentences below with the correct form of *be going to*.

Government to close 12 of the UK's 23 nuclear power plants

China to start exporting cars to Europe

ONE WORKER FOR THREE PENSIONERS BY 2075

1 Well, I'm worried about the effect this will have on jobs in Europe. A lot of my friends have jobs that are connected with the car industry. I (1) _____ buy a Chinese car even if they are a lot cheaper.
2 If fewer and fewer people with jobs have to pay for more and more pensioners, the government will have to increase taxes or cut pensions. My wife and I (2) _____ look into private pension schemes – I think that's the only thing we can do if we want to have enough money to live on later.
3 If electricity prices go up, what (3) _____ do? What can I do? Nothing much – except buy a few energy saving lights. I'm certainly (4) _____ install solar panels, they cost too much.

Internet research

Search for the keywords *what will happen* to read more about what people think the future will hold. Make a note of three ideas that you think will happen and three that you think won't happen.

Test yourself: First conditional

3 Match the beginning on the left with the correct ending on the right.

1	If you buy a dozen,	a)	unless we increase the size of the order.
2	Unless you drop your price by at least 5%	b)	if you want us to print your logo on them.
3	They won't offer us a bigger discount	c)	I'm afraid we will have to reconsider your order.
4	It'll cost another €150,	d)	we'll give you one pair free.
5	OK, we'll replace the parts for free,	e)	they won't be prepared to sell their shares to you.
6	If you buy this car now,	f)	if you can't deliver sooner than that.
7	We will have to look for another supplier,	g)	if you bring the car to us immediately.
8	Unless you are willing to offer them at least €5 million	h)	I'll throw in air-conditioning, winter tyres and a CD player.

Discussion

4 Work with a partner. Look at the topics below and discuss your options.

1 An old aunt of yours has died and left you a luxury villa in the Bahamas.
2 You are both unemployed and want to set up a company together.
3 You are planning a four-week holiday to the USA.
4 You have been asked to organize a one-day festival/event for teenagers in your area.
5 You are going to live on a desert island for three months. Decide what to take with you.
6 You run an organization which helps families who live in poor parts of the world. You have a monthly budget of €10,000 for a new project.

5 Work with a partner. Read these extracts from reports and answer the questions below using the first conditional.

> China's carmakers plan to increase production by over 500% in the next ten years and have also announced that they will open new plants in Eastern Europe.

What do you think will happen to:

a) European carmakers? *If more Chinese cars are produced...*
b) steel prices? _____
c) CO_2 emissions? _____

> The British government has announced that it plans to close 12 of Britain's 23 nuclear power plants over the next ten years. UK power plants currently generate a fifth of the country's electricity.

What do you think will happen to:

a) UK electricity prices? _____
b) the share price of alternative energy companies? _____
c) manufacturing costs in the UK? _____

> Over 25% of the German population is older than 60 and this figure is expected to grow significantly in the next 20–30 years. Some projections show that by 2075 there will be one worker for every three pensioners.

What do you think will happen to:

a) wages and salaries in Germany? _____
b) government spending? _____
c) immigration to Germany? _____

7 The stock markets

7.4 Speaking   Negotiations – making offers, agreeing deadlines

Constrastive stress

1 2:28 Listen to the recording and underline the words that are stressed.

1   a) I don't think their turnover will fall.
    b) I don't think their turnover will fall.
2   a) I told you to buy more shares in UPS if they went above US$ 70.
    b) I told you to buy more shares in UPS if they went above US$ 70.
3   a) The share price hasn't gone up much yet.
    b) The share price hasn't gone up much yet.
4   a) I think profits in the telecom industry will fall this year.
    b) I think profits in the telecom industry will fall this year.

Now listen again and practise saying the sentences.

2 Which of the sentences above means:

1   I don't think their turnover will fall. I know it will fall.
2   I told you to buy more shares in UPS if they went above US$ 70. Not sell them.
3   The share price hasn't gone up much yet. But it soon will.
4   I think profits in the telecom industry will fall this year. But you may not agree with me.

3 Read the sentences below with the correct word stressed.

1   a) Sorry, but I ordered a glass of red wine (not white wine).
    b) Sorry, but I ordered a glass of red wine (not a whole bottle).
2   a) Mario doesn't want to talk about the problem, Pete (he wants to discuss the solution).
    b) Mario doesn't want to talk about the problem, Pete (Julia is the person who wants to talk).
3   a) I don't think their turnover will fall (but maybe our turnover will).
    b) I don't think their turnover will fall (but their profits might fall).
4   a) I didn't ask you to finish the report by Friday (Tom asked you).
    b) I didn't ask you to finish the report by Friday (I asked you to finish the accounts).

2:29 Now listen and check.

Listening for detail

4 2:30 Listen to a negotiation between Antonio and Birgit as they negotiate over the supply of new parts. Fill in the spaces:

Birgit: OK, perhaps we should (1) _____ _____ to business. Well, (2) _____ _____ _____, Antonio, our new CEO is worried about our costs and he expects me to (3) _____ cheaper prices with all our suppliers.
Antonio: Cheaper prices! But you're already getting …
B   Yes, I know, Antonio, you're selling us the parts at cost and you'll be giving them away (4) _____ _____ _____ your prices any more.
A   Exactly, Birgit, wages and salaries have gone up, energy prices have gone up … everything's gone up, but you expect us to drop our prices. It (5) _____ _____ _____, Birgit! No way!
B   OK, Antonio. Let's (6) _____ _____ to prices in a minute and look at some other possibilities. What are our terms of payment? Six weeks?
A   Erm, no, eight weeks. Eight weeks is a long time to wait to be paid, Birgit.
B   Hmm … well, if we shorten the terms of payment to, (7) _____ _____, four weeks, will that help?
A   Hmm … yes, maybe a little, but …
B   But not enough for you to drop your prices. Right?
A   Well …
B   What about delivery times? If (8) _____ _____ _____ another week or two, will that help?
A   Of course it helps, Birgit, but your production department always needs the parts … the day before yesterday!
B   OK, Antonio, (9) _____ _____ this idea? If we agree to pay you 3.5% more for parts delivered within seven days, 2% for parts delivered within 10 days and 1% if they are delivered within 14 days, (10) _____ _____ _____ to drop your prices slightly?
A   OK, maybe we can drop our price by 1%, but only if you pay within 14 days in future.
B   1.5% Antonio and I think we (11) _____ _____ _____.
A   OK, Birgit, if it helps make your new CEO happier, (12) _____ _____ _____ 1.5%, then.
B   Oh, I'm sure our CEO will be delighted Antonio. Now, how about lunch?

DVD-ROM Interactive pronunciation practice on the DVD-ROM 7.4 Speaking

Negotiating language

5 In each set of four match the sentences on the left with the responses on the right.

1 Can we agree on payment within 30 days?
2 Let's come back to price later.
3 Can you deliver within 14 working days?
4 We'd like you to drop your price by 5%.

a) I'm afraid we couldn't agree to that. Our costs have increased by over 3% in the last year.
b) Yes, OK, but only if the price includes the shipping costs.
c) I'm afraid that's not long enough. We need 28.
d) Yes, that's a good idea. Perhaps we should look at delivery times next.

5 So what kind of quantities are we talking about?
6 What about service and maintenance costs?
7 If you pay late, we will charge another 2% for every 30 days.
8 OK, I think we have a deal.

e) They're covered by the guarantee for the first two years.
f) Good! It was great doing business with you.
g) Hmm … 1.5% and I think we have a deal.
h) Well, the first order would only be for 500 units, but if we're happy with the quality …

Negotiation

6 Work with a partner to negotiate the following situation. Student B turn to page 114. Student A read below.

You would like to order some gifts with your company's logo on them for an important trade fair which will take place in 30 days' time.

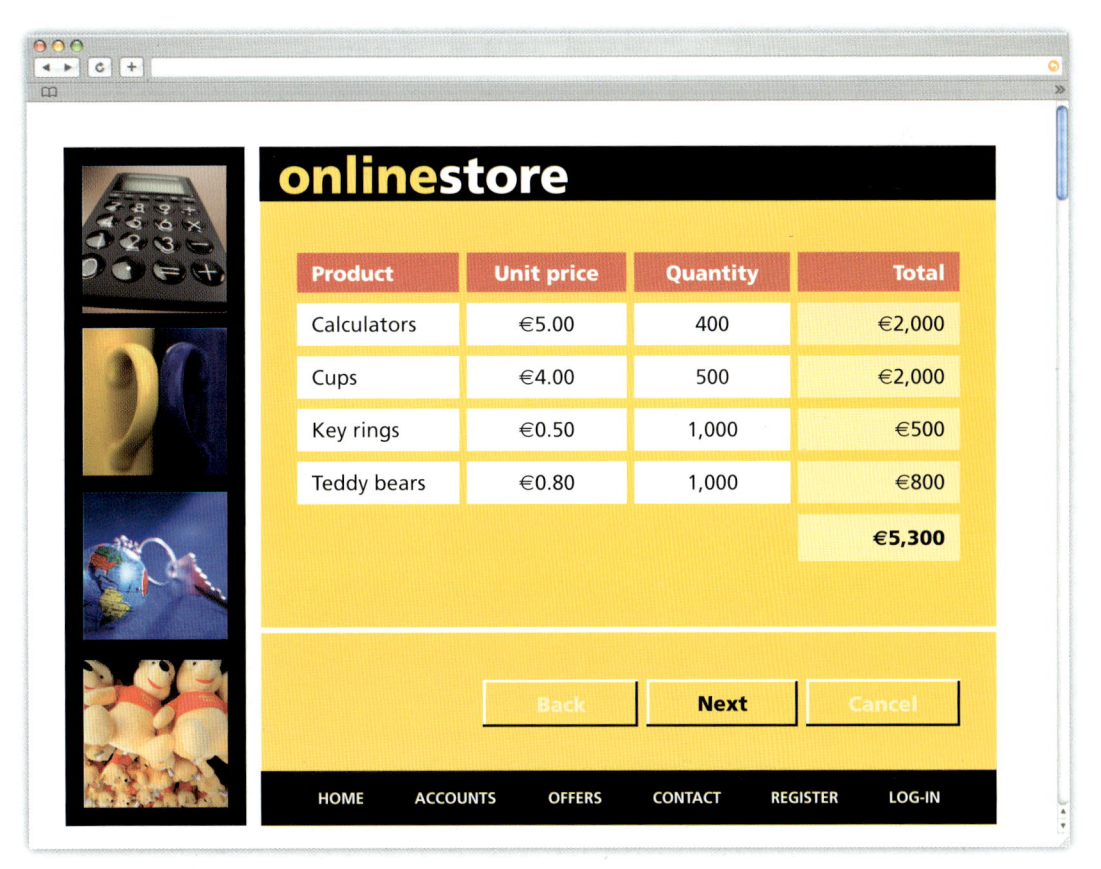

onlinestore

Product	Unit price	Quantity	Total
Calculators	€5.00	400	€2,000
Cups	€4.00	500	€2,000
Key rings	€0.50	1,000	€500
Teddy bears	€0.80	1,000	€800
			€5,300

Back Next Cancel

HOME   ACCOUNTS   OFFERS   CONTACT   REGISTER   LOG-IN

- The catalogue says that discounts for orders of more than 500 items are negotiable, but it is not clear if that means 500 items of one product, or the total order.
- The catalogue price would normally be €5,300. You would like a 10% discount for this order.
- Delivery times are normally 28 days, but you need everything to be delivered in the next 14–21 days. 14 days would be best.
- Payment is normally 10 days, you would like to pay within 28 days.
- The catalogue says shipping costs are €150 for orders over €1,000, but you would like the order delivered free.

Try to negotiate a deal that both you and the seller are happy with.

You start. Phone Student B.

When you reach an agreement Student A turn to page 116, Student B turn to page 117. Work out how good your negotiation skills are.

Internet research

Search for the keywords *successful negotiations* to find out more about negotiating. Make a list of five tips to remember when you are negotiating.

7 The stock markets

7.5 Writing | Describing figures

Discussion

1 Look at the line graph below. What does it show? What other types of graphs and charts do you know?

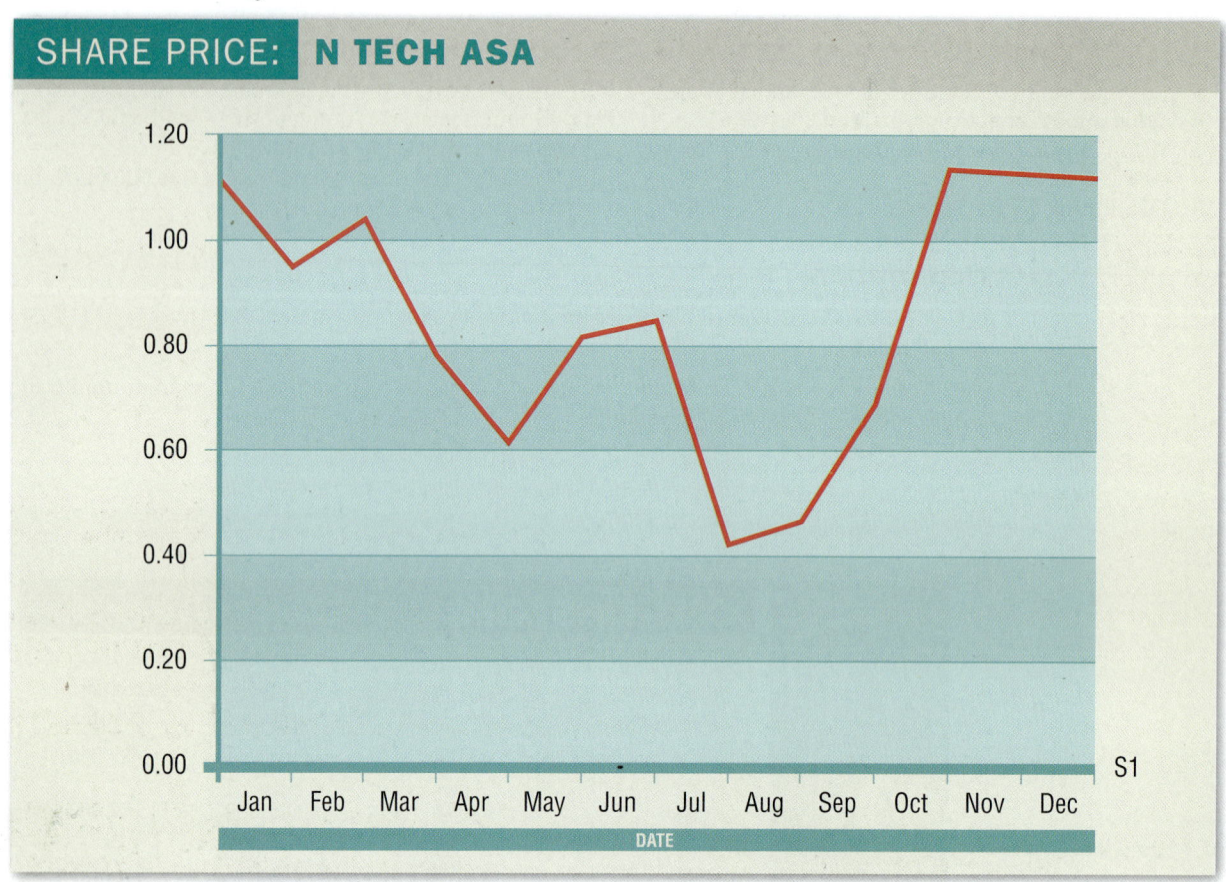

SHARE PRICE: N TECH ASA

Reading for detail

2 Read the description of the graph and mark the sentences *T* (true) or *F* (false).

The Norwegian environmental technology company, N Tech ASA had a turbulent year last year. The share price stood at US$ 1.13 at the beginning of January, but fell significantly in the first five months and stood at US$ 0.63 in May. There was talk of a takeover bid by one of N Tech ASA's competitors, Paterson, at the end of February. This proved to be false however and
5 many speculators lost interest in the company and sold their shares.
　　At the beginning of June, CEO Fredrik Berg announced the closure of one of the factories and plans to lay off more than 1,500 employees at its other plants. Investors saw this as a way of cutting costs and improving the productivity. As a result of this the share price rose to US$ 0.89 in July.
10　　The rise was short-lived. In August, N Tech announced it had lost a US$150 million contract with the Department for Environment, Food and Rural Affairs and its share price plummeted to US$ 0.48. As a result more job cuts were announced in September and the share price rose slightly to US$ 0.56.
　　In the last quarter the share price rose dramatically from US$ 0.70 to US$ 1.15. This was due
15 to the announcement of a massive order for their methane gas-fired power stations from China and the resignation of Fredrik Berg who was replaced by top industrialist, Matilda Inge.

1　The share price rose slightly at the end of February because of speculation that one of N Tech's competitors wanted to buy the company. ☐
2　When N Tech announced job cuts in June, the share price fell. ☐
3　When the company lost the contract with the Department for Environment, Food and Rural Affairs its share price shot up. ☐
4　Fredrik Berg's resignation had a positive effect on the company's share price. ☐

Causes and effects

3 Match the effects on the left with a cause on the right.

	EFFECT		CAUSE
1	Sales of soft drinks increased by 22% last month	a)	as a result of the stronger euro.
2	EU exports to the USA fell slightly last month	b)	due to a strike at the Toulouse plant.
3	Production fell by 150,000 units to 700,000 in June	c)	because of shortages in the supply of oil.
4	Heating costs rose by 10% in the last quarter	d)	because of a heat wave.
5	House prices went up slightly last month	e)	as a result of increasing competition and Internet telephony.
6	Telecom's profits fell by 18.4% last year	f)	due to the fall in interest rates.

Internet research

Search for the keywords *green technology* to find out how companies are making profits from selling environmentally friendly products

4 Complete these sentences with your own ideas. Use *because of*, *due to* or *as a result of* + a noun to explain the cause.

1 Sales of film cameras have fallen dramatically since the 1990s…
2 The number of smokers in the EU has dropped by over 6% in the last 10 years…
3 Sales of convenience foods and ready meals have been growing steadily…
4 Share prices in the airline industry fell significantly last week…

Describing figures

5 Work with a partner. You are going to write two halves of a short report describing the share price of W.B. Rexford over the last year. This company manufactures outdoor clothing.

Student A read below. Student B turn to page 114

Write a report describing January to June. Use the graph below. Include a description of the trend (*it fell from… to…, it fell by… to…*) and a reason for the trend (*bad weather, a strike*, etc). Invent these reasons.

When you finish, swap reports with your partner and read about the other half of the year. Discuss together what actions the management could have taken at key moments.

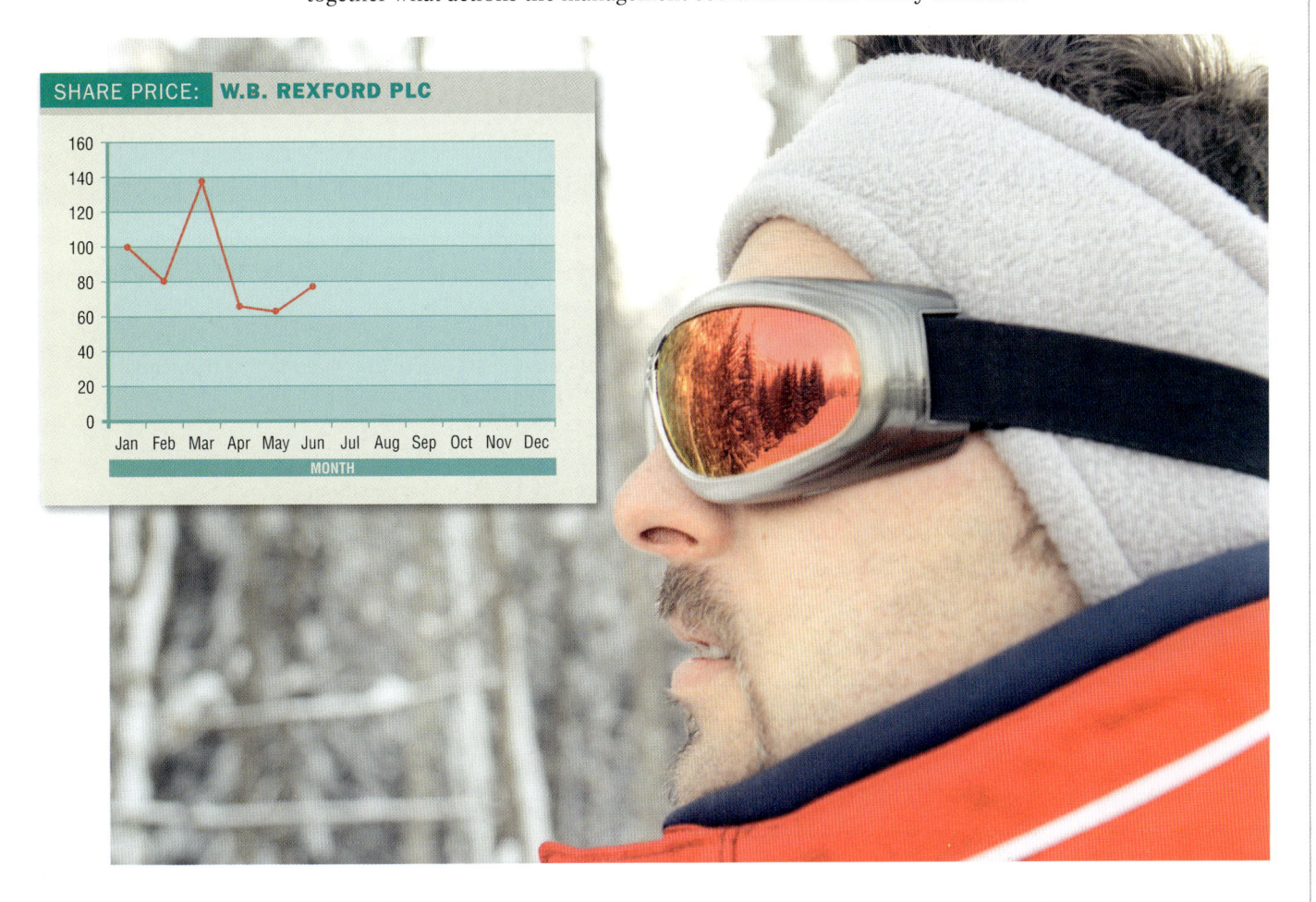

SHARE PRICE: **W.B. REXFORD PLC**

7 The stock markets

7.6 Case study   Trading stocks

Discussion

1 In small groups, discuss the questions about shares.

1 What are the advantages and disadvantages of investing in shares?
2 Are there any types of company you would not want to have shares in?
3 Would you prefer to invest money in:
   a) shares that are risky – i.e. you could make or lose a lot of money?
   b) 'safer' shares of large, well-known companies (blue-chip companies)?
   c) bonds that guarantee fixed interest rates?
   d) a mixture of all of the above? Why/why not?

2 Work with a partner. Look at the companies below.

CanGas Corp. – a Canadian Gas Company
Cyberchip Plc – a British computer chip manufacturer
Zero Emission Cars – a German producer of electric vehicles
Feijão Pretos SA – a Brazilian coffee producer
Genezap Inc. – a US biotech company which produces genetically-modified seed

Decide what kind of opportunities and threats there are for these companies. Think about environmental factors, market stability and competitors.

	Opportunities	Threats
CanGas Corp.		Gas supples will run out soon
Cyberchip Plc	Cost of manufacturing has fallen.	
Zero Emission Cars AG		
Feijão Pretos SA		
Genezap Inc.		

Reading for detail

3 Read the information about the five companies and add any other opportunities or threats they mention to the table above.

Negotiating

4 Shares in the five companies are currently worth €100 each. You have €5,000 to spend on shares. Decide with a partner which companies you are going to invest in.

Company	No. of shares	No. of shares after first report	No. of shares after second report	Value
CanGas Corp.				
Cyberchip Plc				
Zero Emission Cars				
Feijão Pretos SA				
Genezap Inc.				
Total value:	€5,000			

DVD-ROM Further interactive problem-solving on the DVD-ROM

7.6 Case study

Internet research

Search for the keywords *trading basics* to learn more about when to buy and sell shares.

5 🔘 2:31 Now listen to an economic report and decide whether you would like to swap any of the shares you have for other shares. Talk to other pairs and try to exchange shares.

6 🔘 2:32 Listen to a second report and decide whether you would like to make any further swaps.

7 🔘 2:33 Now listen to an interview with stock market analyst Sarah Johnson and find out how much your shares are worth and why.

CanGas Corp. is a medium-sized Canadian gas producer. It owns several gas fields in western Canada and currently produces about 8% of Canada's natural gas output. Some of the smaller gas fields will run out within the next five years, but the company has been investing a lot of money in new pipelines to increase production from its larger gas fields. Environmental groups, such as Greenpeace, are angry at CanGas' plans to start exploiting a new gas field in Alberta and say the planned pipeline will have a negative effect. The increase in oil and gas prices has helped push CanGas' share price up to $100 in recent months. A fall in energy prices would seriously affect CanGas' profitability and investment plans.

Cyberchip Plc has two 'fabs', or fabrication plants, in the UK and recently announced it has developed a new method of manufacturing chips which will reduce production costs significantly. Developing another plant will probably cost Cyberchip several million euros and some investors are worried that Cyberchip does not have the financial resources. FabPro, one of Cyberchip's competitors, has also announced that its new plant in Seoul will also go into full production of its new chip shortly. Many computer chip manufacturers have moved to the Far East where labour costs are significantly lower.

Zero Emission Cars produces small electric vehicles for city driving. It sold 50,000 units last year and plans to increase production by 50% in the next two years. High fuel prices have helped to increase the demand for these cars and new rules and regulations on emissions could push demand even higher. Critics say the car is too expensive and that the 80 km maximum range makes the car impractical for longer journeys. Zero Emission Cars says it is developing a new model which uses a new high-tech battery which could increase the car's range to 180–200 km.

Feijão Pretos SA produces high-quality, organic coffee. Its suppliers are mainly local coffee growers in the southern state of Paraná, Brazil, but it is increasingly buying more coffee from the states of Espirito Santo and Bahia which has helped to reduce the risk of frost because they are further north. Most of the coffee it exports is for the North American markets, but it is hoping to expand to the EU. Coffee prices have been falling on the world's markets, but Feijão Pretos' strategy of targeting the top end of the coffee market has worked well and last year it reported a profit of 42 million Brazilian Real (BRL) – or €15m, up 20% on the year before.

Genezap Incorporated produces genetically-modified seed, such as rice, wheat, maize and potato. Its turnover has increased more than 250% in the last five years and its profits have tripled in the same period. There are signs, however, that the demand for genetically-modified seed is slowing in the USA and Genezap is now hoping to be able to break into the European and Asian markets. Opposition to genetically-modified food is growing, particularly in Europe and the USA.

The **Business** 95

8 Going global

8.1 About business Franchising

Discussion

1 Work with a partner. Discuss the questions about franchising.

1 What is a franchise? Can you define it?
2 What types of businesses tend to be franchises?
3 How much control do you think the owner of a franchise has? Think about salary, uniform, equipment and decoration.

Scan reading

2 Read the article about the Subway franchise and answer the questions below.

1 Who is Fred DeLuca?
2 Approximately how much would you have to invest to open a Subway franchise?
3 Where was the first Subway franchise opened?
4 How many countries have Subway sandwich shops?

Reading for detail

3 Read the article about franchising and mark the sentences *T* (true) or *F* (false).

1 There are more McDonald's restaurants in the USA than Subway sandwich shops.
2 A Hilton Hotel Corp franchise is very expensive in comparison to a Subway franchise.
3 A person who runs a franchise can decide what their employees wear.
4 Fred DeLuca's first franchise shop was very far from his first shop.
5 Subway's first overseas franchise was opened more than 20 years after the first shop was opened.
6 The franchisor is responsible for all tax and legal matters within the country the franchise is operating in.
7 Franchising has had a positive effect on Fred DeLuca's company.

Vocabulary

4 In each set of four, match a word from the article with the correct meaning.

1 rapidly
2 phenomenal
3 furniture and fittings
4 outlet

a) a shop or store that sells goods to the public
b) very quickly
c) extraordinary
d) equipment or fixtures

5 abroad
6 consider
7 subsidiary
8 turnover

e) income or revenue
f) a business which is owned by another company
g) in a foreign country
h) think about

Discussion

5 With a partner discuss the questions.

1 Do you think a franchisee is really his/her own boss? Make a list of the type of decisions a franchisee can and cannot make themselves.
2 If you had the choice of buying a cup of coffee or a hamburger from a no-name company or a well-known franchise, which would you choose? Why?
3 If you wanted to start your own business would you think about buying a franchise? Why/Why not?
4 Do you think there any types of businesses that would not work as franchises? What are they and why do you think they wouldn't work?

Internet research

Search for the keywords *subway franchise* to find out more about Subway and franchising opportunities.

Join a leader in a high-growth industry. Low investment, no experience needed. Find out more today! Be your own boss tomorrow.

Going global with a SUBMARINE

If you would like to be a global player with outlets in hundreds of countries, perhaps you should think about setting up a franchise business.

FRED DELUCA, the CEO of Subway, opened his first Subway restaurant in Connecticut in 1965 with just US$1,000 borrowed from a friend of the family. Subway now has more outlets in the USA and Canada than MacDonald's. And the company is growing rapidly with eight new outlets opening worldwide every day.

One of the reasons for Subway's phenomenal growth is that the franchise fee is relatively cheap. A Subway franchise fee costs less than €10,000 and unlike a franchise with Hilton Hotels Corp, for example, you do not have to invest a small fortune in furniture and fittings. A subway shop can cost less than €100,000 to equip.

What exactly is a franchise and how does it work?

Once a company like Subway has established itself and can show that its business model works, it can offer its trademark or name to other companies or individuals. They pay an initial franchise fee to use the name and a certain percentage of the gross profit or turnover. The franchisee also has to fulfil the franchisor's CI* standards, for example, the stores and outlets have to be equipped and fitted in a certain way or the staff may have to wear a special uniform. But the risk for the franchisee is minimized - they are buying a well-known and established brand with tried and tested products or services which consumers can identify with. They know what to expect whether they are in Beijing, Bombay or Boston.

Franchising is a simple, but effective way of expanding rapidly, however, as Fred DeLuca discovered it takes time and a great deal of hard work to establish your company's name and reputation. It took Fred DeLuca nine years before he felt the time was right to open the first franchised Subway sandwich shop … and it wasn't on the other side of the globe, but just a 40-minute drive from Fred's first shop. It wasn't until 1984, almost 20 years after going into business, that the first Subway franchise opened abroad – and not in Canada, Mexico or Europe as you might expect, but Bahrain.

As Subway soon discovered, franchising is an excellent business model if you are thinking of going global. A franchisor does not need to worry about the laws or taxes of the foreign countries it operates in; it doesn't need to relocate staff to set up and run subsidiaries abroad; nor does it need to offer language training or cross-cultural courses to staff. The franchisee is responsible for running the business on a day-to-day basis and making sure it complies with the legislation of the country it operates in.

Subway currently operates in more than 86 countries … so if you have a good idea, such as how to make and sell a submarine sandwich, perhaps you should consider franchising if you want to go global.

They know what to expect whether they are in Beijing, Bombay or Boston

* CI = Corporate Identity

8 Going global

8.2 Vocabulary Setting up a franchise

Discussion

1 With a partner, put these stages of researching a franchise into the correct order.

a) Shortlist two or three franchises and talk to some of the franchisees running these businesses. How have these franchises developed? Are the franchisees happy with the support their franchisor provides? ☐
b) Decide how much money you can afford to invest and how much money you feel you can borrow. Be realistic! [1]
c) When you are happy that you have all the information you need to make a decision, complete the application form of the franchise you think is the most suitable for you. ☐
d) What are you good at? What do you enjoy doing? Identify the type of business you would like to operate in. ☐
e) Contact the franchises operating in that business and ask them to send you information about their franchising agreements. ☐
f) Do some market research. Do the franchises you have shortlisted already have outlets in your area? Is there a lot of competition? Does the area have enough customers or clients for the product or service you want to sell? ☐

Listening for gist

2 🔊 2:34 Listen to Maria Coelho talking to business journalist Dave Townley about her experience of running a franchise. Answer the questions.

1 What kind of business does Maria run?
2 Where is her business?
3 Is the business successful?

Listening for detail

3 Listen to Maria again and complete a summary of her franchise.

Maria returned to Portugal and decided she wanted to be her (1) _____ _____ and (2) _____ a teashop.
Maria flew to the UK four or five times to select the right (3) _____. She paid a franchising (4) _____ of £12,000.
She took part in a two-week (5) _____ _____.
The franchiser's European agent was unhappy about the location of the (6) _____ Maria had chosen. She spent another three months trying to find a more central outlet she could afford to (7) _____.
The bank agreed to (8) _____ Maria €50,000 and she (9) _____ another €50,000 from the three Fs.
Maria persuaded the franchisor to let her have the (10) _____ and (11) _____ made locally.
The business is now very successful; the (12) _____ has increased by 50% over the same period last year.

Internet research

Search for the keywords *global advertising campaign* to find out more about why companies use global advertising.

Collocations

4 In each set of four below, match a verb on the left with a noun on the right.

1 run   a) money
2 fill in   b) customers
3 raise   c) a business
4 attract   d) the paperwork
5 equip and fit e) a course
6 attend   f) an agreement
7 sign   g) an expense
8 budget for   h) a shop

5 Now use the collocations in 4 to say what these people are doing. Use the present continuous (*is / are* + *–ing*).

1 A: Do I have to write my tax number in this box or the name of the tax office?
   B: Erm, I'm not sure. Where is that list of instructions they sent?
   She is _____

2 A: We can't put the drinks machine there because it'll block the fire escape.
   B: Yes, that's true, but we can't put it over there either, unless we move the display.
   They _____

3 A: I think we'll need to spend about €1,000 a month on advertising.
   B: OK, so I'll put €12,000 down for that.
   They _____

4 A: What about offering free coffee for orders over $5.00?
   B: No, I think we should offer something that will appeal to kids.
   They _____

5 A: It is very informative and I am learning a lot about customer care and the importance of corporate identity.
   He _____

6 A: So the bank will only give us £25,000.
   B: Yes, but maybe my grandfather will lend us the rest.
   He _____

6 Below are words that are often used with the verbs *do*, *make* and *take*. Put them into the correct column in the table.

a profit   a phone call   homework   business   market research   a decision
somebody a favour   a break   a chance   an arrangement   a risk
overtime   a recommendation   an excuse   an exam   serious work

make	do	take

Discussion

7 Use the verbs *do*, *make* and *take* to fill in the questions.

1 When was the last time you _____ an excuse?
2 Have you _____ a chance recently?
3 When was the last time somebody _____ you a favour?
4 Do you usually _____ your homework?
5 Do you ever forget about arrangements you've _____?
6 Which companies do you think are _____ the biggest profits at the moment?

Now take it in turns to ask your partner the questions.

8 Going global

Refresh your memory

Past simple
They opened their first shop in 2003.
completed actions

▶ Grammar reference page 124

Present prefect
He has worked at most of the major banks in Rome
have/has + past participle
actions that started in the past and continue into the present
Peter Brozek has run the business for ten years.
for + length of time
for ten years, for half an hour
We have sold more than 160,000 copies of the DVD since 2007.
since + time the action started
since 2007, since 1st March, since I left college

▶ Grammar reference page 132

8.3 Grammar   Past simple and present perfect

Test yourself: Present perfect with *for* and *since*

1 Complete the dialogue between Ruth and Paolo by putting *for* or *since* into the spaces.

R: So, Paolo, you're a sales manager at BD International, aren't you?
P: Yes, that's right. I'm responsible for international sales. I've been with BD International (1) _____ I left university in 1990.
R: How long have you been in London?
P: I've been here (2) _____ almost ten years. I worked in our Madrid office before that.
R: I guess you have to do a lot of travelling.
P: Oh yes, I've had to fly to Paris, New York and Shanghai (3) _____ the beginning of the month.
R: Shanghai?
P: Yes, we have had a subsidiary in Shanghai (4) _____ 2001. I usually have to fly there two or three times a year.
R: That sounds like hard work! Can you speak any Chinese?
P: A little, but most of my colleagues there speak English quite well. Actually, I'm trying to learn Russian at the moment.
R: Russian?
P: Yes, we've had an office in Petersburg (5) _____ more than ten years.
R: Is your Russian good?
P: It's not bad, but I haven't had any lessons (6) _____ the last two months.
R: Language must be a big problem for an international company.
P: Yes, language and inter-cultural training have been key issues for us (7) _____ we lost a very important contract in Dubai in 1999 because of misunderstandings there.

Test yourself: Past simple and present perfect

2 Read an interview about Siemens' recent history between Peter Davis, a business journalist, and Chris Frank, a business analyst. Underline the correct tense.

Peter (1) **Have there been / Were there** a lot of changes at Siemens since 1970?
Chris Yes, of course, Peter, but most of them (2) **happened / have happened** under the leadership of Heinrich von Pierer and his successor Klaus Kleinfeld who (3) **resigned / has resigned** as CEO of Siemens in 2007.
Peter What sort of changes (4) **did they make / have they made**?
Chris Well, they (5) **have moved / moved** Siemens out of certain business areas such as defence systems and mobile phones. They (6) **sold / have sold** the defence business in 1997 and BenQ (7) **bought / has bought** Siemens' mobile phone subsidiary in 2005.
Peter (8) **Has Siemens moved / Did Siemens move** into any new areas?
Chris Yes, of course. Since 2000 they (9) **took over / have taken over** 20 new companies in areas ranging from wind power to industrial automation.
Peter Siemens is sometimes called a sleeping giant. Do you think that is still true?
Chris (10) That **was / has been** true in the past, but not any more, Peter. There (11) **was / has been** some radical restructuring in the last few years.
Peter And, do you think that will continue?
Chris Yes, I'm sure that subsidiaries and divisions which (12) **were / have been** performing badly will be sold off and Siemens will buy into other companies with high growth potential.

100 *The* Business

DVD-ROM Further interactive grammar practice on the DVD-ROM

8.3 Grammar

Internet research

Search for the keywords *company history* to find out more about a company you are interested in. Tell your partner what you find.

Asking questions

3 Use *how long* + the present perfect to make questions.

	Question	Answer
1		He's been the European agent for the franchise since 2005.
2		We've had outlets in Asia for over 15 years.
3		Sue's known the CEO of the American division for about five years.
4		They've been in the oil business since 1897.
5		We've had an agreement with them for ten years.
6		I've seen this problem with the European market coming for some time.

Describing companies

4 Read the facts about global companies and use the present perfect (*have/has done*) or past simple (*did*) of the verbs in brackets.

1 McDonald's _____ (open) its first foreign outlet in Richmond, Canada in 1967. It now has outlets in 120 countries.
2 The Bank of Tokyo-Mitsubishi UFJ, Ltd _____ (be) the world's largest bank since 2006. It has assets of over US$1.7 trillion.
3 Lufthansa _____ (take over) Swiss Air in March 2005. It is now Europe's third largest airline after British Airways and Air France.
4 De Beers _____ (has) a monopoly of the world's diamond market for decades. It controls about 60% of the market.
5 Exxon Mobil, the world's biggest oil company, _____ (announce) revenues of over US$298 billion in 2004. That is more than the GDP of a country such as Austria.
6 Wal-Mart _____ (be) a family-owned business since Sam Walton opened his first Wal-Mart store in Arkansas in the USA in 1962. It is the world's largest retailer.
7 Levi's _____ (close) most of its factories in the USA and Canada and _____ (move) production to low-cost countries in the 1990s.
8 Apple Inc. _____ (decide) to drop the word 'computer' from its name Apple Computer, Inc. in January 2007. Since the success of its iPod, Apple _____ (focus) on expanding its range of products in the consumer electronics market.

Asking for information

5 Siemens AG is one of the world's biggest technology conglomerates. It has subsidiaries in 190 countries and employs almost half a million people worldwide.

Work in pairs. Ask your partner questions to complete the first 120 years of the company's history.

Student A: use the information below.
Student B: turn to page 115.

- Werner von Siemens established the Siemens and Halske Construction Company in Berlin in _____. (When?)
- The company constructed the Indo-European telegraph line between London and Calcutta in 1870.
- Siemens presented _____ at the Berlin Trade Fair in 1879. (What?)
- In 1919 Siemens formed a joint venture with two other manufacturers of light bulbs. The joint venture company was called Osram.
- The company installed the first automatic traffic lights in _____ in 1924. (Where?)
- Siemens started producing the electron microscope in 1939.
- Reconstruction of the company began. Over 80% of the company's assets were destroyed in WWII.
- Siemens developed a method to produce _____ and entered the data processing industry in 1953. (What?)
- In 1964 construction of the world's largest satellite communications station in Bavaria, Germany began.
- Siemens became a German public limited company; Siemens AG in _____. (When?)
- Siemens set up the company _____ to produce household appliances in 1967. (Which?)

The Business 101

8 Going global

8.4 Speaking   Presentations - handling questions

Discussion

1 Work with a partner. Read the quiz about airports and decide what the correct answer is.

1 The world's busiest airport is:
   a) Beijing, China
   b) Atlanta, USA
   c) Heathrow, UK.

2 The longest runway in the world is at:
   a) New York JFK, USA
   b) Edwards Airforce Base, USA
   c) Dubai International Airport.

3 The highest airport in the world is:
   a) Svalbard Airport, Norway
   b) Lima, Peru
   c) Bangda, Tibet.

4 The biggest passenger plane is:
   a) the Boeing 747
   b) the Airbus A380
   c) Antonov 225.

5 In 2005 the longest non-stop commercial flight was:
   a) from London to Sydney
   b) from Hong Kong to London
   c) from Beijing to New York.

6 The world's oldest airline is:
   a) KLM, the Netherlands
   b) Easyjet, UK
   c) Northwest, USA.

Listening for detail

2 🔊 **2:35** Listen to the first part of a presentation by Ingo Anspach, the press officer at Munich airport. Complete the sentences below with the information you hear.

1 The decision to build the new airport was made in _____.
2 The construction work began in _____.
3 The airport was officially opened in _____.
4 It has been voted the "Best Airport in Europe" for _____.
5 Last year there were 30.8 million _____ and more than 400,000 _____ and landings.
6 The number of passengers has increased by _____ and the number of flights by _____.
7 5% of the passengers fly _____ class and 95% fly _____.
8 52% of the passengers say they are flying for _____ purposes and 48% for _____ purposes.

102 *The* Business

Internet research

Search for the keywords *Heathrow Airport* to find out more about one of the world's busiest international airports.

3 🔊 2:36 Now listen to the question and answer (Q&A) session at the end of the presentation and match the information on the left with the numbers and figures on the right.

1 Over _____ people work at the airport.
2 A second terminal was opened in _____.
3 A new runway is planned for _____.
4 The hotel will have _____ rooms.
5 The hotel will be ready in _____.
6 In the last two and a half years _____ new jobs have been created.
7 Night-Flight, the disco, is big enough for _____ guests.
8 Half a litre of beer at the Airbräu brewery costs €_____.

a) 2003
b) 250
c) 27,400
d) 2011
e) 3,000
f) 2009
g) 2.10
h) 4,000

Handling questions

4 Put the press officer's answers to the questions into the correct order.

1 You said that over 27,400 people work at the airport. What do they all do?
   → a good That's very question.
2 What have been the most important developments at the airport since it opened?
   → OK, glad asked I'm me you that.
3 Do you think the new runway that's planned for 2011 is really necessary?
   → it isn't say people Some that, but...
4 Are you planning anything else?
   → Yes, of course. I my mentioned As in talk...
5 Have a lot of jobs been lost since September 11, 2001?
   → No, the on contrary...
6 What has the airport done to tighten security and make flying safer for passengers?
   → I'm afraid can't I the details go into here.

Listen to the Q&A session again and check your answers.

5 Answer the questions about the phrases for handling questions.

1 Which phrase can you use when you don't want to say any more about something?
2 Which two phrases can you use to introduce a negative answer?
3 Which two phrases can you use to introduce a positive answer?
4 Which phrase can you use to refer back to something that you talked about earlier?

Speaking

6 Work in pairs. Prepare to talk for two minutes about your studies, qualifications and work experience. Prepare a list of questions to ask your partner. When you are talking use the phrases in exercise 4 to deal with the questions.

A: I graduated from university in 2005.   B: What did you study?
A: That's a very good question, my main...

Roleplay

7 At the moment your local airport only offers domestic flights, but it plans to expand and become an international airport.

Your local newspaper has reported that:

- the number of flights could increase by 30 a day to over 300 a day within the next five years.
- a new railway line and motorway from the nearest city will have to be built.
- two international hotels and a conference centre are planned.
- a 24/7 shopping centre is planned.
- the runway will be extended and a small forest will have to be cut down.
- the groundwater in the area will have to be lowered because of the problem of fog in spring and autumn.
- a new town may have to be built for all the extra employees the airport will employ.

8 Work in groups of three. Student A turn to page 114, B turn to page 113, student C turn to page 116

8 Going global

8.5 Writing Reports of recommendation

Discussion

1 Work with a partner. Have you ever had to write a report or make a written statement? What was it about? What kind of information or facts did you include?

Reading and analysis

2 Read these extracts from a report of recommendation. Find answers to the questions.

1 What locations does the report cover?
2 How many selection criteria were used?
3 Which location does the report recommend?

> This first part of this report looks at the advantages and disadvantages of relocating production to various locations in Poland, the Czech Republic, Hungary, Bulgaria and Romania.
> The second part of the report looks at....

> The selection criteria we used to compare the different locations were:
> - local salaries
> - availability of skilled staff
> - land prices/rents
> - local infrastructure
> - availability of local suppliers
> - transportation costs

> ... land prices and rents are likely to rise and this could result in demands for higher wages and salaries. However, we forecast that these costs are likely to increase far more quickly in locations in the countries bordering Austria and Germany.

> The main disadvantages of setting up a production facility in Romania are the higher transportation costs to the western European markets. We would also be almost totally dependent on one local supplier for the electronic components we need. These could be shipped from suppliers in Germany, Austria or the Czech Republic if there were a major disruption at the supplier's factory.

> The biggest advantages of the Romanian sites are clearly the cost savings for skilled staff and the local authorities' offers of a free 99 year lease for the sites.

> ... the cost of moving production to Romania could be covered by selling the UK and French factories. We suggest locating the plant in either Bucharest or Constanta ...

3 The points below are typical of a report of recommendation. Which order would you expect them to be in?

☐ list which points were taken into account
☐ outline the structure of the report
☐ make a recommendation
☐ identify possible future risks
☐ identify the pros and cons

Now read the extracts again. Does their order on the page match your order?

4 Match the phrases on the left with those on the right with a similar meaning.

1 This first part of the report looks at...
2 The selection criteria we used were...
3 ... are likely to (rise / fall) and this could result in....
4 We forecast that....
5 The main disadvantages are...
6 The issues we looked at were...
7 The biggest advantages...
8 We suggest...

a) Factors used to select were...
b) We predict that...
c) The initial part of the report examines...
d) ... could (increase / decrease) and this may lead to...
e) The most significant benefits...
f) The questions we examined were...
g) We recommend...
h) The biggest drawbacks are...

104 *The* **Business**

Listening for detail

5 🔊 2:37 Listen to Ajit Singh, a relocation consultant, talking about the problems of building an electric motors factory in the location David Green has visited.

Make some notes about the positive or negative points you hear.

Notes:

	Positive points	Negative points
Location		
Infrastructure (Roads, railways)		
Staff		
Suppliers		
Constructing the factory		

Writing

6 Work with a partner and use the information in the table above to write a short report to David Green's boss about the pros and cons of building the plant at this location and make a recommendation.

Internet research

Search for the keywords *report* + (a subject you are interested in) to find some reports that have been written about it.

8 Going global

8.6 Case study Choosing a franchise

Discussion

1 Work in small groups. Would you like to set up and run your own business? Why/Why not?

2 Read the statements below and decide whether they would most likely be said by the owner of a small business, an employee or both. Write O (owner), E (employee) or B (both) next to each.

1 I haven't had a holiday for almost two years. ☐
2 I've had to do a lot of overtime since the beginning of the month. ☐
3 We had to close the company for ten days last May because I was ill. ☐
4 Being a good listener is very important. ☐
5 There's no point in having good ideas, they just get ignored. ☐
6 If I didn't take risks, nothing would ever change. ☐
7 I often have to take work home with me. ☐
8 I didn't get a Christmas bonus last year. ☐

Reading for detail

3 Read what franchisees had to say about their franchises and complete the table opposite with the information that is missing.

FINNLEY'S

Lewis and I set up a Finnley's franchise in Malaga, Spain two years ago. We work from home, so the only costs we had were for equipping the office. We probably paid less than £7,000 for the PCs, phones, fax and furniture.
　Lewis does all the paperwork and I organize the staff.
　We have a dozen care workers and almost 200 clients.
　A lot of elderly people retire to Spain and they don't normally have family or friends to support them, so there is a big demand for home care here.
　If you enjoy working with people, home care is a great business opportunity and a very rewarding job.

TOASTIES

When Sally and I left college we decided we wanted to work together and run our own business. We looked into several franchises, but most of them were too expensive for us.
　Our outlet has done really well. We were lucky; we found a shop near the university, so nearly all our customers are students.
　Finding the right location is key in this business. Several of the Toasties franchisees we know have had difficulties because they opened outlets in locations where there were already a lot of fast food restaurants and cafes.
　The fast food market is very competitive so if you don't find the right location, you won't survive for long.

CLASSIC COTTON CLOTHES

Laura and I love what we are doing. We both care about the environment and feel that what we are doing is helping the planet. Lots of people buy clothes without thinking about where the products come from and we aim to provide pure cotton clothes that are made in a completely natural and environmentally-friendly way.
　The business has grown quickly since we started and we now have over 200 customers who regularly order clothes from us. Most of them are in their late twenties or thirties.
　Most franchises open in small towns, away from the big shopping centres, but we also deliver products to people's homes. The clothing market can be difficult to break into because lots of big chains are already well-established so if you don't find a gap in the market, you won't survive for long.

DVD-ROM Further interactive problem-solving on the DVD-ROM

8.6 Case study

Name of franchise	Finnley's	Toasties	Classic Cotton Clothes
Established	2000		
Business area		Convenience food	
Franchise fee			£18,000
Cost of fittings and equipment, etc.	?		
No. of franchises		530	
Typical customers	Disabled and/or older people		?
Growth potential		?	High

Internet research

Search for the keywords *presentation tips* to find out how you can make your presentations better in future. Choose three tips which are useful for you. Tell your partner.

Listening for detail

4 2:38–2:40 Listen to three presentations about the different franchises and add any information you hear to the table above.

Discussion

5 With a partner, decide which franchise above you would like to run and why.

6 Imagine that you are running the franchise you chose in 5. Look at the questions below and fill in the table about the opportunities and threats that you face.

Opportunities:
1 What are your strengths and why do you think they would help you to run this business?
2 What are the trends that will help your business grow (changes in politics, technology, lifestyles, population, etc.)?

Threats:
1 Is there a lot of competition in this market?
2 What changes (in politics, technology, lifestyles, population, etc.) could have a negative effect on your business?
3 Could you have problems financing the business?
4 What weaknesses do you have that could have negative effects on your business?

Opportunities	Threats

Presenting

7 With a partner, prepare a short presentation about the franchise you have chosen and what the opportunities and threats are. Use the prompts below to help you.

Student A
1 Thank the audience for coming.
2 Say who you and your partner are.
3 Tell the audience what the topic of your presentation is.
4 Tell the audience how long the presentation will take and how it is structured.
5 Present the opportunities you think your franchise offers.
6 Hand over to your partner.

Student B
1 Thank your partner.
2 Present the threats you think this franchise has.
3 Sum up the key points.
4 Thank your audience for listening.
5 Ask if there are any questions.
6 Answer any questions you are asked.

Review 7

7 The stock markets

1 Complete each sentence with a pair of items from the box. The items may not be in the same order.

> venture capital/bank loan   go public/make an IPO
> share/stake   turnover/expenses   assets/liabilities

1 The part of a business that you own is your _____ in the company. The word is also used more generally to mean 'the degree to which you are involved in something'. One part of the ownership of a business, which can be bought and sold, is a _____.
2 A small company can obtain funding from two sources: a _____, which it has to pay back, or _____, which means giving a large part of the shares to outside investors in exchange for their money.
3 One type of company report is a Balance Sheet. Here, the _____ are everything that a company owns, and the _____ are all its debts.
4 Another type of company report is an Income Statement (= Profit and Loss Account). Here, the _____ (= income) appears at the top, and the _____ (= costs) are taken away to give the profit.
5 The phrases _____ and _____ have the same meaning. Another synonym, in the right context, is 'list' used as a verb.

2 Write these numbers as words, exactly as you would say them:

1 2/3   _____
2 199,184   _____
3 200,000m²   _____
4 0.52%   _____

3 Complete each sentence with a pair of items from the box. The items may not be in the same order.

> decline/be stagnant   shoot up/drop   fall/rise
> fluctuate/remain stable

1 The words _____ and _____ have the same meaning as 'increase' and 'decrease'.
2 If profits _____, they increase quickly. If profits _____, they decrease quickly.
3 To _____ means 'to go down'. To _____ means 'to not grow or develop'.
4 If sales _____, they don't go up and down very much. If sales _____, they go up and down a lot.

4 Match the adverbs in sentences a-f with their best definitions below.

a) Sales rose considerably.
b) Sales rose dramatically.
c) Sales rose fractionally.
d) Sales rose gradually.
e) Sales rose slightly.
f) Sales rose steadily.

1 by a very, very small amount ☐
2 a little ☐
3 a lot ☐
4 suddenly and surprisingly ☐
5 slowly and in small stages ☐
6 slowly and at the same constant speed ☐

5 Match the questions to the answers.

1 Have you seen this article? ☐
2 Do you know what day it is next Friday? ☐
3 The printer cartridge needs changing. ☐
4 What do they intend to do? ☐
----
a) → Yes, I do. It'll be the 10ᵗʰ anniversary of the stock market crash.
b) → Okay. I'll do it.
c) → They're going to sell all their shares.
d) → Yes, it says that the stock market is probably going to rise this year.

6 Look back at the use of *will* and *going to* in the answers in exercise 5. Write the correct letter a-d below.

1 *will* used for a spontaneous decision made at the moment of speaking _____
2 *going to* used for a decision made before the moment of speaking (i.e. it is a plan) _____
3 *will* used for a fact in the future _____
4 *going to* used for a prediction in the future with evidence in the present situation _____

7 Complete the sentences with the correct form of the verb in brackets. All the sentences are first conditionals.

1 If the share price _____ (go up) by more than 10%, all the senior managers _____ (get) a bonus.
2 Their profits _____ (not/go up) unless they _____ (cut) costs dramatically.

8 Complete the sentences used in negotiating with the best words and phrases in the box.

> by the guarantee   charge another 2%
> drop your price   have a deal
> kind of quantities   payment within 30 days
> we couldn't accept that   we should look at

1 Can we agree on _____?
2 We'd like you to _____ by 5%.
3 So, what _____ are we talking about?
4 If you pay late, we will _____ for every 30 days.
5 I'm afraid _____.
6 Perhaps _____ delivery times next.
7 These issues are covered _____.
8 Okay, I think we _____.

9 Make three linking phrases with the same meaning using each of these words: *because, result, due, a, as, of, of, to*.

The price of oil went up by 5% yesterday _____ / _____ / _____ the threat of a serious hurricane in the Gulf of Mexico.

108 *The* Business

Review 8

8 Going global

1 Complete this text about franchising with the items in the box.

brand	business model	day-to-day
fee	furniture and fittings	laws and taxes
outlets	risk	standards	turnover

If you want to be a global player with your ¹_____ name in hundreds of countries, perhaps you should think about setting up a franchise business. Franchising is now very common, from small retail ²_____ like Subway, to large businesses like Hilton Hotels.

How does franchising work? First, the company has to show that its ³_____ works. Then it can offer its trademark or name to another company or individual (the 'franchisee'). They pay an initial ⁴_____ to use the name, and also agree to pay the parent company a certain percentage of the ⁵_____. The franchisee also has to fulfill certain corporate identity ⁶_____, such as those relating to the ⁷_____ inside the store, or to staff uniforms. But the advantages to the franchisee are many: they are buying a well-known brand and the ⁸_____ is minimized.

For the franchisor, there are also many benefits. They don't have to worry about the ⁹_____ of the foreign countries they operate in, and they can leave all the ¹⁰_____ running of the business to the franchisee.

So, franchising works for both sides. It's a genuinely win-win situation!

2 Fill in the missing letters in these sentences.

1 If you complete some forms, then you f___ in the p____ work.
2 If you prepare an empty store before opening it to the public, then you equ__ and f__ it.
3 If you decide how much money something will cost, then you bu___t for an ex____e .
4 If you think of ways to get customers to enter your store, then you att____ them.
5 All the day-to-day activities of keeping a business going are called __nning the business.
6 If you go on a course, then you a____d it.
7 If you try to get money for a project or business, then you r___e the money.
8 Before you s___ an ag_____nt you should show it to your lawyer.

3 Complete each sentence with one of these words: *do*, *make*, *take*.

1 I hope we _____ a profit, not a loss.
2 I'll be there in five minutes, I just have to _____ a phone call first.
3 I've meet them and they seem honest. I think we can _____ business with them.
4 We have to _____ a lot of market research before we launch the product.
5 We're about halfway through the agenda. I think we should _____ a short break now.
6 I hate the end of the tax year. There is always so much paperwork to _____.

7 We don't have all the information we need, but we have to move quickly. I think we should _____ a risk and go ahead with the project.
8 We've been discussing this for half an hour. I'd like to _____ a recommendation.
9 We don't have the goods from our suppliers yet. I could phone them to complain but they always _____ some excuse or other.
10 I'm on an MBA course. I _____ my final exams next June.

4 Put the verb in brackets into either the past simple or the present perfect. Use contractions where possible (*I've* instead of *I have*).

1 So far this year _____ (they/sell) more than 500 franchise licenses worldwide. That's a big increase on last year, when _____ (they/only/sell) 300.
2 Last week _____ (I/see) the new Bond film. I think it's one of the best action movies _____ (I/ever/see).
3 "How long _____ (you/be) in this job?" → "About two years. Before doing this _____ (I/be) a burger-flipper at McDonalds."
4 I know what happened last week and I understand why _____ (you/do) it. In fact _____ (I/do) it myself many times before.

5 Fill in the gaps with either *for* or *since*.

1 I've been in this job _____ the beginning of the year.
2 I've been in this job _____ about nine months.
3 I've been in this job _____ a long time.
4 I've been in this job _____ leaving university.

6 The phrases below are used for handling questions after a presentation. Match the beginnings to the ends.

1 That's a very   asked me that.
2 I'm glad you   go into the details here.
3 As I mentioned   on the contrary.
4 No,   good question.
5 I'm afraid I can't   in my talk, …

7 Complete the sentences taken from a business report with the words in the box.

| benefit | drawback | issues | recommendations |
| forecast | lead to | likely to | looks at |

1 The first part of this report _____ the need to build a new factory.
2 The selection criteria we used to make our _____ were location, cost and timescale.
3 In terms of location, the _____ we examined were cost of labour and distance from our main suppliers.
4 Labour costs are difficult to quantify. They are _____ rise and this may _____ a loss of competitive advantage in the long term.
5 In relation to timescale, we _____ that the whole project will take around 15 months from beginning to end.
6 The biggest _____ of this proposal is its complexity in terms of planning. The most significant _____ is its greater flexibility for our future needs.

The **Business** 109

Additional material

1.4 Speaking
Making small talk (page 13, exercise 7)

Student A

You are at an international conference and it is the break between two presentations. You don't know any of the other people in your group and so need to make small talk.

Get ready to make small talk about the weather.

You have five minutes to talk to **all** of the other members of your group. Use phrases for beginning and ending small talk so that you speak to everyone in your group.

6.4 Speaking
Discussion (page 76, exercise 1)

1	yes 2	no 0
2	yes 0	no 2
3	yes 2	no 0
4	yes 0	no 2
5	yes 0	no 2
6	yes 2	no 0
7	yes 0	no 2
8	yes 0	no 2
9	yes 0	no 2
10	yes 2	no 0
11	yes 2	no 0
12	yes 2	no 0

Your score

0-8
You are a terrible listener! You need to work on your listening skills. Perhaps you need to slow down and make time to listen to people or you may need to pay more attention to what people are saying and react to what they tell you. You will probably find that your conversations are more successful if you do this.

9-16
You're an average listener. With a little extra effort you could become a really good listener. Why not try using body language a bit more when you are talking? Make sure you keep eye contact with the person you are talking to and always remember to smile, people always respond well to a smile.

17-24
Well done! You are an expert listener! Your listening skills are well developed and you always pay attention to what other people are saying.

3.2 Vocabulary
Describing trends (page 35, exercise 10)

Student B

Graph 3 Road accidents

- Notes: most of the accidents occurred at the weekends, especially at night, or on Tuesdays when the airport is busiest.
- There were a few tropical storms in April and May.

3.2 Vocabulary
Discussion (page 35, exercise 11)

Student B

The road between the airport and the town is full of holes. There are no traffic lights or street lighting in the town or on the airport road.
The town only has six police officers – they are all male.

1.4 Speaking
Making small talk (page 13, exercise 7)
Student B

You are at an international conference and it is the break between two presentations. You don't know any of the other people in your group and so need to make small talk.

Get ready to make small talk about where you are from.

You have five minutes to talk to **all** of the other members of your group. Use phrases for beginning and ending small talk so that you speak to everyone in your group.

2.6 Case study
Discussion (page 29, exercise 6)
Student B

1 Read the hotel's explanations for three of the problems and then tell your partner.

1 Regular buses were provided to take guests to and from the conference facilities. The buses only took ten minutes and were completely free of charge.
2 All of the rooms in the hotel are non-smoking. The guests from Electronics EDC were all together on the same floor of the hotel. The air-conditioning system connects all rooms and any smoky smells came from other rooms on the same floor.
3 Electronics RDC only booked eight rooms and did not tell the Panorama hotel that they needed another one. The hotel was completely full when they arrived.

2 With your partner discuss what action the hotel should take.

4.4 Speaking
Roleplay (page 51, exercise 9)
Student A

You are the manager of the IT department at EMF engineering. Student B is one of your programmers and today you are meeting for an appraisal.
Use your notes on Student B and the questions in 5 to help you.

- Has worked for the company for three years.
- Always punctual
- A little disorganized
- A number of important deadlines have been missed recently.
- Other members of the department complain that Student B is unhelpful.
- Very creative and always has good ideas.

4.6 Case study
Debate (page 54, exercise 6)
Aristotle Onassis

But

Onassiss' family money came from the tobacco business. His own personal fortune was made through unscrupulous and illegal whaling. He liked whaling and killed as many whales as possible regardless of what kind they were, including protected Blue Whales. He got into trouble for whaling too close to the coast in Peru, and for starting the hunt a month before the season began.

Lakshmi Mittal

But

In 2002 he was involved in a political scandal with British Prime Minister Tony Blair: Mittal made a £2 million donation to the Labour party in return for business favours.

Gianni Versace

But

Although the Versace label has increased sales since his death, profit increase is at a much slower rate and the company had to announce a cost cutting programme. Gianni's bother and sister, Santo and Donatella now run the company, but the sole heiress is Donatella's daughter, Allegra.

Coco Chanel

But

She had an affair with a Nazi officer in occupied Paris during World War 2. He allowed her to stay in the Paris Ritz with him. After the war she lived in exile in Switzerland until her comeback into the fashion world in 1954.

1.4 Speaking
Making small talk (page 13, exercise 7)
Student C

You are at an international conference and it is the break between two presentations. You don't know any of the other people in your group and so need to make small talk.

Get ready to make small talk about the hotel you are staying in.

You have five minutes to talk to **all** of the other members of your group. Use phrases for beginning and ending small talk so that you speak to everyone in your group.

4.4 Speaking
Roleplay (page 51, exercise 9)
Student B

You are a programmer in the IT department at EMF engineering. Student A is your manager and today you are meeting for your annual appraisal.
Below are some notes to help you.

- Always arrive on time.
- Really enjoy my job and I am very good at it.
- Very hardworking and creative.
- Colleagues in my department always disturb me with questions which stop me from working. I try to help them as much as I can but sometimes I have too much of my own work to do.
- The company needs to offer more training.

5.2 Vocabulary
Roleplay (page 61, exercise 8)
Student A

You are a salesperson in a large computer showroom. Student B is a customer who wants to buy a new laptop. You need to:
ask why the customer needs this product and how much he or she wants to pay.
ask questions to find out what your customer wants to buy.
recommend some models to the customer because they are not sure which model they want.
offer some alternatives.
answer any questions the customer asks.

5.4 Speaking
Roleplay (page 65, exercise 7)
Student A

1 The company needs to save money

You think a good and easy way is that the company canteen should no longer be subsidized. At the moment employees only pay €4.50 per meal, but the real cost is €8. With 20,000 employees that's a saving of €40,000

2 The offices will be painted

You have read that pink is calming and makes you feel happy and secure. To reduce stress and illness at work you suggest all offices are painted pink.

3 Company sponsorship

You want the company to sponsor the local ice-hockey team, although it's not playing well this season. It's an engineering company and the tough image is a good fit.

3.2 Vocabulary
Describing trends (page 35, exercise 10)
Student A

Graph 2 Car hire

- Notes: 12% of people who hired cars had small accidents.
- 8% of hire cars were stolen or broken into.
- There was a lot of rain in April.
- Many tourists came for beach holidays in July.

3.2 Vocabulary
Discussion (page 35, exercise 11)
Student A

The airport roof leaks and the arrival hall is very small. There are no security-controlled car parks in the town. The rail link from the town to the airport is very slow.

1.4 Speaking
Making small talk (page 13, exercise 7)
Student D

You are at an international conference and it is the break between two presentations. You don't know any of the other people in your group and so need to make small talk.

Get ready to make small talk about the journey here.

You have five minutes to talk to **all** of the other members of your group. Use phrases for beginning and ending small talk so that you speak to everyone in your group.

5.2 Vocabulary
Roleplay (page 61, exercise 8)
Student B

You are a customer in a large computer showroom. Student A is a salesperson.
You need to:
decide why you want this product and how much you want to pay.
ask questions because you are not sure which model you want.
answer all the questions the salesperson asks you.
think about the alternatives the salesperson offers you.
ask any more questions you can think of about the product.

5.4 Speaking
Roleplay (page 65, exercise 7)
Student B

1 The company needs to save money
You think the company canteen should stay subsidized as a good meal at midday is very important. You think you can save the same amount of money by installing vending machines for drinks. At the moment drinks cost nothing.

2 The offices will be painted
You want the offices to be white as usual, you could go along with a pale yellow, but pink is out of the question.

3 Company sponsorship
You want the company to sponsor the local ballet school. It's very successful and sponsoring culture is always good. The local hockey team is bottom of the league.

6.5 Writing
Reporting (page 79, exercise 5)

Minutes of meeting – 4th September
Venue: Main conference room
Present: Cristina (chair), Firat, Lena and Adrian
Apologies for absence: Birgit

1 Matters arising from previous meeting.
   Hot desking.
   Lena reported that the staff were still not happy about this and warned that the atmosphere in the office was bad and was getting worse. Firat agreed with this. Lena agreed to write a report and promised to have it ready for 8th September.

2 New quotations for building new canteen.
   Firat presented quotations from Turnbull Construction Ltd and Haines Ltd. Everybody agreed that the Haines proposal was better. Firat agreed to draw up a schedule for the building work and to bring it to the next meeting.

3 Changes to staff newsletter
   Adrian pointed out that a lot of work was needed for the staff newsletter and that the quality was decreasing. He suggested producing the newsletter every quarter. Lena disagreed with the idea. Adrian agreed to write a proposal of the pros and cons of a quarterly newsletter.

4 AOB
   Christmas party
   Lena wondered if the Christmas party could be held in the canteen. She agreed to check the schedule and to report back at the next meeting.

Next Meeting: September 11th in the main conference room.

8.4 Speaking
Roleplay (page 103, exercise 7)
Student B

You live close to the airport and are the manager of a supermarket. The plans to expand could be very good for your business, but they could also create problems for you. Think of questions to ask C, the airport's press officer.

7.4 Speaking

Negotiation (page 91, exercise 6)

Student B

You work in the sales department. Your company specializes in printing logos on gifts that companies give away to their customers or clients.

You normally offer a discount for orders of more than 500 items of one product, but you can be flexible there if you think the total order is large enough.
Your delivery times are normally 28 days.
Your terms of payment for smaller orders (up to €2,500) are normally 10 days.
Shipping costs for orders over €1,000 are €150, but again you can be flexible.
Your orders were down 10% last month.

The standard prices in your catalogue for up to 500 items of the following products are:

Product	Unit price	Quantity	Total
Calculators	€5.00		
Cups	€4.00		
Key rings	€0.50		
Teddy bears	€0.80		
	Discount ___%		

Try to negotiate a deal that both you and the customer can live with. Your partner phones you.

7.5 Writing

Describing figures (page 93, exercise 6)

Student B

Write a report describing June to December. Use the graph below.

Include a description of the trend (*it fell from … to …, it fell by … to …*) and a reason for the trend (*bad weather, a strike, etc*). Invent these reasons.

When you finish, swap reports with your partner and read about the other half of the year. Discuss together what actions the management could have taken at key moments.

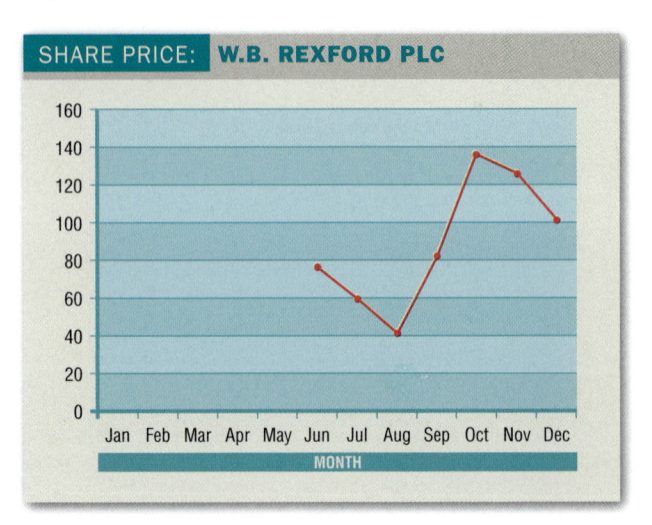

6.4 Speaking

Handling interruptions (page 77, exercise 6)

Student B

Prepare a short talk on a company that is successful all over the world. Make some notes. Think about what the company does, why you think they are successful and who their main rivals are.
When you are ready give your talk to the other two members of the group. Be prepared to answer any questions that they might have.
When the others give their talks try to ask a question and interrupt once or twice

8.4 Speaking

Roleplay (page 103, exercise 7)

Student A

You live close to the airport and your house is between the airport and the city. You are very worried about these plans. What kind of negative impacts could these plans have for you and family? Think of questions to ask C, the airport's press officer.

6.4 Speaking
Handling interruptions (page 77, exercise 6)
Student C

Prepare a short talk on the kind of company you would like to set up. Make some notes. Think about what your company would specialize in, why you want to set up this kind of company and what you would do to make sure it is successful.

When you are ready give your talk to the other two members of the group. Be prepared to answer any questions that they might have.

When the others give their talks try to ask a question and interrupt once or twice

8.3 Grammar
Asking for information (page 101, exercise 5)
Student B

Ask your partner questions to complete the first 120 years of the Siemens' history.

- Werner von Siemens established the Siemens and Halske Construction Company in Berlin in 1847.
- The company constructed the Indo-European telegraph line between London and Calcutta in _____. (When?)
- Siemens presented the first electric railway at the Berlin Trade Fair in 1879.
- In 1919 Siemens formed a joint venture with two other manufacturers of light bulbs. The joint venture company was called _____. (What?)
- The company installed the first automatic traffic lights in Berlin in 1924.
- Siemens started producing the electron microscope in _____. (When?)
- Reconstruction of the company began. Over _____ per cent of the company's assets were destroyed in WW II. (How many?)
- Siemens developed a method to produce ultra-pure silicon and entered the data processing industry in _____.
- In _____ construction of the world's largest satellite communications station begins in Bavaria, Germany began. (When?)
- Siemens became a German public limited company; Siemens AG in 1966.
- Siemens set up the company Bosch-Siemens to produce household appliances.

3.2 Vocabulary
Describing trends (page 35, exercise 10)
Student C

Graph 4 Crime
- Notes: the police know that pickpockets are working at the markets and on the beach.
- The island's festival week was in July.

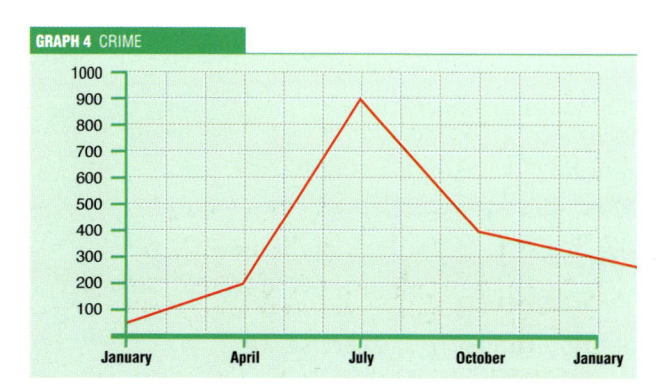

3.2 Vocabulary
Discussion (page 35, exercise 11)
Student C

There are no lifeguards or security patrols on the beach.
The island only has one ambulance.
You should have everything ready before the music festival.

7.4 Speaking
Negotiation (page 91, exercise 6)
Student A

Use the table below to see how good your negotiation skills are.

	0 Points	1 Point	2 Points	3 Points	Score
Discount	-	2%	5%	10%	
Delivery within	28 days	24 days	21 days	18 days	
Payment	10 days	14 days	21 days	28 days	
Delivery costs	150	100	50	Free	

8.4 Speaking
Roleplay (page 103, exercise 7)
Student C

You are the airport's press officer. You have the following information:
The motorway is planned to go very close to A's house, but no definite decision has been taken yet.
The train line will be in a tunnel and will not have any environmental impacts for A.
The motorway and train line will make it easier for local residents to get to the city.
About 12,000 new jobs will be created.
4-5,000 new houses and flats will be needed in the area.
The products and goods in the 24/7 shopping centre will probably be 5-10% more expensive than elsewhere.
Lowering the groundwater could have negative impacts for local plants and animals and an environmental study is being done. You do not have the findings yet.
The new town will probably be located close to B's supermarket, but a final decision has not been made yet.
House and land prices are expected to increase in the next few years.

6.4 Speaking
Handling interruptions (page 77, exercise 6)
Student A

Prepare a short talk on an organization that you would like to work for. Make some notes. Think about what the organization do, why you would like to work for them and what you imagine working there would be like.
When you are ready give your talk to the other two members of the group. Be prepared to answer any questions that they might have.
When the others give their talks try to ask a question and interrupt once or twice.

116 *The* **Business**

7.4 Speaking
Negotiation (page 91, exercise 6)
Student B

Use the table below to see how good your negotiation skills are.

	3 Points	2 Points	1 Point	0 Points	Score
Discount	-	2%	5%	10%	
Delivery within	28 days	24 days	21 days	18 days	
Payment	10 days	14 days	21 days	28 days	
Delivery costs	150	100	50	Free	

2.6 Case study
Discussion (page 29, exercise 6)
Student A

1 Read the hotel's explanations for three of the problems and then tell your partner.
1. The prices of the rooms at the hotel often change. Rooms booked a long time before they are needed are cheaper. Cheaper rooms are also available if you have no booking and just walk into the hotel. These prices are the ones shown in reception.
2. As part of the hotel's environmental policy, the heating in the rooms cannot be changed by guests. There is one central thermostat which is controlled by the hotel to stop guests turning the heating up and wasting energy.
3. All of the attendees of the Panorama conference from Electronics RDC were in the same part of the hotel. The noise that some of the guests complained about was probably caused by their colleagues from Electronics RDC.

2 With your partner discuss what action the hotel should take.

Grammar and practice

1 Living abroad

Present simple

1 Complete the dialogue. Use contractions (*I'm* not *I am*; *don't* not *do not*) where possible.

A: Where ¹_____ you work?
B: I work in Lyon.
A: Lyon? But I thought you said you worked in Paris?
B: No, I ²_____ work in Paris, I work in Lyon.
A: Okay, so you work in Lyon. And ³_____ you married?
B: Yes, I ⁴_____ . My wife's name is Zsi-Zsi.
A: That's an unusual name. ⁵_____ she French?
B: No, she ⁶_____ French, she ⁷_____ Hungarian.
A: And ⁸_____ she have a job?
B: No, she ⁹_____ have a job at the moment. We have two young children and she stays at home to look after them.
A: Two children! How wonderful! How old ¹⁰_____ they?
B: The girl is six, and the boy is just two years old.
A: Two years old! I imagine that you ¹¹_____ get much sleep!
B: Yes, you ¹²_____ right. I must look tired!
A: And what about the girl? ¹³_____ she go to school?
B: Yes, she ¹⁴_____ .

Present simple
Positive
I/You/We/They work.
He/She/It works.
Negative
I/You/We/They don't work.
He/She/It doesn't work.
Questions
Do I/you/we/they work?
Does he/she/it work?

Present simple: *to be*
Positive
I'm Hungarian.
You're/We're/They're Hungarian.
He's/She's/It's Hungarian.
Negative
I'm not Hungarian.
You're/We're/They're not Hungarian.
  Or You/We/They aren't Hungarian.
He's/She's/It's not Hungarian.
  Or He/She/It isn't Hungarian.
Questions
Am I Hungarian?
Are you/we/they Hungarian?
Is he/she/it Hungarian?

---

2 Correct the mistakes in these sentences.
1 Do you working for Siemens?
2 I doesn't work for Siemens, I work for Bayer.
3 And your wife, do she work?
4 My wife work as a teacher.
5 She is German?
6 No, she not German, she's Hungarian.

3 Look back at the last two lines of the dialogue in exercise 1:

Does she go to school?
*Yes, she **does**.* (NOT *Yes, she goes.*)
Complete the replies to the questions below.

1 A: Do you enjoy your work?
  B: Yes, I _____
2 A: Do you know this restaurant?
  B: No, I _____
3 A: Does your wife work?
  B: No, she _____
4 A: Does your daughter go to school?
  B: Yes, she _____
5 A: Are you Hungarian?
  B: Yes, that's right, I _____
6 A: Are you Hungarian?
  B: No, I _____ . I'm Romanian.

4 Match examples 1-3 with the uses of the present simple a)-c). Choose the best answer if several are possible.

1 Most days I **leave** home around 7.00. ☐
2 The Rhine **meets** the sea in the Netherlands. ☐
3 Our company **offers** a range of investment products. ☐

a) present simple for facts such as what or where things are
b) present simple for habits and routines
c) present simple for actions and situations that are generally true (i.e. not temporary)

Adverbs of frequency

5 Put the time adverbs on the frequency scale.

| always | nearly always | never | not very often |
| sometimes | often | rarely | usually/normally |

100% ¹_____
 ↑   ²_____
      ³_____
      ⁴_____
      ⁵ *sometimes*
      ⁶_____
 ↓   ⁷_____
0%   ⁸_____

6 Fill in **one** of the gaps with the word *often*. Leave the other gap empty.
1 He _____ works _____ late.
2 He _____ is _____ late.

Adverbs of frequency come <u>before</u> the verb. The exception is ***to be***, where they come <u>after</u>.

---

7 Fill in the missing letters.
1 Instead of saying 'one time a year' we can say 'o___ a year'.
2 Instead of saying 'two times a year' we can say 't____ a year'.

118 *The Business*

Times of the day

8 Study how Brits and Americans say the time. Look at the differences in **bold**.

	UK	USA
10.00	ten o'clock	ten o'clock
10.10	ten **past** ten ten-ten	ten **after** ten ten-ten
10.15	a quarter **past** ten ten-fifteen	a quarter **after** ten ten-fifteen
10.30	half past ten half ten ten-thirty	half past ten **(not used)** ten-thirty
10.40	twenty to eleven ten-forty	twenty to eleven ten-forty
10.45	a quarter to eleven ten-forty-five	a quarter to eleven ten-forty-five

Complete the table below.

	British English	American English
8.10	ten ^{1}...... eight	ten ^{2}...... eight
8.45	a quarter ^{3}...... nine	a quarter ^{4}...... nine

Yesterday, today and tomorrow

9 Read the information in the box then do the exercise below.

We say:	the day before yesterday, yesterday, today, tomorrow, the day after tomorrow
We say:	the week before last, last week, this week, next week, the week after next
And for parts of yesterday, today and tomorrow we say:	
yesterday:	yesterday morning, yesterday afternoon, yesterday evening, last night
today:	this morning, this afternoon, this evening, tonight
tomorrow:	tomorrow morning, tomorrow afternoon, tomorrow evening, tomorrow night

Try to remember the phrases. Then cover the table above with a piece of paper before continuing.

The phrases in *italics* below are not English. Correct them by writing a more appropriate phrase.

1 I'm busy tomorrow, but I can see you *tomorrow plus one day*.
2 No, not last week, the week *previous to last week*.
3 We went to a great bar *yesterday night*.
4 Would you like to come to the restaurant with us *today in the evening*?
5 The metro stops running at midnight *this night*.

Dates

10 Compare the UK and the USA:

	UK	USA
saying a date	the third of July July the third	July third
writing a date	3 July 3rd July July 3rd	July 3
writing a full date	DD/MM/YY	MM/DD/YY

Now write **today's** date:

1 As a Brit would say it: _____
2 As a Brit would write it in full: _____
3 As an American would say it: _____
4 As an American would write it in full: _____

Prepositions of time: *in, on, at*

11 Fill in each gap with *in, on, at*, or ~ (no preposition).

1 _____ 2007
2 _____ ten o'clock
3 _____ yesterday
4 _____ Christmas
5 _____ Christmas Day
6 _____ 28 July
7 _____ last week
8 _____ winter
9 _____ next April
10 _____ Saturday
11 _____ the end of the year
12 _____ New Year's Day
13 _____ the 1990s
14 _____ a few days ago
15 _____ July
16 _____ the afternoon
17 _____ the week after next
18 _____ the day before yesterday

The rules for these prepositions are given below. But many people think it is easier to just see if they 'sound right' rather than try to learn the rules. Use:
- *In* with parts of the day, months, seasons, years
- *On* with dates, days of the week, special days
- *At* with religious festivals, hours of the clock, particular points in time
- No preposition for *yesterday/today/tomorrow, last/next, the day before/after*

Some speakers of American English use other forms such as:
- no preposition for days of the week (*I'll see you Wednesday*)
- *on the weekend*.

2 Dealing with customers

Countable and uncountable nouns

1 Read the information in the box then do the exercise below.

> **Countable nouns**
> Countable nouns can be singular or plural: *house(s), colleague(s), file(s), team(s), man (men), person (people)*. We use countable nouns for separate things that we can count. Many countable nouns are concrete (*one product/ three products*) but some are abstract (*one idea/two ideas*).
>
> **Uncountable nouns**
> Uncountable nouns only have one form, without -s: *air, electricity, health, information, money, success*. We use uncountable nouns for things that do not divide into separate units. Many uncountable nouns are abstract (*happiness*) but some are concrete (*water*).

Put these words into the correct column below: *dollar, money, luggage, bag, furniture, chair, hotel, accommodation, job, work, wine, litre, time, week, machine, machinery, information, fact, suggestion, advice*.

countable nouns	uncountable nouns

2 If the sentence is correct, put a tick (✓). If it is incorrect, put a cross (✗).

1. Accommodation are difficult to find in this city.
2. Accommodations are difficult to find in this city.
3. Hotels are difficult to find in this city.
4. Time is money.
5. The time is money.
6. I had several part-time works while I was at university.
7. I had several part-time jobs while I was at university.
8. I'll go now. I know you have work to do.
9. I'll go now. I know you have a work to do.
10. She gave me an advice.
11. She gave me some advice.
12. She gave me a suggestion.
13. She gave me some suggestions.
14. I don't have much information to give you.
15. I don't have many information to give you.
16. I don't have a lot of information to give you.
17. I don't have much facts to give you.
18. I don't have many facts to give you.
19. It only cost a little dollars.
20. It only cost a few dollars.
21. Would you like a little wine?
22. Would you like a few wine?

> Uncountable nouns take a singular verb, not a plural verb (so 1 and 2 are wrong).
> Uncountable nouns do not have an –s form (so 2 is wrong).
> Uncountable nouns used in a general way do not have *the* or *a* (so 5, 9 and 10 are wrong).
> Uncountable nouns cannot be counted (so 6 is wrong).
> Uncountable nouns go with *much*, not *many* (so 15 is wrong).
> Countable nouns go with *many*, not *much* (so 17 is wrong).
> Countable nouns go with *a few*, not *a little* (so 19 is wrong).
> Uncountable nouns go with *a little*, not *a few* (so 22 is wrong).

> Summary
> - With countable nouns we use **a, some, a lot of, many, a few**.
> - With uncountable nouns we use **some, a lot of, much, a little**.
> - We do not use *the* before an uncountable noun used in a general way.
>   ~~The~~ life is beautiful. ✗ Life is beautiful. ✓
> - In positive sentences, **a lot of** is common.
> - In negative sentences and questions, **many/much** and **a few/a little** are common.

some and *any*

3 Read the information in the box then do the exercise below. Note that this information is true for both countable and uncountable nouns.

> **Some** is common in positive sentences.
> *I got some paper for the photocopier.*
> **Any** is common in negative sentences and questions.
> *I didn't get any paper for the photocopier.*
> *Did you get any paper for the photocopier?*

Complete each sentence with the most likely word, *some* or *any*.

1. Do you have _____ questions to ask me?
2. Yes, there are _____ questions that I'd like to ask.
3. Okay, that's all. I don't have _____ more questions to ask you.

> There are some exceptions. For example, we can use **some** in a question if it is an offer or a request.
> *Would you like **some** more wine?* (offer)
> *Could I have **some** more wine?* (request)
> And we can use **any** in a positive sentence if it means 'no limit'.
> *You can come **any** time – morning or afternoon.*

Can, could & would for polite questions

4 Read the information in the box then do the exercise below.

> To request that someone else does something, we use *can/could* and *would*.
> (informal) Can you pass the salt?
> (neutral)   Could you open the window, please?
> (polite)   Would you help me move this desk?
>
> To request something for ourselves (permission), we use *can/could* and *may*.
> (informal) Can I ask a question?
> (neutral)   Could I borrow your pen?
> (polite)   May I come in?

Rewrite the first sentence in a more polite way using *could*, *would* or *may*. There are two answers each time.

1 Can I ask who is calling?
   Could I ask who is calling?
   May I ask who is calling?
2 Can you give her a message?
   _____ ?
   _____ ?
3 Can I write down one or two details?
   _____ ?
   _____ ?
4 Can you explain that again?
   _____ ?
   _____ ?

> Tip. Don't tell people to do things, ask them.
> *Give me a hand, please.* (not polite, even with 'please')
> Could you give me a hand? (better)
> Could you give me a hand, please? (much better)
> It is usually safer to use *could* in requests, particularly in a business context where the person is not a personal friend. *Can* is sometimes too direct and *would* is sometimes too formal.

5 Read the information in the box then do the exercise below.

> To ask for something, use *I'd like*, not *I want*. The word want can sometimes be impolite in a request.
> To offer something, use *Would ... like...?*
> These uses of *would like* (meaning 'want') are not the same as *like* (meaning 'enjoy').

If the sentence is correct and polite, put a tick (✓). If the sentence can be made more polite with *like*, or if it is grammatically wrong, correct it.

1 Does anyone want a drink?
2 Yes, I want a beer, please.
3 Yes, I like some mineral water, please.
4 Yes, I'd like a herbal tea, please.
5 Generally, I like white wine with fish.
6 Generally, I'd like white wine with fish.

Requests with 'mind'

6 If the sentence is correct, put a tick (✓). If it is incorrect, correct it.

1 Do you mind to call back later? ☐
2 Would you mind to call back later? ☐
3 Do you mind calling back later? ☐
4 Would you mind calling back later? ☐

Put a tick (✓) by correct and polite replies to the question in italics. Put a cross (✗) by incorrect or impolite replies.

Would you mind calling back later?

5 _____ Yes, I mind.
6 _____ Yes, I mind calling.
7 _____ No, not at all.
8 _____ No, of course not.

> - Requests with *mind* are followed by *–ing*.
>   Would you **mind waiting** for a moment while I get my coat?
> - This means *Is it a problem for you?*. So an answer with *yes* is impolite: it means *yes, it is a problem*. Instead, use an answer with *no* like **No, not at all**.
> - We can also use **Would you mind if I ...** to ask for permission.
>   **Would you mind if I** sat here?

Polite requests and negative responses

> If we have to give a negative response to a request, we don't usually use the word *no*. Instead, we can follow this formula:
> **I'm afraid/Actually/Sorry/I'm sorry but** ... + reason + suggest an alternative
> The phrase *I'm afraid ...* is not used in this way in American English.

7 After each polite request 1-4, write the two letters that go together to make a full response.

1 Can I ask you a few questions about this report? [a] [g]
2 Would you mind working late on Tuesday? ☐ ☐
3 Could you give us a discount if we order 1000 units? ☐
   ☐
4 Would you mind opening the window? ☐ ☐

a) I'm sorry but I'm really busy right now.
b) Actually, the air conditioning is more efficient.
c) I'm afraid I can't, it's my daughter's birthday.
d) Sorry, we only offer discounts to regular customers.
e) Why don't you ask Mariana? She said she was looking for some overtime.
f) But we could give you more convenient terms of payment – perhaps another 30 days credit.
g) Ask me again tomorrow. I'll have more time.
h) I'll turn it on now.

3 Operations

Present continuous

1 Study the form of the present continuous in the box. The contractions shown (*I'm* for *I am*, *You're* for *You are*) are the forms used most often in speech and informal writing.

Present continuous
Positive
I'm working
You're/We're/They're working
He's/She's/It's working
Negative
I'm not working
You're/We're/They're not working
  Or *You/We/They aren't working*
He's/She's/It's not working
  Or *He/She/It isn't working*
Questions
Am I working?
Are you/we/they working?
Is he/she/it working?

Complete each sentence using the present continuous form of the verb in brackets. Use contractions where possible.

1 We _____ (redesign) our website.
2 _____ (you/enjoy) the conference?
3 The photocopier _____ (not/work) at the moment. Try again later.
4 Is that Stephanie on the phone? _____ (she/call) from Paris?
5 I _____ (read) a great book about solutions to the energy crisis.
6 They _____ (not/stay) at the Novotel this time, they've chosen the Mercure instead.

2 Match examples 1-3 with the uses of the present continuous a-c. Choose the best answer if several are possible.

1 Let's go for lunch. I'll tell you about my news – **I'm working** on a big project in Turkey. ☐
2 I'll finish the spreadsheet in about half an hour. **I'm working** as fast as I can. ☐
3 Developments in communication technology mean that more people **are working** from home. ☐

a) present continuous for an action happening right now, at the moment of speaking
b) present continuous for an action happening around now, but not at the exact moment of speaking
c) present continuous for a current trend or slow change happening over a longer time period

Note that uses a)-c) above are really just variations on the one basic use of the present continuous: a temporary activity in progress now.

Present simple and present continuous

3 Study the differences between the present simple (unit 1, module 3) and the present continuous.

Present simple	Present continuous
permanent	temporary
habit	activity in progress now
fact	slow change

Complete each sentence by putting the verb into the present simple or present continuous.

1 We _____ (sell) our products all over the world.
2 Fantastic offer! For one month only we _____ (sell) this product with a 20% discount for new customers.
3 They _____ (change) their advertising agency – they aren't happy with the usual one.
4 Of course, all companies _____ (change) over time.
5 She _____ (work) for SAP.
6 Today she _____ (work) from home.

4 The present simple and present continuous are associated with different time phrases. Underline the correct alternative in italics.

1 *This year/Every year* we're building a new factory in Turkey.
2 *This year/Every year* we increase our market share in the Turkish market.
3 *At the moment/Usually* we're recruiting a lot of new staff – business is going very well.
4 *At the moment/Usually* the factory closes for two weeks over the summer for maintenance.
5 *Right now/Twice a year* we're getting a lot of orders from the Middle East.
6 *Right now/Twice a year* we organize a special event for all our employees.

State verbs

5 Put a tick (✓) if the sentence is possible, put a cross (✗) if it is not possible.

1 I know exactly what you mean.
2 I am knowing exactly what you are meaning.
3 That Lexus belongs to our Marketing Director.
4 That Lexus is belonging to our Marketing Director.
5 It costs €49.
6 It is costing €49.

There are a number of verbs that describe states, not actions. These verbs are not usually used in a continuous form. State verbs include:
agree, know, remember, think, understand
hate, like, need, want, wish
belong to, contain, own
appear, look like
be, exist
cost, depend, mean, measure, owe, weigh

122 *The* **Business**

Adverbs

6 Read the information in the box then do the exercise below.

- Adjectives describe nouns. Adverbs describe verbs.
  *There was **a significant** increase in sales.*
  *Sales increased **significantly**.*
- Most adverbs can be formed by adding *-ly, -y, -ally, -ily*.
- Some adverbs and adjectives have the same form: *daily, early, fast, hard, late, quarterly*.
- *Good* is an adjective. *Well* is an adverb.

Make adverbs from the following adjectives. Think about the spelling.

1 slow *slowly*   5 full _____
2 dramatic _____   6 fast _____
3 hard _____   7 good _____
4 happy _____   8 bad _____

Passive: present simple and modals

7 Underline the correct forms in italics in the following text about beer.

What is beer? Beer ¹*makes/is made* from just four ingredients: water, barley, hops and yeast. We'll look at the last three in more detail.

First there is barley, which is a grain. Before it ²*can use/can be used* to make beer, the barley ³*goes/is gone* through a special process. The seed grows a little but then this growth process is stopped.

At this point the barley ⁴*calls/is called* 'malt'. The malt is dried by raising the temperature. The flavour and colour of the beer depends a lot on the temperature during this drying process.

Next we have hops. Hops are a type of flower and they ⁵*give/are given* flavour to the beer. Interestingly, the hop plant ⁶*closely relates/is closely related* to the marijuana plant. Hops ⁷*contain/are contained* acids, which give beer its bitter taste, as well as oils that give beer some of its flavor and aroma.

Finally, there is yeast. This is a micro-organism and is responsible for creating the alcohol and carbon dioxide found in beer.

Beer ⁸*can find/can be found* in two forms: 'lager' like Heineken, Carlsburg and Budweiser, and 'ale' like the darker and less bubbly varieties that ⁹*drink/are drunk* in the UK.

Compare sentence a) and b):
a) People make beer from just four ingredients.
b) Beer is made from just four ingredients.
Sentence a) is called 'active'. The person or thing doing the action is the subject: *people*.
Sentence b) is called 'passive'. The person or thing affected by the action is the subject: *beer*.

Here are the forms with the present simple:

Active	Passive
I do it./He does it.	It is done.
I don't do it./He doesn't do it.	It isn't done.
Do I do it?/Does he do it?	Is it done?

Here are the forms with modals (*can, must, will* etc):

I/She can do it.	It can be done.
I/She can't do it.	It can't be done.
Can she do it?	Can it be done?

8 Complete each sentence using the words in brackets and the passive. Use contractions where possible (*it's* not *it is*, *can't* not ~~can not~~).

1 No, no, it's all wrong. _____ (It/not/do) like that, _____ (it/do) like this.
2 a: _____ (ale/drink) in continental Europe?
   b: Not very much. _____ (It/mainly/drink) in the UK.
3 a: _____ (any Korean cars/manufacture) in the Czech Republic?
   b: Yes, Hyundai cars _____ (produce) at Nosovice, although they _____ (still/not/make) in large numbers.
4 a: You say that you need this item by the end of the week. But _____ (will/it really/need) so soon? The end of the week is difficult for us.
   b: It _____ (must/deliver) by the end of the week, Friday at the latest. I'm sorry.

9 Match examples 1-3 with the uses of the passive a-c. Choose the best answer if several are possible.

1 First, the barley **is soaked** in water, then it **is drained** and **kept** at a temperature of 15 degrees. This allows the seed to grow. ☐
2 The barley seed grows. At this point **it is called** 'malt'. ☐
3 Beer **is made** from just four ingredients. ☐

a) passive used because the subject refers back to a noun in the previous sentence
b) passive used to describe part of a process or procedure
c) passive used because the person who does the action is not important or not known

Saying who does the action: *by*

10 Read the information in the box then do the exercise below.

If we want to say who does the action we use *by*.
*The car plant at Nosovice is run **by Korean managers**.*
But in many cases it sounds strange or unnecessary to mention this.
Ale is drunk ~~by people~~ mainly in the UK.

Cross out any phrases that are not necessary. If every phrase is necessary put a tick (✓).

1 The quality of the manufacturing process is checked by quality control inspectors every day.
2 The quality of the manufacturing process is checked by a team of twenty people.

4 Success stories

Past simple

1 There are three different pronunciations of the regular –ed past simple. First check that you can say the six examples in the table below the box. Then write the words in the box in the correct column.

> developed   started   realized   discussed
> closed   finished   constructed   complained
> accepted   prepared   introduced   visited

/d/	/t/	/ɪd/
moved	focussed	decided
opened	asked	wanted

There is a 'rule' for these endings, but you have to know a little about pronunciation to understand it.
- A voiced sound at the end of a verb is followed by a /d/ sound for -ed. 'Voiced' means that your vocal chords vibrate as you produce it. Try tapping your fingers lightly on your throat as you say the 'v' of 'move' and listen for the vibrating sound.
- An unvoiced sound at the end of a verb is followed by a /t/ sound for -ed. 'Unvoiced' means that your vocal chords do not vibrate as you produce it. Try tapping your fingers lightly on your throat as you say the 's' of 'focus' – there is no vibrating sound.
- The sounds /d/ and /t/ at the end of a verb are followed by an /ɪd/ sound for -ed. It would be impossible to make either of the other two sounds.

2 How many irregular past simple forms do you know? Write the missing forms below.

infinitive	past simple	infinitive	past simple
become	1 _____	leave	16 _____
begin	2 _____	lose	17 _____
bring	3 _____	make	18 _____
buy	4 _____	meet	19 _____
choose	5 _____	pay	20 _____
cost	6 _____	see	21 _____
fall	7 _____	sell	22 _____
find	8 _____	set	23 _____
forget	9 _____	speak	24 _____
give	10 _____	spend	25 _____
go	11 _____	take	26 _____
grow	12 _____	tell	27 _____
have	13 _____	think	28 _____
keep	14 _____	understand	29 _____
know	15 _____	write	30 _____

3 Complete the questions and answers about Google. There are a mixture of past simple forms: positives, negatives and questions.

1. a: What _____ (be) the names of the founders of Google?
   b: Their names were Larry Page and Sergey Brin. According to the company myth, they _____ (not/like) each other when they first _____ (meet).
2. a: So when _____ Larry and Sergey _____ (meet)?
   b: They _____ (meet) in 1995 at Stanford University.
3. a: And where _____ they _____ (start) their business?
   b: They _____ (start) in a garage with a staff of just three – themselves and one other person. This first 'office' _____ (not/be) very luxurious – it also _____ (contain) a washing machine and a dryer for clothes.
4. a: When _____ Google _____ (make) a profit for the first time?
   b: It _____ (make) a profit in 2001, although they _____ (not/have) a stock market listing until 2004.
5. a: What _____ (be) their source of income?
   b: The company _____ (grow) by developing a 'cost per click' model of advertising. Advertisers _____ (pay) to have their names on the search page, and then paid again when users _____ (click) on the link.
6. a: And why _____ Google _____ (have) so much success compared to other search engines?
   b: They _____ (have) a lot of success for two main reasons. First, their search technology _____ (find) better results than the competitors. And second, in the year 2000 they _____ (introduce) an innovative tool called Google Toolbar. This was a browser plug-in that _____ (make) it possible to use Google search without going first to the Google homepage. The Toolbar also _____ (highlight) key words in search results, and _____ (block) annoying advertising pop-ups.

> **Past simple**
> Positive
> *I/You/He/She/It/We/They worked.*
> Negative
> *I/You/He/She/It/We/They didn't work.*
> Questions
> *Did I/you/he/she/it/we/they work?*

Past continuous

4 Match the examples of the past continuous 1–4 with their uses a) or b).

1 **I was working** at Estée Lauder from 2004 to 2006.
2 It was the summer of 2005 and **I was working** at Estée Lauder.
3 That evening I decided to stay late at the office. Anyway, it was 7pm and **I was writing** a report.
4 **I was writing** the report yesterday afternoon. I was exhausted by the end!

a) An activity in progress in the past. The past continuous shows that we were in the middle of something. ☐☐
b) An activity in progress in the past. The past continuous is used for the whole period. ☐☐

In which examples above could the past continuous be replaced with the past simple? ☐☐

- The form of the past continuous is *was/were + –ing*.
  Positive: *I was working. We were working.*
  Negative: *I wasn't working. We weren't working.*
  Questions: *Was I working? Were we working?*
- We use the past continuous for an activity in progress in the past.
- Usually the past continuous shows that we were in the middle of something. But it can also be used for the whole period.

5 Complete each sentence with the correct form of the past continuous.

1 I _____ (walk) to the station after work when it suddenly started to rain very heavily.
2 Yesterday, in the office, why _____ (you/look) at me in that strange way? Did I do something wrong?
3 Miguel came to the presentation but he seemed very distracted and he _____ (not/listen) to anything that the speaker said.

Past continuous and past simple

6 Look at the sentence in *italics* then choose the best answers below.

While I was working at my computer, I saw Rita fall to the floor.

1 Which happened first: a) working at my computer or b) seeing Rita fall? ☐
2 Which took longer: a) working at my computer or b) seeing Rita fall? ☐
3 Is it likely that a) I continued working at my computer or b) I stopped working? ☐

Now continue in the same way.

While I was working at my computer, I saw Andy and his expensive new suit.

4 Which happened first: a) working at my computer or b) seeing Andy's suit? ☐
5 Which took longer: a) working at my computer or b) seeing Andy's suit? ☐
6 Is it likely that a) I continued working at my computer or b) I stopped working? ☐

- We often use the past continuous (*I was working*) together with the past simple (*I saw*). The past continuous gives the background to a story, and the past simple gives the individual events that happened.
- We often use *while* with the past continuous, and in this case the meaning is the same as *when*:
  While/When I was working at my computer, I saw Andy fall to the floor.
- The background activity (*working*) is interrupted by another shorter action (*saw*). Sometimes the activity continues, sometimes not – we only know by the context.

7 Complete each sentence by putting one verb into the past continuous and one into the past simple. These two tenses might be in any order.

1 While I _____ (check) the figures on the spreadsheet, I _____ (notice) that the sales total for June was incorrect.
2 When I _____ (join) the company, they _____ (expand) their activities in Central Europe.
3 The negotiations _____ (go) very well until their boss _____ (arrive) on the scene.
4 Incredible! Someone _____ (take) my bag while I _____ (sit) at the table outside the café.

Used to

8 Read the information in the box then do the exercise below.

- *Used to* describes a long-term situation or a repeated habit in the past. It suggests that the situation or habit is no longer true.
  *I **used to** live in Dusseldorf, but now I live in Koln.*
- With negatives and questions *used to* becomes **use to**.
  *There didn't **use to** be so much crime.*
  *Did you **use to** drive to work before they opened the new metro line?*

Complete each sentence with a form of *used to*.

1 Where _____ (you/work) before you became a freelance consultant?
2 In my twenties I _____ (play) tennis most weekends, but now I'm married and I don't play at all.
3 To be honest, I _____ (not/like) him very much, but now I know him better and we get along very well.

The **Business** 125

5 Selling

Comparatives

Comparatives and superlatives
- We use the comparative form of an adjective to compare two separate things. Note the use of *than*.
  This is a newer model than the one you're currently using.
- We use the superlative form of an adjective to compare one thing in a group with all the others. Note the use of *the*.
  This is the newest model on the market. Our competitors don't have anything similar.

1 Each sentence has a mistake. Cross out the wrong words and write the correct version.

1. Internet speeds are more fast than with the old model.
2. This perfume is expensiver than the other one.
3. This year we made a much biger profit than last year.
4. It's most expensive to fly to Brussels than to go by train.
5. Please make your desk look a bit tidyer - the CEO is visiting our offices this afternoon.
6. Every year the situation is getting badder.

Comparatives
short adjectives: *small – smaller*
doubling of consonant (when word ends in one vowel + one consonant): *hot – hotter*
long adjectives: *convenient – more/less convenient*
-y changes to *-i*: *heavy - heavier*
irregular forms: *good – better; bad – worse; far - further*

Superlatives

2 Each sentence has a mistake. Cross out the wrong words and write the correct version.

1. Of all the perfumes in this shop, this one is the expensivest.
2. That type of engine has the most high fuel consumption.
3. The most far place from here that we sell our products is Turkey.
4. This is the more powerful engine we've ever produced.
5. Their head office is amazing – it's one of the most beautifulest buildings in the city.
6. The design looks like something from the seventies – it's one of the worse I've ever seen.

Superlatives
short adjectives: *small – the smallest*
doubling of consonant (when word ends in one vowel + one consonant): *hot – the hottest*
long adjectives: *convenient – the most/least convenient*
-y changes to *-i*: *heavy – the heaviest*
irregular forms: *good – the best; bad – the worst; far – the furthest*

3 The information in the boxes above is true. But some rules are more flexible than others! Try the following exercise.

Put a tick (✓) if the form in italics is correct, put a cross (✗) if it is not.

1. The new system is a lot *safer*.
2. The new system is a lot *more safe*.
3. The improved graphics make this computer game *realer*.
4. The improved graphics make this computer game *more real*.
5. Customers who get good after-sales service are always *the pleasedest*.
6. Customers who get good after-sales service are always *the most pleased*.
7. In Japan you should give people your business card using two hands – it's *more polite*.
8. In Japan you should give people your business card using two hands – it's *politer*.

- Some short adjectives can have either *–er/–est* or *more/most*. These include: **clear, fair, free, proud, safe, sure, true**.
  (So 1 and 2 above are both ✓)
- We do not use *–er/–est* with the word 'real' and with short adjectives ending in *ed* like 'pleased'. Instead, we use *more/most*.
  (So 3 is ✗ and 4 is ✓; and 5 is ✗ and 6 is ✓)
- Some longer adjectives can have either *–er/–est* or *more/most*. These include: **clever, common, handsome, likely, narrow, polite, quiet, secure, simple, stupid, tired**.
  (So 7 and 8 above are both ✓)

4 Complete each sentence using a form of the word in brackets. Extra words like *the/than/more/less/most/least* will also be needed.

Product:	Handi	Regula	Apex
Price:	35	65	80
Weight:	2kg.	4kg.	5kg.
Delivery time:	1 week	4 weeks	3 weeks

1. Regula is _____ (cheap) Apex.
2. Of all three products, Handi is _____ (cheap).
3. Regula is _____ (expensive) Handi.
4. Handi is _____ (expensive) Regula.
5. Of all three products, Apex is _____ (expensive).
6. Of all three products, Handi is _____ (expensive).
7. Apex is _____ (heavy) Regula.
8. Handi has _____ (good) delivery time of all.
9. Regula has _____ (bad) delivery time of all.
10. Apex is too complicated for our needs. Let's order Regula – it's _____ (simple).

Question forms

5 Put the words in the correct order to make a question. Write your answers below – decide if it is a 'Yes/No' question or a 'Wh' question.

1. it does cost a lot of money?
2. how much it does cost?
3. use a Blackberry do you why?
4. use a Blackberry you will?
5. I at your office can park?
6. where park I can?
7. our best salesperson who is?
8. Benedicte is our best salesperson?
9. always you do buy DVDs online?
10. do you how often buy DVDs online?

Yes/No questions
_____
_____
_____
_____

'Wh' and How questions
_____
_____
_____
_____

6 Complete the table. Choose from these words: *are, are, can, did, did, do, does, has, have, is, is, will*.

Yes/No questions		
'to be'	1_____	you a marketing specialist?
	2_____	he a marketing specialist?
Present simple:	3_____	you like this product?
	4_____	she like this product?
Present continuous:	5_____	you coming with us?
	6_____	he coming with us?
Past simple:	7_____	you buy it here?
	8_____	she buy it here?
Present perfect:	9_____	you ever been to Zurich?
	10_____	he ever been to Zurich?
Modals:	11_____	you speak German?
	12_____	she be late?

7 Change each affirmative sentence into a 'Yes/No' question.

1. David is a communications consultant.
   Is David a communications consultant?
2. Marketa is arriving tomorrow.
   _____
3. Roberto thinks it's a good idea.
   _____
4. Fernanda has already given her presentation.
   _____
5. Pierre made a backup copy of the file.
   _____
6. Petra will be at the meeting tomorrow.
   _____

8 Complete each question with an item from the box. Look at the reply for a clue.

| How much | How often | What | When |
| Where | Who | Whose | Why |

1. a: _____ did you meet during your trip?
   b: I met all our colleagues from the Paris office.
2. a: _____ do you travel abroad on business?
   b: Oh, three or four times a year I suppose.
3. a: _____ are you going to do about it?
   b: I'm going to call them in the morning.
4. a: _____ did they cancel their order?
   b: Because we didn't have the items in stock.
5. a: _____ does your flight leave?
   b: Nine o'clock tomorrow morning.
6. a: _____ did you pay for those shoes?
   b: About 150 euros. But I really like them.
7. a: _____ exactly is the meeting?
   b: In the conference room on the second floor.
8. a: _____ newspaper is this?
   b: It's mine, but you can read it if you want.

Questions
- A yes/no question is formed with auxiliary verb + subject + main verb:
  Do you live here?
  Did she pay a lot of money for her flight?
- A Wh- or How question is formed in exactly the same way, but with a question word in front:
  Where do you live?
  How much did she pay for her flight?
- The question word *whose* is used to ask who something belongs to.
  Whose glass is this? Is it yours?
  Whose idea was it? Was it Peter's?

9 Study the information in the box, then complete the sentences below with *What* or *Which*.

What or Which?
What is more common
a) for things and activities
b) where there is a wide choice.
Which is more common
a) for people and organizations
b) where there is a limited choice.

1. _____ time does the meeting begin?
2. _____ room is the meeting in – room 207 or room 208?
3. _____ salesperson won 'employee of the month'?
4. _____ do you do in the evening?

6 The organization

Reported speech

Read the information in the box.

> You hear Marta say 'sales are rising'. You can report this comment to a colleague in two ways:
> (1) *Marta says (that) sales are rising.* (no tense change)
> (2) *Marta said (that) sales were rising.* (tense change)
> There is no rule about whether to change tense or not, but if we think Marta's original statement is still true and relevant then we are likely to use no tense change (1). By using a tense change (2) we can sound more formal and objective – we are distancing ourselves from the statement.
> Making a tense change like in (2) is called 'reported speech'; some people call this 'indirect speech'.
> The word *that* is in brackets in the examples above because we often leave it out.
> With reported speech the original verb 'moves back' in time. Study the verb tenses:
>
> ---
> Actual words: *'It's a great idea.'*
> Reported: **He said (that) it was a great idea.**
>
> ---
> Actual words: *'I work part-time.'*
> Reported: **She said (that) she worked part-time.**
>
> ---
> Actual words: *'Sales are rising.'*
> Reported: **He said (that) sales were rising.**
>
> ---
> Actual words: *'Jeff started his own company.'*
> Reported: **She said (that) Jeff started/had started his own company.**
>
> ---
> Actual words: *'Market share has grown.'*
> Reported: **He said (that) market share had grown.**
>
> ---
> Actual words: *'We will expand the business.'*
> Reported: **She said (that) they would expand the business.**
>
> ---
> Actual words: *'We can deliver next week.'*
> Reported: **He said (that) they could deliver next week.**

1 Now read this extract from a presentation, then complete the reported version below.

Actual words: 'I'm very pleased to tell you that sales this quarter have increased by 6% compared to the same period last year, and I am confident that we can maintain that rate of increase going forward. We have an ambitious expansion plan, and we are moving rapidly into the new markets of Central and Eastern Europe. We will open new branches in Bucharest and Sofia next year.'

Reported: Did you go to the presentation? No? Let's see if I can remember what he said. Oh yes, he said that sales this quarter ¹*had increased* by 6% compared to last year, and he ² _____ confident that the company ³ _____ the same rate of increase. What else? Oh, yes, I remember. He said that they ⁴ _____ some ambitious plans, and that they ⁵ _____ into Central Europe in a big way. I think he said they ⁶ _____ new branches in Romania and Bulgaria next year.

2 In all the examples above the reporting verb is *say*. Study the information in the box.

> **Say, tell, and ask**
> We **say** something.
> We **say** to someone. (NOT ~~say someone~~)
> We **tell** someone something. (NOT ~~to someone~~)
> To report a question we can use **ask**.

Now fill each space with *said*, *told* or *asked*.

1 She _____ me she was leaving the company.
2 She _____ she was leaving the company.
3 She _____ me if I was happy working here, and I _____ 'yes'.
4 She _____ to Michael that she was leaving the company.
5 She _____ Michael that she was leaving the company.
6 She _____ Michael what he thought about the company, and he _____ her that he was happy here.

3 There are many other reporting verbs. Match each verb 1-8 to its closest meaning a-h below. Be careful – some are very similar!

1 He stated that … [b]
2 He added that … ☐
3 He continued that … ☐
4 He explained that … ☐
5 He claimed that … ☐
6 He insisted that … ☐
7 He stressed that … ☐
8 He pointed out that … ☐

---
a He said something in a way that helped us to understand it better.
b He said something in a definite and formal way.
c He said something more (and different).
d He kept talking about the same thing.
e He kept saying very firmly that something is true.
f He said that something is true, even though there is no definite proof.
g He said something that we had not noticed or thought about.
h He emphasized something such as an idea, fact or detail.

> We often use **should/shouldn't** to report an imperative:
> Actual words: *'Call back tomorrow, please.'*
> Reported: **She said (that) I should call back tomorrow.**

4 Complete the reported version of these imperatives.

1 'Include your mobile number on your CV.'
   She said I _____
2 'Don't list all your hobbies on your CV.'
   He said I _____

Phrasal verbs

5 Read the information in the box.

A phrasal verb is a verb + 'a particle'. Don't worry about the word particle – it just means adverb or preposition. Compare these two sentences:
(1) *I took off my jacket because it was so hot.*
(2) *The plane took off.*
In sentence (1) the verb 'take' and the adverb 'off' are being used with their normal, literal meanings.
In sentence (2) the meaning of 'take' changes when it is followed by 'off'. The meaning is non-literal.
You probably already know some phrasal verbs, at least passively:
I woke up at 6 o'clock this morning.
I'm looking for a new job.
I deal with customers from all over the world.
Many phrasal verbs are easy to understand, either from the individual words or from the context:
We're going the wrong way – turn round.
The factory is going to close down next year.
We ran into trouble with our controversial advertising campaign.
But other phrasal verbs are not so obvious and you just have to know them:
Don't worry about this problem. I'll sort it out and get back to you tomorrow.
(= I'll find an answer and contact you again)
Phrasal verbs are used a lot by native speakers. But don't worry if you don't use them yourself – there is nearly always another, simpler way of saying the same thing.

Complete each sentence with a phrasal verb from the box. The definitions are in brackets.

| keep on | keep to | look after | look into |
| put forward | put off | set back | set up |

1 I made a complaint and they promised to _____ the matter. (investigate)
2 It's hard work to _____ three children all day. (take care of)
3 I don't like working for a large, bureaucratic organization – I want to leave and _____ my own business. (start)
4 The production problems in the factory are going to _____ our plans by several weeks. (delay)
5 At the last meeting she _____ a very interesting idea. (suggest something so that other people can discuss it)
6 I'm sorry, I'm busy on Friday. Can we _____ the meeting until next week? (arrange to do something at a later time)
7 Costs are increasing all the time and it's difficult to _____ our budget. (do what you agreed to do)
8 Don't worry if you're not successful at first – just _____ trying. (continue)

6 Sometimes the phrasal verb is separable, other times non-separable. Look at the words in bold and write a tick (✓) if the word order is possible, or a cross (✗) if it is not.

1 Hello? Is that Citibank? Can you **put me through** to the mortgage department please. ☐
2 Hello? Is that Citibank? Can you **put through me** to the mortgage department please. ☐
3 Can you **pick up Patricia** from the airport? ☐
4 Can you **pick Patricia up** from the airport? ☐
5 Don't worry, I'll **deal with it**. ☐
6 Don't worry, I'll **deal it with**. ☐
7 Just give me a little more time – I'll **figure out the answer** soon. ☐
8 Just give me a little more time – I'll **figure the answer out** soon. ☐

The easiest way to know if you can separate a phrasal verb is just to say it and see if it sounds right. If you want to know more about phrasal verb grammar, read the following bullet points.
- Some phrasal verbs are intransitive – that means they have no object. Here the phrasal verb cannot be separable because there is no object to put in the middle!
Suddenly the lights went out.
I grew up in Hamburg.
- Some phrasal verbs are transitive. This means that they must have an object:
I deal with customers from all over the world.
I'll sort out the problem.
- And some phrasal verbs can be used both with and without an object:
We closed down the factory last year.
We closed down last year.
- Usually, a phrasal verb with an object can be separated:
Can you pick up Patricia?
Can you pick Patricia up?
We closed down the factory.
We closed the factory down.
- But sometimes a phrasal verb with an object cannot be separated:
I'll deal with it.
(NOT *I'll deal it with.*)
- If the phrasal verb is separable, and the object is a pronoun, then it must come in the middle:
Can you pick her up? (NOT *Can you pick up her?*)
We closed it down. (NOT *We closed down it*)
- When the object is a long phrase, then the phrasal verb is not separated:
Can you pick up a colleague from our Warsaw office who is arriving at 7 this evening?
(NOT *Can you pick a colleague from our Warsaw office who is arriving at 7 this evening up?*)

7 The stock markets

will

1 Read the information in the box then do the exercise below.

> ***Will*** is used in several ways:
> To talk about a future fact, something we cannot control.
> *The company **will** celebrate its twentieth anniversary next year.*
> To make a prediction (here we often use *I think* …).
> *I think the share price **will** be much higher one year from now.*
> To make an instant decision (something we decide at the moment of speaking).
> *It's raining. **I'll** take an umbrella.*
> To make a promise.
> *Don't worry, **I'll** speak to my boss about this tomorrow.*
> To make an offer of help (to say that we are willing to do something).
> ***I'll** carry your bags for you.*
> To make a request (to see if the other person is willing to do something).
> ***Will you** give me a hand with these bags?*

Look at the six sentences below and decide how *will* is used. After each one write one of these: *fact, prediction, instant decision, promise, offer of help* or *request*.

1 Isn't it hot in here? I'll open the window. _____
2 She'll be in Toulouse all next week, so there's no point calling her at the Hamburg office. _____
3 **Will** you call a taxi for me? Thanks. _____
4 I'll look after your things while you go to the bathroom. _____
5 I'll love you for ever. _____
6 I think sales **will** probably improve next quarter. _____

> Some of the examples above could have more than one answer (e.g. 4 is probably an offer of help, but it could be an instant decision or a promise). The important thing is to realize that *will* is much more than just a simple future.
> Notice from the examples how *will* is often shortened to *'ll* in speech, particularly after pronouns (*I'll, he'll* etc.).

2 Read the information in the box then do the exercise below.

> - The negative of *will* is **won't** (will not).
>   *I **won't** be in Toulouse – I'm going to Lyon instead.*
> - Notice that we don't use **won't** after *I think*:
>   NOT: *I think the name won't appeal to Italian customers.*
>   INSTEAD, SAY: *I **don't think** the name **will** appeal to Italian customers.*
> - Be careful! Use a present tense, NOT *will*, after these words: *if, when, before, after, as soon as.*
>   NOT: *I'll give her your message when I will see her.*
>   INSTEAD, SAY: *I'll give her your message when I see her.*

Cross out the error in each sentence and write the correct form.

1 Sorry, I not be able to come to the meeting next week.
2 I think we won't make a profit next year.
3 I will call you as soon as I will get the information.
4 I should know whether we have funding for the project after I will meet the bank manager.

be going to

3 Read the information in the box then do the exercise below.

> ***Be going to*** is used in two main ways:
> - To make a prediction.
>   *See that fence at the end of the garden? I'm sure **it's going to** fall down soon.*
> - To talk about a plan or intention.
>   ***I'm going to** start my own business.*

Look at the four sentences below and decide how *be going to* is used. After each one write either *prediction* or *plan/intention*.

1 Joelle wants a salary increase – she**'s going to** speak to her boss about it next week. _____
2 Have you seen the most recent opinion poll? I think the Social Democrats **are going to** win the election. _____
3 Unemployment **is going to** increase if the government cuts its spending program. _____
4 I got some money from an inheritance. **I'm going to** invest it in stocks and bonds. _____

4 Read the information in the box then do the exercise below.

> ***will* and *be going to***
> **Predictions:** *Will* and *be going to* are both used to make predictions, and in many cases a native speaker could use either one. But if there is strong evidence in the present situation, then *be going to* is more likely.
> *Look at the clouds. I think it's going to rain.*
> **Decisions:** Note that *will* is used for instant decisions, whereas *be going to* is used for a plan or intention where the decision has already been made.

Complete each sentence with a form of *will* or *be going to* and the verb in brackets. In every case both are possible, but decide which form is most likely.

Predictions
1 Look at the time! We _____ (be) late.
2 I'm sure it _____ (be) nice weather at the weekend.

Decisions
3 Okay! That's agreed! We _____ (give) you a 2% discount. But you have to place a minimum order of 1000 pieces.
4 I was talking to my wife about this last week. We _____ (give) our daughter €500 a month while she's at university.

First conditional

5 Read the information in the box then do the exercise below.

> - A sentence beginning with *If ...* is called a conditional. There are different types of conditional. By far the most common is called a first conditional. It is used when a future event is reasonably likely to happen:
> *If the venture capital company likes our business plan, they'll invest in our company.*
> *If we decide to buy shares, we'll have to accept some risk.*
> - Notice the form of the examples above:
> *If + **present simple**, ... will **(+ simple infinitive)***
> A common mistake is to use *will* in the *If ...* clause. NOT *If the venture capital company will like our business plan, ...*
> - The *If ...* clause can come at the end.
> *We'll have to accept some risk if we decide to buy shares.*
> - We can use negatives.
> *If the venture capital company likes our business plan, we won't have to invest so much of our own money.*
> *If the venture capital company doesn't like our business plan, we'll have to take out a second mortgage on the house.*

Correct the errors in these sentences. Each sentence has two errors.
1 If the company will be successful, they list on the stock market.
2 If I don't will hear from them soon, I will to send them an email.
3 Don't worry, I don't will say anything about your new job if your colleagues will be in the bar with us this evening.

6 Complete these sentences using a first conditional form and the verbs in brackets. Use contractions (*'ll not will*) where possible.
1 If you _____ (sign) today, I _____ (give) you the items at last year's price.
2 If you _____ (take) our extended guarantee, you _____ (not/have to) worry about service and spare parts for four years.
3 We _____ (miss) the deadline if we _____ (not/get) any more money for the project.

7 Match the beginning of each sentence 1-3 with the most likely ending a)-c).
1 If we're seeing the bank manager next week ...
2 If you're looking for a model with more features, ...
3 If you've got a problem, ...

a) ring our Helpline.
b) we should think about how much money we need to borrow.
c) I can show you our new Alpha range.

Variations
- In exercises 5 and 6 you saw that a first conditional often has *If* + present simple followed by *will* in the result clause.
- But in exercise 7 you can see that there are some common variations. *If* can be followed by other present tenses (present continuous 1/2 or present perfect 3).
- And in the result clause we can use an imperative (a), or another modal besides *will* (b/c).

8 Read the information in the box then do the exercise below.

> **Unless** means if ...not.
> **Unless** we employ more part-time staff, we'll miss the deadline.
> **If** we **don't** employ more part-time staff, we'll miss the deadline.

Rewrite the sentences using *unless*.
1 If we don't pay more money, we won't attract people with the right skills.
 _____ , we won't attract people with the right skills.
2 You'll get wet if you don't take an umbrella.
 You'll get wet _____ .

9 Read the information in the box then do the exercise below.

> **by** and **until**
> **By** means on or before.
> *I need your report **by** Friday.*
> **Until** means up to.
> *I'm out of the office **until** Friday.*

Complete the sentences with *by* or *until*.
1 I can give you _____ the end of the month to pay your first instalment.
2 We need the goods _____ the end of the month at the latest.
3 The CEO is over 65. I think he'll retire _____ the end of next year.
4 For a small additional payment we can extend your warranty _____ the end of next year.

8 Going global

1 Complete the table below. The final column is needed to make irregular forms of the present perfect.

infinitive	past simple	past participle
become	became	1 _____
begin	began	2 _____
bring	brought	brought
buy	bought	bought
choose	chose	3 _____
cost	cost	cost
fall	fell	4 _____
find	found	found
forget	forgot	5 _____
give	gave	6 _____
go	went	7 _____
grow	grew	8 _____
have	had	had
keep	kept	kept
know	knew	9 _____
leave	left	left
lose	lost	lost
make	made	10 _____
meet	met	met
pay	paid	paid
see	saw	11 _____
sell	sold	sold
set	set	set
speak	spoke	12 _____
spend	spent	spent
take	took	13 _____
tell	told	told
think	thought	14 _____
understand	understood	understood
write	wrote	15 _____

Cover the right-hand column with a piece of paper and test yourself. Repeat until you have learnt all the forms!

Present perfect

2 Match the examples of the present perfect 1-4 with their uses a)-d) below.

1 I've been to Prague 12 times this year. ☐
2 We've opened a new office in Prague. Our operations in central Europe will be much more efficient now. ☐
3 The Prague office has been open for three months. ☐
4 I've never been to our office in Prague. ☐

a) the present result of a past action
b) life experience up to now
c) repeated actions before now
d) a state lasting up to the present

- The form of the present perfect is **has/have** + past participle (third column of verb tables). Contractions are common in speech.
  Affirmative: *I have (I've) gone, He has (He's) gone.*
  Negative: *I have not (I haven't) gone, He has not (He hasn't) gone.*
  Questions: *Have I gone?, Has he gone?*
- The present perfect is neither a past tense, nor a present tense, but both. It 'looks back' from the present to the past.
  Study examples 1-4 again. Notice how they all look back from the present to the past.
- We can use the past simple as well as the present perfect for 'the present result of a past action'. This is very common (a) in American English and (b) with the words *just* and *already*.
  We have just opened a new office in Prague.
  OR *We just opened a new office in Prague.*

3 Complete the sentences by putting each verb into the correct form of the present perfect. Use contractions where possible.

1 _____ (we/make) the right decision?
2 I had a headache but I _____ (take) an aspirin and I feel better now.
3 Do you know where Marta is? I _____ (not/see) her since lunchtime.
4 Do you think our Marketing Director is making the right decisions? She _____ (spend) half the advertising budget on internet ads.
5 Don't worry, you're not late. The meeting _____ (not/begin) yet.
6 We need to see Peter's market report. _____ (he/write) it?
7 _____ (anyone/lose) their keys? I found these by the water cooler just now.
8 Yes, I know I need to enter all the sales data into the spreadsheet. Don't worry, I _____ (not/forget).

4 The present perfect is often used with *ever* and *never* to talk about general life experience. Write sentences using the words in brackets.

1 you/ever/work/abroad?
   Have you ever worked abroad?
2 I/never/be/to Istanbul. What's it like?
   _____. What's it like?
3 you/ever/forget/a client's name?
   _____
4 Christine/never/tell/me about her family
   _____
5 you/ever/have/an argument with your boss?
   _____

132 *The* Business

Grammar and practice

Present perfect and past simple

5 Put the verb into either the past simple (*I did*) or the present perfect (*I have done*). Decide whether the speaker sees the action as completely in the past, or as linked to the present.

1. a My PC _____ (crash) last week and so I'm using my laptop.
   b On no! My computer _____ (crash)! What am I going to do now?!?
2. a News is just coming in. There _____ (be) a serious earthquake in San Francisco.
   b There _____ (be) a small earthquake just outside San Francisco while we were there on holiday.
3. a She _____ (act) in more than thirty movies during her career, but now she's retired and spends her time working for charity.
   b She _____ (act) in more than thirty movies, but this is her best film yet.
4. a _____ the meeting _____ (start) yet? I hope I'm not late.
   b _____ the meeting _____ (start) on time? I wasn't there so I don't know.

6 It is very common to ask a question with the present perfect and then reply with the past simple. Use this pattern to complete the sentences.

1. a: How many customers *have you served* (you/serve) this week?
   b: Oh, loads. On Monday alone we *had* (have) over 500 people in the shop.
2. a: _____ (you/ever/be) to Germany?
   b: Yes, I _____ (be) in Frankfurt last year for a trade show.
3. a: How long _____ (you/know) Roberto?
   b: For ages. We _____ (work) together in London for a long time.
4. a: Why _____ (you/come) to this talk? It's not really your field.
   b: You're right. But it _____ (look) interesting on the program.
5. a: _____ (you/finish) yet?
   b: Yes, of course, I _____ (finish) ages ago.
6. a: _____ (not/we/meet) somewhere before?
   b: Yes, I remember you from the conference in Chicago last year. You _____ (give) a talk on direct marketing.

7 If there is a time expression, then it controls the verb tense. Complete the sentences by putting the verb into either the past simple (*I did*) or the present perfect (*I have done*).

1. a **Last year** we _____ (make) a profit of €4 million.
   b **This year** we _____ (make) a bigger profit – something close to €6 million.
2. a **So far this month** we _____ (have) 15,000 hits on our new website.
   b **A few months ago** we only _____ (have) an average of 8,000 hits per month.
3. a I _____ (**never**/visit) Rome, but I hope to go there one day.
   b I _____ (visit) Rome **in 2002**, for my honeymoon.
4. a I _____ (not/speak) to my boss **yesterday** – he was really busy.
   b I'm sorry, I **still** _____ (not/speak) to my boss. I'll do it this afternoon.
5. a _____ our lawyer _____ (look at) the contract **yet**?
   b _____ our lawyer _____ (look at) the contract **before** he went away on vacation?

> Notice from the examples above how:
> - Some time expressions go with the present perfect because the time period includes the present: *this year, so far this month, never, still, yet*.
> - Some time expressions go with the past simple because the time period is in the past: *last year, a few months ago, in 2002, yesterday*.

for and *since*

8 We often use *for* and *since* with the present perfect. But we can use *for* with other tenses as well. Read the information in the box then do the exercise below.

> - **for** + length of time
>   present perfect: *I've been here in London **for two weeks**.*
>   past simple: *I lived in London **for a year** just after I finished university.*
>   present continuous: *I'm staying here in London **for a year**.* (= one year in total)
> - **since** + point in time when the action started
>   present perfect: *I've been here in London **since** the beginning of the month.*

Complete a part of Louisa's email to a friend by:
- putting the verb into either the past simple or present perfect
- underlining either *for* or *since*.

> Hi Ana, how are things? I'm writing to you from Paris! It's my second time here. If you remember, the first time was when I ¹_____ (be) here on holiday ²*for/since* two weeks with Paulo. It seems like a long time ago!
>
> Anyway, now I'm here for work experience, and I'm staying ³*for/since* a year. Actually, I ⁴_____ (arrive) at the beginning of January – more than two months ago! Sorry that I ⁵_____ (not/write) ⁶*for/since* then.
>
> Things are going well. I have a job in a bookshop and I'm learning French – I speak it all the time. I ⁷_____ (meet) all sorts of interesting people ⁸*for/since* I got here, including a really nice guy called Alain. Let me tell you about him. We ⁹_____ (meet) for the first time a couple of weeks ago. He ¹⁰_____ (come) into the shop and …

Recordings

1 Living abroad

1.1 About business Working abroad
🔊 1:01–1:04

Kiki
My name's Kiki and I spend two months every year in India buying supplies for my jewellery business. When I come to India I spend time meeting local manufacturers in different parts of the country, talking with them and looking at their jewellery. India is such a big country that it can sometimes take two days to go from one city to another. I'm in Jodhpur at the moment and tomorrow I'm going to Delhi. When I find some jewellery that I like, I buy it from the manufacturer to sell in my shop in Hong Kong. I have a lot of very good contacts here in India, and this is my tenth visit here. I always visit the same companies and I know a lot of the managers very well. When I first came here I thought the food was very strange, there wasn't very much meat and the flavours were very different to the food in Hong Kong. But now I love the food and I always buy lots of spices to add to my cooking back at home!

Anil
My name's Anil and I'm a software analyst for LOG Software Systems. My company often sends me abroad and I usually spend more than half of each year away from home. I go to companies around the world and help them to install our software systems. I then stay there to train the employees how to use the new system and to help with any problems that the company have. This process usually takes about six months from beginning to end. Last year I was in Venzuela for seven months and at the moment I'm in Thailand so I see some very different and interesting places. I'm staying in a really nice hotel in the centre of Bangkok, it's got five stars and has everything that I need. I really enjoy my job because I meet a lot of people and I learn a lot about how different countries do business.

Jean Marc
My name's Jean Marc and I work abroad for ten months every year. I work as a doctor and I travel around the world giving medical help after natural disasters such as droughts and tsunamis. I never know where I am going next and that's what makes my job really exciting. At the moment I'm working in Indonesia, on a very small island. I'm going to be here for about ten months. The journey here takes four days because there are no roads, you have to fly and then get a boat. I work in a health centre giving medical treatment to local people and I'm also teaching the young children about how important clean water is. I love working with the children and the people here are all very friendly. When my work here finishes I am going to spend six weeks travelling around Indonesia before I start my next job, I don't know where it will be though!

Marika
My university has links with engineering firms in Germany. As part of my degree I'm spending a year working for a petroleum company near Munich. I'm working in their labs helping them develop new equipment. At first it was difficult because I had to learn a lot about the job and I also missed my friends and family. I soon made lots of new friends though and stopped feeling homesick. There are people from all over the world working for the organization and I made lots of German friends. I'm staying with a local family and this really helped me when I first arrived. They made me feel at home. They showed me around the city and gave me lots of help with any problems that I had. I'm really enjoying working here and my manager says that I am doing a good job. Hopefully I will get a good reference when I leave and this will help me find a good position after university.

1.2 Vocabulary Living abroad
🔊 1:05–1:08

Conversation 1
Bank manager: Come in, Mrs Silvera. Please sit down.
Carmen: Thank you.
BM: Now, what can I do for you?
C: I'd like to open an account.
BM: Well I can hear that you're not from New Zealand.
C: No, I'm not, I'm from Brazil but I'm going to be in New Zealand for a year, my company has sent me to work at their subsidiary here.
BM: Oh, great, you're going to love it here, is this your first visit to New Zealand?
C: Yes it is, but everyone at work is very friendly and the countryside is so beautiful.
BM: That's good. Now, before I can open an account I need to see some important documents, do you have your passport?
C: Yes, here it is. It's all in Portuguese though.
BM: That's OK, I just need to check the address and the photo. I also need to see a letter or a contract from your company. Do you have one?
C: Yes, here you are.
BM: Great. Does it give details of your salary? Oh yes, I can see it here. Good and it's got your address in New Zealand too. Now, I need you to fill in these forms and then we can open the account for you. I'll go and make a copy of your documents while you fill in the form. I'll be back in a couple of minutes.
C: OK.

Conversation 2
Landlord: OK, so this is the apartment. If we go through this door you'll see the living room.
Petra: Wow look at the view, you can see right across the harbour!
Kris: Yes, it's beautiful.
L: Yes, the views are good. You can see that the apartment is fully furnished so you won't need to buy any furniture or equipment.
P: That's good, and the kitchen?
L: Yes, through here is the kitchen.
P: It's bigger than our old kitchen at home!
K: And it's much more modern. How many bedrooms are there?
L: There are two bedrooms in the apartment, the door behind us opens into one of the bedrooms, the other is back through the hall.
K: Two bedrooms, that means we can have visitors to stay!
P: I suppose the most important question is about the rent. How much is it?
L: Well, it's €1,500 per month but that includes all of the bills.
P: And how much is the deposit?
L: One and a half month's rent, so that's €2, 250.
K: That's a lot of money, but my company says that they will help us with the deposit and the rent for the first month.
L: It might seem like a lot of money but it's a lovely apartment. I don't think you'll find anything cheaper in this area.
P: We need to think about it. Can we call you back tomorrow?
L: Of course, but don't take too long, another couple are coming to view the apartment later. You wouldn't want to lose it, would you?
K: No, we'll be in touch soon, bye.

Conversation 3
Doctor: Come in, Mr Goodman, have a seat.
Mr Goodman: Thanks.
D: So what can I do for you today?
Mr G: Well, I arrived in Greece last week. I'm working for Athens Bank on a year's placement and they told me that I need to come and register with a doctor.
D: Yes, it's definitely a good idea. Before we start the examination, do you have a European Health Insurance Card?
Mr G: No, I don't.
D: OK, here's the form. Fill this in and you won't have to pay so much for your medical treatment. You can give it to the receptionist on the way out.
Mr G: OK.
D: Now there are a number of questions that I need to ask you. Are you taking any medicine at the moment?
Mr G: No I'm not.
D: Good, now I need to check your weight and your height, how tall are you?
Mr G: I'm one metre 65.
D: And your weight?
Mr G: I'm not sure.
D: Well if you can stand on the scales we can check, they're just over there...

Conversation 4
Sales assistant: Good afternoon, can I help you?
Yuki: Yes, I'd like to buy a mobile phone.
SA: Well, you're in the right place, we are the largest mobile phone shop in Copenhagen. What kind of phone do you need?
Y: I don't have a landline in my apartment here so I need a cheap phone. Also I'm not sure how long my company need me to stay here and so I don't want a phone with a contract.
SA: OK, we have a lot of phones that come with prepaid packages, there's a lot of choice.
Y: And is buying top-ups easy?

DVD-ROM The recordings are available as MP3 files on the DVD-ROM, to be downloaded or played back with interactive script.

Recordings

SA: Yes, lots of the phones come with free minutes so that you can use them as soon as you buy them. This one, for example comes with 400 minutes free talking time. When you need to top the phone up you can come back to this shop to buy some more credit or you can call the provider with your credit card and they will put more credit on the phone for you. It's very easy.
Y: And what happens when I go back to Japan?
SA: Well there is no contract so you don't have to pay when you don't want the phone any more.
Y: That's just what I need, can you show me some of the prepaid phones, please?
SA: Of course, the most popular one is this one.....

1.3 Grammar Present simple and prepositions of time

🔊 1:09–1:15

1. January the 26th is Australia's official national holiday. It marks the day that the first ships landed in Sydney Cove in 1788. On that day the prime minister makes a special speech on the TV and people set fireworks off in the evening.
2. Boxing Day in the UK is the day after Christmas Day and so is the 26th of December. It is a public holiday and in the UK it is common for sports events to take place.
3. Groundhog Day is a traditional festival that is celebrated in the United States and Canada on February the 2nd. A groundhog is a small animal that lives in a hole in the ground. People believe that if a groundhog sees its shadow on this day there will be six more weeks of cold weather.
4. Bastille Day is the French national holiday and it is celebrated each year on the 14th of July. On this day in 1789 the Bastille, a prison in Paris, was attacked by the local residents. Every year there are military parades.
5. April Fool's Day, is not a real holiday, but is celebrated in many countries on April the 1st by playing jokes on friends and neighbours.
6. In Japan, April the 29th is Showa Day. This was the Emperor's birthday and it begins a week of festivals, called Golden Week.
7. The Day of the Dead in Mexico is the 1st of November. On this day people visit the graves of their families and they also build and fly large kites.

1.4 Speaking Making small talk

🔊 1:16–1:18

Conversation 1
A: Hi there.
B: Oh hi, how was your weekend?
A: Oh, it was great, we took the kids camping.
B: Wow, that sounds lovely. Did you have good weather?
A: Well, no, on Saturday it rained all afternoon but it was much better on Sunday, it was sunny and warm all day.
B: So where did you go?
A: We went up into the mountains and camped on the shores of Lake Garda.
B: And did the children enjoy it?
A: Oh yes they love it when we go camping. They didn't want to come home!
B: Well, that sounds really nice, if you'll excuse me I've got to make an important phone call. See you soon.
A: OK, see you later.

Conversation 2
C: I can't believe how busy it is.
D: No, me neither. I didn't know so many people would be able to take the time to travel to Thailand for this conference.
C: Did you have a good journey here?
D: Well I left home in Helsinki on Monday but I had to stop in Abu Dhabi for a meeting so I arrived here on Wednesday.
C: Abu Dhabi, wow! What was it like?
D: Well the weather was really hot but it's a really interesting place.
C: Was it your first visit there?
D: No, we do a lot of business out there actually.
C: Oh, really, where did you stay?
D: In a really nice hotel, right in the centre of Abu Dhabi.
C: Was it called the Continental?
D: Yes, I think it was. Why do you ask?
C: Oh I stayed there last month
D: Really? I didn't know you did business there.
C: Yes, we do. I go there about three times a year. Well, enjoy the rest of the conference.
D: Yes, you too, bye.

Conversation 3
E: Where do you want to go?
F: The Royal Hotel please.
E: OK, no problem. Are you here in Paris for work or on holiday?
F: It's work actually.
E: Oh, what do you do?
F: I'm an engineer, I work for a large Spanish engineering company. I'm the research and development manager. I'm in charge of a group of six scientists who work in the lab. We're responsible for developing new ideas and products for the company.
E: That sounds really interesting. Do you like your job?
F: Well, every day is different, so yes, I love it. Some days I'm in the lab while others I'm out doing research. We're always working on new and exciting products so I never have a chance to get bored. At the moment we're working on a new software program for the Indian market.
E: That sounds very exciting. Are you going to visit India?
F: Yes, I'm flying out there next week. Have you been there?
E: Yes, last year I…

1.6 Case study Global Recruit

🔊 1:19–1:22

Tomas
My name is Tomas. I'm 25 years old and come from the Netherlands. I finished a degree in Business Studies in Eindhoven one year ago. I really enjoy working with people, in my last job I worked for a mobile phone company in Germany but I finished there last month. I had to offer advice to customers and help them when they had a problem with their phone. I'm pretty good at languages. I speak English, Flemish & French. My hobbies? Well I go running everyday. In fact, I try to run in at least two marathons a year. I'd love to run a marathon in another country one day. I want to go and work abroad so that I can learn about living and working in a different culture because I want to experience something totally different and I want to see the world.

Panayota
Hi, my name's Panayota, but that's a bit difficult so everyone calls me Pana. What can I tell you about myself? Hmm, well, I come from a large traditional Greek family. I studied geography at university in Athens but at the moment I'm working in my family's taverna. I mostly serve in the restaurant, I love chatting to the customers because I can practise my languages, I can speak English, French and German and even a little Chinese. I also keep the accounts and organize the orders and the deliveries. I'm good with figures and I'm very well organized. I'm nearly 28 years old and in Greece that means that all my aunts keep asking 'When are you getting married?' I'm not ready for that yet. I would like to see something of the world first, although one day I'd like to have a big family with lots of children. My hobbies? Well, I come from an island so I have to say sailing and swimming.

Miroslav
Hello, my name is Miroslav. I'm 27 years old and single. I have a diploma in information technology from the technological college in Bratislava. In my current job I design websites for expensive boutiques across Slovakia. It is important for the shops that their websites look good because most of the customers shop online. As far as languages go, I speak English and also Portuguese because my mother is from Portugal. When I'm not working I love computers and spend lots of my free time keeping my own website up-to-date. The address is www.miroslavparty.sk. I also love parties and going out, I have a lot of friends who are designers and so we spend a lot of time at nightclubs, discos and parties. I really want to go and work abroad somewhere exciting.

Francesca
Ciao, my name's Francesca and I'm 28 years old. I learnt to speak English, Spanish and a little bit of French and Portuguese at one of the best universities in Italy. I studied modern languages and as part of my degree I spent a year studying in Spain. I had a fantastic time. You learn so much when you live away from home, that's why I want to do it again. After I graduated I spent four years working as a senior computer programmer for an IT company in Rome. I was responsible for a team of twenty other programmers but to be honest it was a little bit boring so last month I left. Now I want to try living in another country. In my free time I love to be outside, I love walking in the mountains and cycling so I'd like to go to a country where I can continue to do those things.

🔊 **1:23**

Heidi: Hi there Dana, this is Heidi from the recruitment department.
Dana: Hi there, how are you?
H: I'm fine thanks, I'm calling with regard to the applications for job numbers TC / 428 and WA / 926. I've got the references for all of the four candidates that you shortlisted. I thought you'd like to hear about them immediately.
D: Oh, excellent, that's great. Can we start with the Call Dubai job?
H: OK, first of all there was Mr Visser.
D: Oh, yes Tomas. He was a very nice young man. What did his reference say?
H: Well it says that he was very hardworking in his last job and he was popular with the other members of staff.
D: That's good.
H: Yes it is but the reason he left was because there was a problem with a customer. The reference doesn't give any more information. It just says 'Tomas left the company after a complaint from a customer.' Maybe the customer was very difficult or maybe Tomas did something wrong, I don't know.
D: That sounds a bit worrying, we'll have to talk to him about it. Now what about Ms Mitropoulos, the lady from Greece?
H: Well this is a little bit strange but because she left university and worked in her father's taverna there was no professional reference for her. The reference that we have is from her university professor. It says that she was a very good student but it doesn't say anything about whether she would be suitable for a job in Dubai.
D: OK, we need to have a think about her too. What about WA / 926, the job at MTM in Brazil?
H: Well, the first person was Miroslav Kalata. At the moment he is working as a web-designer in Slovakia. His reference says that he is very creative and he produces some really great things on his website but unfortunately he is often late for work and is often tired. Last month he was more than half an hour late on six occasions.
D: That's quite a lot, but it's a problem that isn't difficult to fix. And what about Francesca, I think her surname was Di Ponti.
H: Well she has a lot of experience as a manager, her reference said that she was really good at her job. She was a senior computer programmer for an IT company in Rome.
D: Yes, I remember her. I thought she would be ideal for the job in Brazil.
H: She has a lot of strengths but her reference says that she was very unpopular with the other employees. She worked well on her own but when she had to work as part of a team the results were not good.
D: Well that's not great either. OK, thanks for letting me know. Can you email the references to me?
H: Yes, I'll do it straightaway.
D: Thanks a lot Heidi, that's great.
H: Not a problem, Dana. Bye now.
D: Goodbye.

2 Dealing with customers

2.1 About business The shopping experience

🔊 **1:24**

Interviewer: Good afternoon and on Modern Business today I am joined by Rafael Fernandez. He is a market analyst and an expert on luxury customer spending. Good afternoon Rafael.
Rafael: Good afternoon Emilia.
I: So, Rafael could you start by telling us what a typical consumer looks for when shopping in a luxury department store?
R: Well, the first is the product itself. They want to know that the product they are buying is of a high quality and that it is reliable. Sales assistants have to remember to tell the consumer this. The second important factor is the experience of buying these products. They want to enjoy the experience and don't want to have any problems. Sales assistants need to make the experience of shopping as pleasurable as they can so they need to make the consumer feel special. This could involve giving them personal attention, calling them by their names and carrying the shopping to the car. It also means that the assistants need to be able to deal with problems quickly and carefully. You've heard the expression 'the customer is always right?'
I: Yes.
R: Well here it is really important. If the customer doesn't feel they are getting the service they are paying for they will go to another store. That leads me onto the final thing that these consumers look for, value for money. Even though they are spending a lot of money they still want to feel that the things they are buying are worth the money that they are spending.
I: Wow, it sounds like luxury consumers are very difficult to please.
R: Well, yes they can be, but remember, if they come to your store and are pleased with the service, they will come back again and again.
I: Wow, it sounds like they love to spend! OK, thank you very much Rafael, now it's time for…

2.2 Vocabulary Telephoning and customer care

🔊 **1:25–1:27**

Conversation 1

A: Good morning, Custom Computers, how can I help you?
B: Hello, I'm calling about my new computer that was delivered last week.
A: OK, can you tell me more about the problem?
B: Yes, the computer was delivered to the office last week, but we had some problems setting it up. Lots of the cables are missing.
A: Right, so the computer was delivered last week but some parts are missing. This is a problem for our deliveries department. Can you hold while I put you through?
B: Well I'm actually very busy, do you think somebody could call me back?
A: Of course sir, I'll get somebody from deliveries to call you back later this morning, goodbye.
B: Oh, goodbye.

Conversation 2

A: Good afternoon, Simpson Stationery, How can I help you?
B: Hello, I'm calling about my delivery of stationery.
A: OK sir, what seems to be the problem?
B: We ordered 25 boxes of paper for an SX 279 laser printer. The delivery was supposed to arrive this morning but it didn't. We've run out of paper for our laser printer and so we can't print any documents. This is going to have a huge effect on our business!
A: OK, so you ordered 25 boxes of printer paper for an SX 279 printer and the order was supposed to arrive this morning. Do you have a reference number, sir?
B: Yes it's 482 / 917.
A: OK, 482 / 917 and what was the delivery address?
B: 27a Delta Avenue
A: I'm just checking on the computer now sir. Oh, I see what the problem is. Our computer has the delivery address as 37a Delta Avenue. It must be our driver's fault; he is always doing things like this. He took your paper to 37a Delta Avenue. I'll arrange for another driver to come and deliver it later today, would that be OK?
B: Yes that would be great, thank you very much.
A: Thank you for calling, goodbye.
B: Goodbye.

Conversation 3

A: Good morning, Inter-Europe hotels. How can I help?
B: Good morning, I'm calling about a reservation that I made with you last week. My name's Mr Lalo.
A: Oh, do you have the details of the reservation, Mr Lalo?
B: Yes, I reserved six single rooms for employees of my company as we are…
A: No, I mean do you have a booking reference number?
B: Hold on, let me have a look, yes, it's WA 8628.
A: OK, can you tell me which of our hotels the reservation was made for?
B: Well we were going to stay at your hotel in Warsaw…
A: Yes and when did you need the rooms?
B: Well, we needed six rooms for three nights…
A: Yes, I know that, but when did you need the rooms?
B: We need the rooms from Tuesday the seventeenth, and it was for three nights
A: OK, so what's the problem?
B: Well, one of our employees can't come to the conference so I need to cancel one of the rooms.
A: Right, I see. That's no problem. We can change your reservation from six single rooms to five. Your new reference number is WA 8629.
B: WA 8629. Thanks for all your help.
A: You're welcome.
B: Goodbye
A: Goodbye Mr Lalo.

2.4 Speaking Telephoning- Handling complaints

🔊 1:28–1:31

Conversation 1

Luca: Good morning HF Precision Engineering, Luca speaking. How can I help?
Paul: Hi there, this is Paul Rossi and I'm calling about a delivery of five hundred head cleaners.
L: I see, what's the problem?
P: Well, the delivery date was yesterday but nothing arrived. It's very inconvenient because it's holding up production at my plant.
L: I'm sorry about that Mr Rossi, do you have the reference number?
P: Yes, it's AJ/96241
L: OK, I'm just checking it now on our system. Ah, here it is, delivery AJ/96241 should have arrived yesterday but there was a problem at our distribution centre. Unfortunately the wrong label was put on your delivery so it was put on the wrong lorry. Your delivery is currently in our distribution centre in Milan but we can deliver it to you before the end of the week.
P: Well, this is very unsatisfactory, this is delaying production and my company is losing money because of this.
L: I understand Mr Rossi and I am very sorry. We are working hard to try and solve this problem for you. Can we do anything to help you with this?
P: I think that you could give me a discount on the delivery to make up for all the trade that I have lost.
L: I think that's reasonable. Would a discount of 10% be OK?
P: Yes, I'd be happy with that.
L: OK. I'll put a 10% discount on the delivery notes and the parts will be with you before the end of the week. I'm sorry for the inconvenience.
P: That's OK. Thanks for all your help. Bye.
L: Goodbye.

Conversation 2

IT support: Good morning IT support, how can I help?
Bruna: Hi there, this is Bruna Perez and I'm calling from the Finance department. I'm having problems with our computer system this morning. I can't access the accounts for the Asia group.
IT: That must be very frustrating, can you give me some more details?
B: Well, when I start the computer everything is OK and all of the other programs run without any problems. When I try to open the program that I use to run the accounts for the Asia group I can't get into them.
IT: Can you access the accounts for the other groups?
B: I don't know, I haven't tried. I only ever use the Asia accounts.
IT: Do you get a message on the screen?
B: Yes, it says 'Error 27c, unknown command.'
IT: OK, let me see what I can do. Are you OK to hold the line for a minute?
B: Yes.
IT: Right I've found the problem, we need to install the program again on your PC. I'll come up and do it now, are you on the third floor?
B: Yes.
IT: OK, I'll be there in a minute. Goodbye.
B: Bye.

Conversation 3

Restaurant Manager: Hello, Restaurant Exclusivo, how can I help?
Mr Langenburg: Hi, my name is Mr Langenburg and I came to your restaurant last night with some very important guests from Japan.
RM: I see.
Mr L: Well, the service was absolutely terrible! It was really embarrassing.
RM: What was the problem?
Mr L: Well we waited more than an hour for the food to be brought to the table. It was great food but it wasn't hot enough. When we complained to the waiter he said that the restaurant was very busy and there was nothing he could do.
RM: Oh dear.
Mr L: Also when I asked to speak to the manager he said that there was no manager working last night. My guests were very important and so I didn't want to upset them by becoming angry but I want to let you know that I am very disappointed.
RM: This is the first time that I have heard about this but I'll look into it straight away to find out which waiter it was.
Mr L: Good.
RM: Also to make things better what we could do is give you a free meal for eight people in our VIP section next Friday night.
Mr L: That would be great. Thank you.

Conversation 4

Jon: Good morning Laboratory Products, Jon Lauffman speaking.
Ingrid: Hi there Jon, this is Ingrid Heller calling from Scitech.
J: Oh, hi, Ingrid how can I help?
I: Well, Jon there's a bit of a problem with the machine that we ordered from you.
J: Really, what's the problem?
I: Well, you said that it would arrive on Monday but it's now Thursday and it still hasn't arrived.
J: I'm sorry to hear that, that's very strange.
I: Yes it is, we really need the machine so that we can move on with our research. It's really urgent.
J: OK, let me see what I can do. Will you be in the office all morning?
I: Yes, I will.
J: Right, I'll make some phone calls and I'll get back to you on that.
I: Alright, thanks for your help Jon.
J: No problem Ingrid, bye.
I: Goodbye.

2.6 Case study The Panorama conference

🔊 1:32

Receptionist: Good morning sir, welcome to the Panorama Hotel, how can I help?
Van Der Vaart: Hi there, my name's Jan Van Der Vaart. I'm from Electronics RDC and I made a reservation for myself and some colleagues. We're here for the Panorama Conference.
R: Ah, Mr Van Der Vaart, it's nice to see you, let me check the details of your reservation.
V: OK
R: So, you booked our eight premium class rooms on the top floor of the hotel and you're staying for the conference, that's from the 5th to the 8th of February, is this correct?
V: Well, the dates are correct but there are nine of us. We booked eight rooms on the Internet but we had to bring another colleague to the conference. Do you have another premium class room available?
R: Well we only have eight premium class rooms in the hotel. Let me see if there are any other rooms available. I'm really sorry Mr Van der Vaart but the hotel is completely full because of the conference. I'm very sorry. We don't have any rooms available in the whole hotel.
V: Are you sure nothing is available? We have never had a problem like this and we've brought extra guests before. Electronics RDC use your hotels regularly, we stayed in the Grand Hotel in Singapore last month and last week we stayed in the Grand Hotel in Lisbon. We are Gold Class members and expect good service.
R: I understand what you are saying, sir but all our rooms are fully booked. This is a very busy time of year and the conference also means that our luxury rooms are full.
V: What do you suggest we do then? I can't send one of my colleagues back to Holland.
R: The only solution I can think of is for two of your party to share a room. In each of the premium class rooms there are two king size beds and they are our most luxurious rooms. Your colleagues will be very comfortable.
V: Well it's not perfect but I suppose we don't have any choice if all of the rooms are taken.
R: I really am sorry sir, now can I ask you to fill in these forms with your passport numbers and the names of your colleagues. I'll organize for your bags to be taken to your rooms.

3 Operations

3.1 About business Lean manufacturing

🔘 1:33

Good afternoon and welcome to the first of our lectures on the history of the organization of work in the UK. Throughout this course we are going to focus on how working trends have changed throughout history.

I'd like to start today with an overview of the period, it's important that you all understand this. There are four main stages in this introduction and they are the domestic system, the workshop system, the factory system and the post-factory system. Let's look at each of them in a little more detail.

First of all was the domestic system. During this time most people worked from home, a bit like today but without the computers! It was a very simple process and everything was very basic. People bought the materials that they needed and then made whatever products they could, most people made clothes or cloth products. The whole family worked from home and then sold what they made at market each week. Most families were also farmers and so this was a way that they could make extra money, working part-time. One result of this though was that production was very slow.

The second stage was what we call the workshop system. This was very similar to the first stage, people still worked from home and still worked part-time. The main difference was that the people were organized by a subcontractor, a bit like a manager. The people didn't buy their own supplies, they used the subcontractor's. The subcontractor paid the families to make the products but kept any profit that was made when the products were sold.

In the eighteenth century work moved from the home into factories. The first factory in the UK was built in 1769 by Richard Arkwright. Around this time a lot of new machines were developed. These were usually large and so couldn't fit inside people's homes. One advantage of the factories was that production was much quicker but people had to leave their homes to go to work. Working conditions in the factories were also quite bad.

We still use the factory system today but they are much nicer places to work in. Many people refer to this as the post-factory system. The system is largely the same but we use much more advanced technology. This reduces the need for humans because today our computers can do almost anything! Many people think that one day nobody will work to produce things in this way but I don't think this is true, we need humans to check the machines and we always need engineers to mend them when they break down.

Now, who knows what I mean by……

🔘 1:34

Back in the 1990s our company decided to send a team of managers over to Japan to learn about the TPS, or lean management system. They came back full of enthusiasm about this wonderful efficient system and they wanted to implement it in our company immediately. Well, the first thing we did was to send all of our employees to a series of workshops on *kaizen* and lean manufacturing. Six months later we introduced the system to our factory floor.

At first the employees were very keen on the system. They could see the benefits immediately. They liked being more involved, they began to take more pride in their work, and it was clear to them that their work was less stressful than before.

But soon the problems began. One or two employees felt uncomfortable having to make decisions about production; decisions which had previously been made by their supervisors or managers. We had to repeat the workshops, and this cost a lot of time and money. Then a rumour went around the company that one of the owners was thinking about moving the factory to Eastern Europe in order to save on wage costs. Faith in the company was lost, and when some of the employees decided to go on strike, well, the end to working to a lean management system was in sight.

Maybe employees in the West are unable to identify with their companies in the way that Toyota's employees are able to in Japan. I don't know. Whatever the reason, although our experience of lean manufacturing was wonderful while it lasted we're now back to mass production.

3.2 Vocabulary Trends and planning

🔘 1:35

Mr Ruby: … and if we look at recent trends we can all see that the number of international airports is increasing, and at the same time, the number of people who are subjected to aircraft noise is rising. Now, we all know that as the cost of airfares goes down, the demand for flights goes up. Therefore we cannot ignore the problems of aircraft noise any longer. This is why we're interested in hearing about the silent plane. Ms. Bloom, can you tell us a bit more about the project?

Ms Bloom: Thank you, Mr Ruby. Yes, we're currently working on producing a silent aircraft. Admittedly, the plane would not be completely silent, but we are aiming to decrease noise levels by 99%.

R: That's a significant amount.

B: Indeed, and it's a big challenge. Most people think that a plane's engines produce all the noise, but that's not entirely true. At the moment almost half the noise comes from the body of the plane, although the other half does come from the engines. Traditionally, a plane's engines are situated below the wings; we intend to situate the engines *above* the wings. This would keep the noise up in the air and shield the people on the ground from the noise. Of course, innovative design and research costs money. And while costs are growing, unfortunately our level of funding is shrinking. And that's why I'm here.

R: Could you tell my colleagues what the benefits would be for us as an airline company?

B: Well, apart from turning you into a good neighbour to the people who live near airports, the silent plane could completely change your pattern of operations. You would, for example, be able to land at night time. This would increase the utilization of the aircraft and at the same time decrease your overall costs. More flights into and out of an airport would increase the amount of jobs in the area and that means that the local economy would grow. So, good news all round.

R: And when will this silent plane be finished?

B: As long as we can get funding, we hope to have a plane ready and flying by the year 2020 …

🔘 1:36

Councillor: In the past, an average of 2,000 tourists visited our island every year. This number stayed the same for many years. Then, this year, with flights arriving from six new destinations, the number of tourists rose dramatically. In January we welcomed 550 tourists, which was normal for the time of year, but then, after that television programme about our island, more and more tourists came. There was only a slow increase at first; by April the number rose to just over a thousand. However, the numbers grew throughout the summer and peaked in September at 7,000! From September the number of tourists fell, but the numbers didn't go down that much. At the moment, in November we still have about 3,000 tourists on our island. Now, on the whole this is a good thing. We are very happy about the money they bring to our island, our economy is growing, but we also have some problems. To make matters more urgent, the first island music festival is going to take place next August. As this was also announced on the television programme we can expect more visitors during that week. Ladies and gentlemen of the council we currently have 2.5 million dollars in the bank and it's time we put that money to good use.

3.4 Speaking Presentations – signposts and stepping stones

🔘 1:37

1 I'd like to start by …
2 First of all …
3 Moving on to …
4 Let's go back and look at …
5 I'd like to finish by …
6 Are there any questions?
7 Thank you for coming.

🔘 1:38

Good afternoon everyone. I'm glad you could all make it. My name's Sonia Padron Perez and I'm the sales manager here at DMC Wood. I'd like to start by giving you a short overview of today's presentation.

First of all we're going to look at the sales figures for last year. Then we'll see how our competitors did during the same period. After that we'll look at how this has affected our share prices, and finally we'll see what we intend to do about this in the future.

If you have any questions, I'll be happy to answer them at the end of my presentation.

OK, so let's start with the sales figures. On the first slide, you can see that our sales figures fell dramatically last summer. As you can see, the biggest fall was in June, sales went up slightly in September, but then fell again in October. Last summer was very unusual because that is usually when we sell most of our products. We think that this was because of the bad weather that we had during the summer. We expected people to buy much more of our garden furniture for barbecues and garden parties but there was a lot of rain in June and so people weren't interested in being outdoors. The sales went up in September and that was because the weather was a little better. The summer was a little late but it eventually arrived! Our sales did go back down again though in October which was a bit of a surprise.

Let's take a closer look at that last point: on the next slide you can see that our competitors brought out a new product in May …

Moving on to our share prices: the next slide shows us how our shares performed over the last year. As you can see, it wasn't a very good year for our shareholders.

But it's not all bad news, we can see that the share prices didn't increase very much but we can see that at the end of last year they were slightly higher than they were at the start. This is a very promising sign for next year.

Now, let's go back and look at the first slide again. Here you can see that our sales figures rose in September. This is an indication that we still have a chance to regain our position as the market leader and that we can close the gap.

I'd like to finish by showing you how we aim to reach this target. Ladies and gentlemen, let me introduce you to the new GTQ luxury model … Welcome to the future!

3.6 Case study ScotAir
1:39–1:44

1 I've been working for EvanAir for the past 19 months and in that time I've seen the company change in such a big way! When I did my training we were told that safety was the main concern for EvanAir. Not any more! Some cabin crew don't even have security passes! I don't mind so much the tea and coffee being taken away from us but they won't even provide water for us. They hire cabin crew whose first language is not English and they make us pay £25 a month for our uniforms. We work on average 10 and a half to 11 hours a day and very often don't have a break.

2 I worked for EvanAir for three months and had to give up because I was extremely tired. I often felt ill when I had 12 hours flying per day without a break plus three hours per day just travelling to and from home to work. Can you imagine starting work at five o'clock in the morning and spending 15 hours per day in uniform? I was sad when I left because I really like this job, but I think your health comes first.

3 I can understand that for the employees it might be better to work for larger traditional airlines where they are treated better, receive better salaries and lots of benefits. But EvanAir has revolutionized air travel and enabled everybody to fly, not only the rich. It is EvanAir which gives us this possibility, not the airlines which provide all the extras for the employees. There is a reason why EvanAir are one of the most profitable airlines in Europe.

4 EvanAir may be uncomfortable, but they're cheap and they get me to my meetings quicker than travelling by train or car ever did. I fly with them nearly every week. For me, it's just like taking the bus. It gets me from A to B in a short time, and that's good for my business.

5 EvanAir of course, wants to make a profit, but when the cabin crew gets so tired that passengers start to notice, that's going too far. Nobody forced these people to work for EvanAir, but I imagine cabin crew employees can't just leave their jobs, given the economic state of many airline carriers today. I'm not going to fly with budget airlines again. Safety and security is more important than saving a few euros.

6 Britain's CO_2 emissions from aircraft doubled between 1990 and 2000, and they are likely to double again by 2030. And it's not just us; other European countries are no better. One long-haul return flight - say, from London to Sydney - will, by itself, double most people's carbon footprint for the entire year. But short flights are even worse as they use proportionally more fuel for take-off and landing, so, for the environment, flying short distances is the worst way to travel.

4 Success stories
4.1 About business Business leaders and success stories
1:45

Presenter: Hello and welcome to today's three-minute podcast in the series 'Great business leaders of the twentieth century'. Today we're going to hear about a beauty-industry icon who literally changed the face of the cosmetics industry: Estée Lauder.

Josephine Esther Mentzer, known as Estée, was born in Queens, New York in 1908, the daughter of Hungarian and Czech immigrants. From an early age she was fascinated by the lotions and potions developed by her uncle, a chemist. She began her business career in the 1930s, selling his skin care products to New York beauty salons and hotels.

In the 1940s, she founded the Estée Lauder Company together with her husband, Joseph Lauder. Her first major breakthrough was in 1948, when she managed to get counter space at New York's prestigious Saks Fifth Avenue department store.

Estée Lauder had a combination of ambition and stubbornness that enabled her to get ahead in the business world. A risk-taker, she was the first sales person to pioneer the idea of giving away free product samples. This risk paid off, and she was able to expand her range of skin care products and introduced other cosmetics and perfumes. In the 1960s, she ventured into the male cosmetic market, and brought out the very successful Aramis product line. Another of her brilliant business ideas was the medically tested and fragrance-free Clinique line.

Today, the Estée Lauder Company consists of many well-known brand names such as M.A.C, Bobbi Brown, Tommy Hilfiger, Donna Karan, and many, many more. The products are sold in 130 countries around the world and the company has a turnover of over six billion dollars.

Her family was always very important to Estée, and although the company went public in 1995, the majority of the stock is held by Lauder family members and the company is currently headed by one of her grandsons.

Sadly Estée died in 2004, but she will be remembered by all as an entrepreneur who was never willing to settle for anything but the best.

4.2 Vocabulary Describing yourself and being successful
1:46

Interviewer: So Alan, your qualifications are all in order and you have already had some experience in sales. Now I'd like you to tell me something about yourself. What kind of person are you?

Alan: Well, I think I'm a positive person, I mean, I always try to look for the best in a situation and I try to focus on the positive things that are taking place around me. For example in my last job the managers introduced a new system for dividing up the sales department. They decided that every member of the sales department was going to be given a new sales region. A lot of my colleagues were angry because they were given a new area with new clients. I thought that it was good though because we could all learn something new and face new challenges.

I: Well, I can understand that, there are lots of people who don't like change. What else can you tell me about yourself?

A: I would probably say that I'm a helpful person, if someone has a problem I try to help them out. In my last company there was a mentoring system. When somebody new joined the company one person was responsible for introducing the new member of staff to their colleagues and helping them with any problems. I often volunteered to do that, I think I did it about four times.

I: Oh, really? And is there anything else?

A: Um, let me think. I am also generally a calm person and I'm able to work well under pressure. I don't get nervous or over-excited easily.

I: How do you manage that?

A: Well, actually, my mother is a yoga teacher and so she taught me and my sister how to do yoga and meditate when we were very young. Just two or three minutes of yoga exercises – you can do them at your desk, no one will notice – can help you deal with everyday stress at work.

I: Hm, I know a lot of people who should learn to do that.

A: Well, if I get the job, I would be happy to teach them how.

I: That sounds like a good idea.

A: Oh and I almost forgot, some people say I'm a lucky person, things often seem to go right for me, but I don't think it's luck. I think I get positive results because I focus on what I do and I'm organized. I always use an online personal organizer so that I never miss meetings or deadlines. I think that it's a really good way to make sure that you know exactly what you are doing and when you need to do it.
I: Yes, I would definitely agree with that, I wish more of our employees thought like you.

4.3 Grammar Past simple, past continuous and *used to*

1:47

Amina: Yes, Grameen Bank has made a really big difference to our lives. My business is making baskets. I work 12 hours a day making baskets. These days I work together with ten other women in the village. We used to work for other people, and they would tell us, "we need 100 baskets by next Tuesday", and we would have to make them. Sometimes I worked in the dark. It was very bad for my eyes. Now, with Grameen's help, we have formed a working group, a cooperative, and this makes our work easier and more fun.

Before I heard about Grameen bank and micro credit, I used to live below the poverty line. Actually, I didn't even know that there was such a thing as a poverty line! Now I'm able to support my family - my husband died two years ago, you see, and so I have to provide food for my children. I used to work for nothing. Things are so much better now. In fact, I even make a small profit each month. It makes such a difference.

When my husband died, I took my children out of school. Because I work all day, my daughters had to look after the home and their little brothers. Now they all go to school regularly, even my two daughters! I hope they will study hard and become doctors or business women. Women in Bangladesh used to have many children. It was the only way to make sure that someone would look after you when you are old and no longer able to work. Now we know that running a small business and saving money is a much better way to plan for the future.

Before we received the loan from Grameen to buy our materials, we always had to borrow from money lenders. Well, it was terrible, the money lenders asked for so much interest that we had to pay nearly all our earnings back to them, if we were lucky we had enough money left over to feed our families, if not.... well, we didn't eat. The start up loan from Grameen released us from this vicious circle and now we are even able to invest our profits back into our business *and* save a little bit of money in the bank.

And it's not only women's cooperatives that receive help. I know a woman called Sufiya. She used to beg on the street; she had a very hard life. Grameen gave her a small loan and now she sells toys and other small items. She's still on the street every day, but she's not begging anymore. Grameen has really made a huge difference to the lives of the people in our village.

4.4 Speaking Appraisals

1:48

Galina: Suki, can you help me with my appraisal preparation form, please?
Suki: Oh, I hate those, they're a waste of time, don't you think?
G: Well no, not completely, they can be useful. I mean, they do make you think about your job and yourself.
S: That's what I mean! Anyway, how can I help?
G: Well, for me, the most difficult bit is talking about my strengths and weaknesses.
S: So, let's be positive and start with your strengths.
G: Well, I think I'm hard-working…
S: That's right. You *certainly* are!
G: And I'm probably a team-player, too. What do *you* think?
S: I'm not sure. You probably *are*, although I think you work better on your own, but put it down anyway.
G: OK, and shall I say that I'm a social person?
S: Oh, definitely. Everyone says how friendly you are. Everyone except Ben, that is.
G: Ben? Why? What did *he* say?
S: Oh nothing. Forget him, he's just annoyed because you won't go out with him.
G: Huh! That's another thing I could put down. I'm always calm, and I'm good at working under pressure.
S: Absolutely. You sure are. Even with Ben in the same office!
G: And what about my weaknesses? Hmmmm, I don't think I'm very creative, I could put that down.
S: I can't agree with that. That's just *not* true. That Christmas card you designed was brilliant.
G: Oh, I forgot about that. Shall I say that I'm forgetful?
S: No, don't be silly. But maybe you're not always focused.
G: Oh, do you *really* think so?
S: I'm afraid so. I mean, sometimes you arrive later than the others.
G: But you all start at 7! That's far too early for me!
S: Maybe, but it takes you a while to get down to your work and that means you can't always finish on time and have to stay late.
G: That's true. So, I'll put down, not very focused, and that I need to improve my time management.
S: That sounds about right.
G: Thanks for your help.
S: No problem. Anytime. Shall we go for a drink now?
G: Sorry, I can't, I've still got a lot of work to do.
S: Focus, Galina, and get that time management under control!

1:49

Manager: OK, so we've talked about your job description, your responsibilities and your duties. Now, moving on to the self-assessment part of your appraisal; can you tell me: what do you consider to be your particular strengths?
Galina: Um, I do think that I'm a hard-working person. I always try to get my job done on time. I stick to deadlines; even if they're tough, in fact I think I'm good at working under pressure; I mean, I always manage to stay calm.
M: From what I've seen, I'd say you get on well with your colleagues. Would you agree?
G: Oh absolutely! People say that I'm a friendly person, always ready to help out. Yes, I think that's true; I think I'm a friendly and helpful person. I'd say that I'm a social person.
M: Your section leader, Alan, thinks that you sometimes have problems working as part of a team. Do you agree?
G: Well no, not completely. I don't really see it that way. I *can* be a team-player, but maybe I'm just better at working on my own.
M: Uh huh. I see. Now, we don't like to talk about weaknesses here in this company, but, as we all know, nobody's perfect, so are there any skills you would like to improve?
G: Yes, there are. Although I'm good at working under pressure, I would like to improve my time management. I often find that I have to stay longer than my colleagues in the evenings in order to get my work finished.
M: And why do you think that is?
G: Well, at home, in my country, people start work later, that's what I'm used to, and so I often come in later than the others. With the flexitime that's not a problem, but then, I often find I can't start work immediately – I allow myself to be distracted too easily. So maybe I also need to be more focused.
M: So would you agree that you need to work on your time-management and learn to be more focused?
G: Yes, I agree with that.
M: Fine. So, how can we help you?
G: Well, maybe we could …

5 Selling

5.1 About business Advertising

2:01

A: Hello everyone. Today we're going to talk about advertising again and in particular USPs. So, to recap, why is advertising necessary?
B: To persuade people to buy products.
C: To reach the right target group.
A: Good. Anything else?
D: To position products.
B: And to create brands.
E: Actually, I don't think advertising is necessary. I hate all the hype. I only buy what I need and I'm one hundred per cent sure that ads don't influence me in any way. They are a waste of money.

A: Well, if more consumers thought like you, then ads would be a waste of money. Experts say that people are in fact influenced by ads and we'll talk about this next time. Right. Last week we spoke about a model of advertising from the 1920s to help us understand what it is. Who can remember?
E: It was the AIDA model which stands for attention, interest and, oh, what comes next?
A: Yes, A stands for attention. Ads must attract attention. I stands for interest, ads must get people interested. The D is for desire. The ad must create the desire to have this product. And, most importantly, the A stands for action – people actually go out and buy the product. So advertising needs to include these points.
D: And to tell customers why a product is good and better than others.
A: Yes, exactly. To tell customers why this product is the biggest, best, most attractive, the one you absolutely must buy if you want to feel happy and successful. But the market is full of good-quality products, so how does the consumer know which one to buy?
D: You need to differentiate your product. You need differentiators so consumers recognize your product.
A: That's right. Products need to be different. They should have a special something. Something that no other product has; something that people want – or think they want – and are happy to pay for. In reality, your product may be almost the same as the other products, but you need to advertise a special something. This special something is called a USP. Does anyone know what it stands for?
E: Unique selling something?
A: Almost right. It's unique selling proposition, but a lot of people say point. It's not a new marketing concept; it was used in the 1940s. In his book *Reality in Advertising* Rosser Reeves gives a definition of a USP. Firstly, each ad must make a clear proposition to the customer which says 'Buy this product and you will get *this* benefit.' Secondly, the proposition you are offering must be unique – no other product can give you this. And thirdly, the proposition must be strong enough to attract new customers, and to make people change brands.
Now, if you open your books at page 53 …

5.2 Vocabulary Buying and selling

2:02

Salesman 1
Salesman: Good morning. My name is Simon Harper. May I help you or would you like to browse a little longer?
Mr Hunt: We're looking for a small car for my daughter here. She's going to university in September.
S: Oh, well done, …?
Julie: Julie.
S: Which university are you going to, Julie?
J: To Nottingham.
S: Nice town. A small car, you say. Which model?
H: We're not really sure. This is the first dealer we've tried.
S: Do you want a new car or a used one?
H: It really depends on the price. We want something economical with low running costs.
S: What about you, Julie?
J: Well I like the BMW Mini, especially that red one over there. It looks great.
S: Yes, it's nice. That one has a lot of optional extras and it is quite pricey. I had the impression you're looking for something more reasonable.
H: Reasonable! Cheaper you mean! Half that price actually!
S: No problem. We have a wide selection of good three-year old used cars with a full guarantee at very competitive prices. And, of course, we have some very interesting customer incentives for you.
H: What, for example?
S: Well, at the moment we're offering an interest-free loan on sales over £12,000.
H: So I can pay every month at no extra cost?
S: Exactly. Now, what about the engine? You mentioned an economical car so maybe a diesel?
J: Does it matter?
S: Well, the diesel is more expensive but more economical in the long term. With the petrol engine you have more fuel consumption. Are you planning to travel long distances?
J: No, not really.
S: Then I think the petrol engine is fine. Two or four doors?
H: Oh, a two-door model is fine.
S: If you'd like to come with me, I can show you a selection of cars which are very good value for money. Would you like a cup of coffee?
J: Could I have a Coke?
S: Of course. So, what are you going to study?
J: I'm going to train to be a …

2:03
Salesman 2
S: Looking for anything in particular?
H: We're looking for a small car for my daughter here. She's going to university in September.
S: New or used?
H: We're not really sure. This is the first dealer we've tried.
S: Most customers have some idea before they come in. They look on the Internet or whatever for information. What do you want to spend?
H: Well, about £10,000.
S: At least you know that. That limits your choice quite a lot. You can forget these cars, they're way out of your price range. Correct me if I'm wrong, but I think you're looking for a three-year old used car, two-door model with a small engine. Basic model with no optional extras. Right?
H: Quite right. What have you got in that price range?
S: Not much, to be honest. If you're prepared to spend more, I could offer you this three-year old Golf for £12,000.
H: What about a discount?
S: A discount! £12,000 is the going rate for this car. You won't find it cheaper anywhere else. If you want value for money, you have to pay for it.
J: What about the colour?
S: Good heavens, the colour! Yes, extremely important. What colour would you like, young lady?
J: Black if possible.
S: Right. The used cars are over there. Go and have a look at them. If you find one that you are interested in, come and tell me. I'm going to speak to those people over there. They look as if they might actually buy something.

5.3 Grammar Comparatives, superlatives and asking questions

2:04
Esengul Badem: Excuse me. My name's Esengul and I'm conducting a customer satisfaction survey. Have you got a few minutes to answer some questions about your shopping experience here?
Shopper: Oh, all right. Fire away.
E: OK, first of all, why do you come here to do your shopping?
S: Well, it's the closest supermarket to my house, and it's not the most expensive.
E: And how often do you do your shopping here?
S: At least once a week.
E: And who normally comes with you? Your husband or your children?
S: Oh, I like to go alone. It takes longer if I have the kids with me.
E: And what do you think about the parking facilities?
S: Terrible! You have to walk so far to put your trolley back.
E: And what about the selection of products? Are you satisfied?
S: I suppose so, although there isn't a good selection of exotic fruit.
E: How about the display of the products? Can you easily find things and reach them?
S: Yes, no problem.
E: Do you think the store is clean and tidy enough?
S: It seems clean enough; it could be tidier, though. There are always a lot of empty boxes in the way.
E: How satisfied are you with the speed of the check out desk?
S: I've never waited longer than five minutes.
E: May I ask you how much you normally spend?
S: Around €200.
E: Where else do you go shopping?
S: You mean to which other supermarket?
E: Sorry, yes, that's what I mean.
S: I find Quidsin very reasonable.
E: What time do you normally go shopping?
S: I like to go quite early in the morning, as soon as the kids leave for school.
E: What do you like the most about this store?
S: Well, it's open 24/7 so I can pop in any time if I've forgotten something.
E: What do you like the least?
S: There isn't a good selection of wine. I always buy my wine somewhere else.
E: Thank you very much for your time.
E: You're welcome.

5.4 Speaking Negotiating
🔊 2:05–2:07

Negotiation 1
Husband: What about Majorca this summer? We should start planning or everything will be booked.
Wife: Oh, not another beach holiday! You want to go to Majorca although you know I hate lying and doing nothing. I'd like to suggest something active like trekking in the Alps.
H: Walking up and down mountains. You can't be serious!
W: You don't know anything about it! Come and have a look at the brochure. There's a lot of sun too in the Alps.
H: I don't want to know anything about it. I need two weeks to relax, eat too much and do nothing. There's no way I'll walk around mountains, in spite of the sun.
W: I'll go to Majorca for a week provided we go to the Alps for a week.
H: No way!
W: We do what you want every year. Can't you compromise this time?
H: I can meet you half way. Let's find an island with a mountain on it. That way you can wander around on it and I can lie on the beach. Can you go along with that?
W: That's out of the question. Either we do something together or I don't want to go. That's my bottom line.
H: That makes two of us. That means that neither of us is going on holiday this year. Great!

Negotiation 2
Man: Thanks for showing me around. It's a beautiful house.
Seller: Yes, I know. I don't want to sell it, but my husband has got a job in New York so we have to move.
M: So, how much are you asking for it?
S: I'd like €500,000.
M: Frankly, I think that's a lot for this house. Is that your best offer?
S: I think it's a fair price. Remember there is a very big garden and a new garage.
M: True, but look at the windows. You need to replace all of them. And the floor downstairs doesn't look good. I would only pay that price on condition that you do all the repairs.
S: You have a point there. I should repair the windows. However, I don't have time to do all of the work. If I understand you correctly, you will take the house if I lower the price because of renovations?
M: Exactly. Look, you want a quick sale, and I really like the house. If you go down to €450,000, I'll take it and you'll have your money at the end of the week.
S: Done! Let's draw up the contract.

Negotiation 3
Modelling agent: If you want Tania to model your winter collection, it will cost €10,000 an hour.
Shop owner: That's far higher than I expected. We only need her for two hours.
A: Fine. That'll cost €20,000 for the evening. It's at your new shop in the centre of town, isn't it? Nice location.
O: Look, the model I booked can't make it. Our new shop opens on Friday and I really need a model but can we talk about the price again?
A: No, I don't want to discuss this. You know Tania is almost a top model. €10,000 is the price if you want a famous face. I can't go any lower than that. Take it or leave it.
O: I have no choice. But can't we take a long term view? If Friday is a success, then I'll book Tania for the spring and summer collection. Surely you can give me a discount for three firm bookings?
A: 'Fraid not. As I said, Tania is in demand at the moment.
O: Look, I'll pay the 20,000 as long as she stays for an extra hour and chats to my regular customers.
A: So what you're saying is you want more than two hours work. No deal. You can have Tania for two hours and not a second longer. If you want extras, you have to pay for them.
O: I think that's very unreasonable, but, OK, it's a deal. €20,000 for the two hours, but I won't do business with you again.

5.6 Case Study Coolhunters
🔊 2:08

Part one
Interviewer: In the latest in our series on new businesses I'm here with the managing director of the company Coolhunters, Gabriella Cortez. Good afternoon Gabriella.
Gabriella Cortez: Hi, it's nice to be here.
I: So why did you set up Coolhunters, Gabriella?
GC: Well after many years working as a marketer I began to realize that young, single people and couples with no children today have more disposable income than ever before, and they want to spend it. A few years ago marketers didn't know what these people wanted to spend their money on.
I: Why was that?
GC: The main problem was these groups were no longer being influenced by traditional methods of advertising, such as commercial breaks on the TV. They wanted absolutely up-to-date products, but the products also had to be as individual as they are. Companies were investing a lot of money in trying to identify new trends to give the right customer the right product but by the time they had identified and produced a new cool product it was already out-of-date. This was when I decided that there was a gap in the market for a cool hunting company.
I: So how do you know what the next big trend is?
GC: Simple! I have a team of brilliant young trendspotters. I have to admit that I find it really difficult to identify what is cool and what's not. Actually, they are led by my nephew, who is 19 and so he has no problems spotting new trends. They use the Internet and track down cool new products before they become too popular and everyone has them. Then they post what they have found on my website. Large companies contact me for more information about the next big thing. Cool hunting is basically the search for what's not popular - yet.
I: How did cool hunters begin?
GC: Many coolhunters started their websites by listing the products they liked, anything from shoes to shampoo. They then received tips from thousands of people visiting the site, and the sites grew. Of course it wasn't long before marketers and big companies started logging on to see which products were generating attention. It is one of the most effective ways for marketers to understand what young people want. The Internet has speeded up the process of trendspotting. As soon as cool hunters spot a trend, they have only a few seconds to tell the world. And companies only have a short time to react and mass produce this item. When the product becomes really popular and thousands of people start buying it, it's time for the cool hunter to identify the next trend.

🔊 2:09

Part Two
I: What does a company need to do if they want to sell a new product?
GC: If you want to introduce a new product or service and sell it, you need to know and describe the buying behaviour of your customers. Selling the right product to the right customer is a complicated business. Not all customers rush out and buy new products as soon as they hit the market.
I: Is this the 'Adoption process?'
GC: Exactly. How and why consumers buy and accept new products is called the "Adoption Process". Let me explain. We have, for example, the laggards. These are consumers who are not interested in the latest technology or complex, multifunctional products. Laggards, also known as traditionalists, take a long time to try out and accept new products, perhaps never buying them – there are still a lot of people who have no PC or only a very basic mobile phone. This group makes up about 16% of consumers.
   Then at the other end of the spectrum we have the innovators. These are individuals who really love anything new or complex. They want to be the first to own the product. Innovators, or enthusiasts as they are sometimes called, account for only 2.5% of consumers and so are not very important for companies.
I: These groups are both quite small, what about the other groups?
GC: The biggest two groups are the early and late majority. They have waited to see if the product works, if it's worth the money and if they really want it. For this reason they are also called pragmatists. These two groups make up 34% each and are very important for mass sales. The early and late majority are very influenced by early adaptors. This group is also quick to buy new products and services and they make up approximately 13%. These people, also known as opinion leaders, can influence a great many people and are very important for companies.

Recordings

6 The organization

6.1 About business Entrepreneurs
🔊 2:10

Robin Hurd: So Ms Patel, you're a consultant for people starting up a business. What's important at the beginning?

Ms Patel: You have to decide which sort of business you want to start. Do you want to work alone, or with a partner? There are advantages and disadvantages for both types. But for both you need to be an entrepreneur.

R: What exactly is an entrepreneur?

P: First of all, we all have the potential to be an entrepreneur. An entrepreneur is someone who has a good idea and sees a chance to start a business with it. This sounds simple, but to do it you need creativity, vision, optimism and, very importantly, you are willing to take a risk. If you are afraid of failure, you can never be an entrepreneur. You need a lot of energy too, because you will work day and night to get what you want. Also, you don't give up easily. If things go wrong at the beginning, you keep trying, even harder than before.

R: I guess there are too many risks for most people. Some countries seem to produce more entrepreneurs than others. Why is that?

P: Well, entrepreneurs usually thrive in countries where there is only a very basic social security system such as in America. This means the individual is responsible for finding and keeping a job, and if you don't work, the state doesn't help you. This drives a lot of people to make something out of their lives, and you have nothing to lose. You have to believe that this can happen – this is the American Dream. It doesn't matter if you have a bad start in life, anyone can become rich and successful. You also need a legal system where you can set up a company easily and quickly without too much red tape. In this sort of system, it's usually easier to get banks to finance you or to borrow money from other people. In America, Britain and Australia, where there is a lot of entrepreneurial activity, people are very mobile. They don't expect to live in the same place all of their lives. They go where the work is.

R: Have you got any advice for would-be entrepreneurs?

P: Yes. Don't sit around thinking about starting a business – get up and do it now.

6.2 Vocabulary Types of companies
🔊 2:11–2:16

1   A company should make good quality products at competitive prices. There should be a good choice of products and services. No company should have a monopoly. If I don't like a product, I'll buy another one the next time.
2   I need my salary every month. I want the company to do well so I can keep my job. The company should give me job security, good working conditions and a fair salary.
3   It's important for companies to grow, create jobs and pay tax. The more people there are in work, the more money they spend and that's good for the economy. And if people are happy with the economic situation, they'll vote for me again.
4   Some companies are too big and powerful. They pollute the environment and test their products on animals. They don't invest their big profits to stop global warming. I think they should show more responsibility to the community.
5   The company should be as profitable as possible so I can earn a dividend when the profit is announced at the Annual General Meeting. If the company does badly, I'll sell my shares or I will try and fire the directors.
6   I want the company to do well so that it buys the components my company makes. If the company doesn't pay me quickly enough, I'll have cash flow problems and I can't pay my workers or I may have to close down.

6.3 Grammar Reported Speech
🔊 2:17

Helen Wang: Well, the first meeting is important. You shake hands with the most senior person in the room first, but not too hard. You use the family name, not the given name, so Lee Peng is Mr Lee.

When you exchange business cards, you use both hands. Always read it and then put it in a card case. Don't write any extra information on it.

In China people don't talk business straight away, they make small talk. Sometimes in the first meeting you don't talk about business at all, you get to know your business partner.

You should be punctual and sometimes people bring a present. A good choice of present is an expensive cognac. Again, give the present with both hands. If you receive a present, take it with both hands and unwrap it later.

The Chinese prefer face-to-face meetings to emails or the phone, as it's better for the relationship. Don't interrupt and don't disagree openly or the other person might lose face. Never say 'No'. This is too direct. Say something like 'We need time.' or 'That will be difficult.' Don't start your presentation with a joke as this is too informal.

Above all you need a lot of patience, especially when you come to the written contract. You may find that the details in the contract get changed all the time. This is normal. A written contract is not as important as in the West.

6.4 Speaking Interrupting in meetings
🔊 2:18

Lisa: As you know, Ms Sanchez, member of the board for HR, has asked us to look into the possibility of having our own company fitness centre and …

John: Not that again! We've discussed this several times already and we always came to the conclusion that …

L: If I could just finish what I was saying! Ms Sanchez is personally very interested in setting up a fitness centre on the company premises because …

Tom: May I interrupt here? This is a new issue for me. I'd like to know why John is against the project.

L: Well, the issue came up last year …

J: Let me speak for myself. Have you any idea what a fitness centre would cost? It's not only the building and equipment, but you need trained personnel working there and working until late in the evening. I …

Mary: Sorry to interrupt, but I'd like to come in here. I realise there's a lot of cost involved, but maybe in the long term we would save money because employees would be fitter, and less often ill and I …

J: Stop right there! What if people injure themselves? We'll have more absenteeism than before, and if it's a serious injury, maybe they'll want to sue us!

T: Could we get back to the first point? I'd like to know what Ms Sanchez has in mind.

L: As I was saying, Ms Sanchez would like to raise this issue again. Now, I'd like to make two points before we all start talking again. Firstly, Ms Sanchez is concerned about the high rate of illness not only in the production area but also among office staff. Secondly, we are talking about a possibility. We may come up with another idea to …

M: I've got something to say here. I've brought some charts with me about illness rates and their causes, which I think is very relevant …

6.5 Writing Agendas and action minutes
🔊 2:19

Cristina: So, let's make a start. Thank you for coming. Present today are Lena, Firat and Adrian. Birgit can't come as she is in another meeting. Firat, I think it's your turn to take the minutes. Right, item one on our agenda today. Lena, I think you want to start with Matters arising.

Lena: The office staff is not happy about the hot desking we agreed last time. The work atmosphere is bad and getting worse. I think we should review the situation.

C: Any comments?

Firat: Yes, I agree with Lena …

…

C: So, Lena, you will write a report to review the situation. How long do you need?

L: I can have it ready by the eighth of September.

C: Good. Let's move on to the next item. Firat, are you ready to present?

The Business 143

F: Yes, we had two quotations for building a new canteen, one from Turnbull Contruction Ltd, and one from Haines Ltd. Now let me show you the facts and figures …
F: So, I believe the Haines Ltd proposal is better.
C: Do we all agree?
All: Yes.
C: We all agree with the Haines Ltd proposal so we will go ahead with it. Firat, please draw up a schedule for the building work and let us have it at the next meeting. OK, our last item today is about the company newsletter. I know you wanted to point out something, Adrian?
Adrian: Let me start by saying the newsletter needs a lot of time and energy. The quality of the articles is no longer very good. Why don't we produce the newsletter every quarter, and not once a month?
L: I'm not in favour of that idea. It's very important to …
C: Right. We can't reach an agreement today. Let's discuss the issue again at the next meeting. Adrian, please write a proposal with the pros and cons of a quarterly newsletter. That brings us to the end of the meeting. Any other business?
L: Would it be possible to hold the Christmas party in the new canteen?
C: Good idea. Check the building schedule and report back next meeting. OK, the next meeting is here on the eleventh of September.

6.6 Case study Soup kitchen vs Gourmet to go

🔊 2:20

Cristiana: OK, you've got a great idea and you're willing to take a risk and be your own boss. That's good, but you need to plan carefully. You need a business plan to show the details of starting and developing your business. Most new business owners need to borrow money from the bank. The bank will want to see a business plan which states how much start-up capital you need, what resources you have, and a cash flow forecast. You need to persuade people that your business is a good investment. So, what should a business plan contain? It should answer a number of questions.

Well, firstly, the personal details of the owner of the company; what are the qualifications and experience? Secondly, you need the name and type of business; where is it? Is it a partnership or a sole trader? Thirdly, the mission statement; what are the general aims of the business? Then you need the objective; what specifically will the company do? You also need a product description; what is your USP; who is your target group and what competitors do you have? Then of course you need details of the production; where and how will you make the product; what equipment do you need? Another important detail is your staff. How many people do you need to do the work? Lastly, and perhaps most importantly for the bank is your finance; how much money do you need to start up the business? What is your cash flow forecast? And what is your estimated profit and loss account? The bank will also want to know what return on investment they can expect.

7 The stock markets

7.1 About business Keep it in the family

🔊 2:21–2:23

Part 1
John: So, Gunter, can you tell us some of the ways companies raise money for new ideas or projects?
Gunter: Yes, of course. There are basically two ways for companies to do this. They can ask for a loan from a bank or they can offer shares in the company to individuals or institutions.
J: OK, so what are the advantages and disadvantages of borrowing the money from a bank?
G: Well, the biggest disadvantage is that banks are not always happy about lending money to new or small companies – especially if the company cannot secure the loan.
J: Secure the loan?
G: Yes, if a company asks for a loan of, let's say $200,000, the bank will want to see the loan can be repaid. It may ask the owners of the company to secure, or guarantee the loan with their own private savings or a house, for example.
J: I see, so what are the advantages?
G: Well, the advantage is that the loan is usually for a certain number of years – maybe five or ten years – and the interest rates are fixed, so a company knows exactly how much it has to pay for the loan every year. There are no hidden costs or surprises.

Part 2
J: Can a company borrow money from other institutions?
G: Yes, of course. They can also ask venture capital companies for a loan. Venture capitalists are often prepared to lend small start-up companies money which no bank would, but they also want more money for the loan than a bank does. Have you heard of two and 20?
J: No, I haven't. Two and 20, what's that?
G: A venture capitalist company usually asks for a management fee of 2% of the loan.
J: 2% – well, that's much lower than most banks ask for a loan.
G: Right, but they also want 20% of any profit the company makes.
J: I see.

Part 3
G: The other way to raise money is through equity.
J: Equity? Yes, what exactly is that?
G: Well, equity is basically money that investors give a company in return for a share of the profits it makes.
J: So they buy a share in the company.
G: Exactly.
J: And what are the advantages and disadvantages for a company there?

G: The main advantage is that the company doesn't have to pay any interest for the equity, just a share of its profits, in other words, a dividend. The main disadvantage is that if the original owners don't have more than 50% of the company's shares, the company can be taken over. Another disadvantage for companies listed on a stock exchange is, of course, the cost of meeting the financial reporting standards.
J: Well, thanks very much, Gunter. It was very interesting talking to you.
G: You're welcome.

7.2 Vocabulary Dealing with figures

🔊 2:24–2:27

1 America
The Federal Reserve announced it would drop its key interest rate by 0.25% to 4.25%. This is the second drop in interest rates in the last six months. Productivity grew by 2.1% in the third quarter, compared with 3.9% in the first six months. Employers reported 123,000 new jobs had been created in July.

2 Germany
Germany's job growth was stronger than expected in March. Unemployment fell by 183,000 to 4,370,000. Its trade surplus grew again in the first quarter to €18.4 bn. up 0.4% over the previous quarter. The German car industry reported that a record 750,000 vehicles were exported in the first three months.

3 Japan
Japanese industrial production increased slightly by 0.7% and unemployment fell by 195,000 to 2,890,000 last year. The yen remains strong at 111 yen to the dollar. Bank lending rose by 2.4% in the year to April, the fastest increase in the last five years.

4 The UK
Jobs in the service industry rose to 2.1 million last year while jobs in manufacturing fell by 315,000. The National Statistical Office reported that the number of jobs paid below the national minimum wage increased to approximately 338,000. It also reported that 57,000 jobs, 3.2% held by those aged 18 to 21 were paid below £4.10 per hour.

7.4 Speaking Negotiations – making offers, agreeing deadlines

🔊 2:28

1 a I don't **think** their annual turnover will fall.
  b I don't think their annual turnover will **fall**.
2 a I told you to **buy** more shares in UPS if they went above US$ 70.
  b I told you to buy more shares in UPS if they went **above** US$ 70.
3 a The **share** price hasn't gone up much yet.
  b The share price hasn't gone up much **yet**.
4 a **I** think profits in the telecom industry will fall this year.
  b I think profits in the **telecom** industry will fall this year.

2:29

1. a Sorry, but I ordered a glass of **red** wine.
   b Sorry, but I ordered a **glass** of red wine.
2. a Mario doesn't want to talk about the **problem**, Pete.
   b **Mario** doesn't want to talk about the problem, Pete.
3. a I don't think **their** turnover will fall.
   b I don't think their **turnover** will fall.
4. a **I** didn't ask you to finish the report by Friday.
   b I didn't ask you to finish the **report** by Friday.

2:30

Birgit: OK, perhaps we should get down to business. Well, as you know, Antonio, our new CEO is worried about our costs and he expects me to negotiate cheaper prices with all our suppliers.
Antonio: Cheaper prices! But you're already getting …
B: Yes, I know, Antonio, you're selling us the parts at cost and you'll be giving them away if you drop your prices any more.
A: Exactly, Birgit, wages and salaries have gone up, energy prices have gone up … everything's gone up, but you expect us to drop our prices. It can't be done, Birgit! No way!
B: OK, Antonio. Let's come back to prices in a minute and look at some other possibilities. What are our terms of payment? Six weeks?
A: Erm, no, eight weeks. Eight weeks is a long time to wait to be paid, Birgit.
B: Hmm … well, if we shorten the terms of payment to, let's say, four weeks will that help?
A: Hmm … yes, maybe a little, but …
B: But not enough for you to drop your prices. Right?
A: Well …
B: What about delivery times? If we give you another week or two, will that help?
A: Of course it helps, Birgit, but your production department always needs the parts the day before yesterday!
B: OK, Antonio, so how about this idea? If we agree to pay you 3.5% more for parts delivered within seven days, 2% for parts delivered within 10 days and 1% if they are delivered within 14 days, will you agree to drop your prices slightly?
A: OK, maybe we can drop our price by 1%, but only if you pay within 14 days in future.
B: 1.5% Antonio and I think we have a deal.
A: OK, Birgit, if it helps make your new CEO happier, let's agree on 1.5%, then.
B: Oh, I'm sure our CEO will be delighted Antonio. Now, how about lunch?

7.6 Case study Trading stocks

2:31

Economic report 1
Oil prices hit an all-time high today. A barrel of oil was up US$ 0.9 on yesterday at US$ 80. Analysts say the price could go even higher if the terrorist attacks on oil refineries in the Middle East continue.

Intel announced it will be introducing a new generation of processors next month. A spokesman for Intel said the new chips will cost under US$100.

The EU has announced that it will tighten controls of imported food. Many consumer groups are unhappy that a lot of processed food contains genetically-manipulated ingredients.

Tropical storms in Kenya have destroyed many of the country's crops this year. Tea and coffee exports could be as much as 80% down on last year.

2:32

Economic report 2
BP Amoco, Britain's largest oil company announced it has found a large oil field 30 km from the Faeroes. A spokesman for the company says the field could contain enough oil and gas to cover Britain's energy needs for the next 25 to 30 years.

The German government announced it will drop road tax for emission-free cars and lorries next year. Mr Braunling, the new German environment minister says the government hopes that 1 in 20 cars will be emission free within the next 7 to 10 years. The authorities in many larger German cities have also announced that they plan to introduce a ban on petrol and diesel vehicles if ozone levels go above 100 milligrams per cubic metre.

India today announced they would subsidize genetically-manipulated crops. They say such crops will help to stop food shortages. Last year heavy rain and flooding destroyed a lot of crops in central and southern India.

China could soon become the world's largest chip producer. At the moment the Chinese semiconductor industry only produces about 10% of the chips used in Chinese computers, but the government says it will increase its financial support to the industry significantly.

Consumers in North America and Europe are worried about a new World Health Organization report that up to 60% of tea and coffee that is imported contains the dangerous pesticide, Endosulfan.

2:33

Part 1
David: So, Sarah, CanGas shares have increased to €110 this week. BP Amoco's announcement hasn't affected CanGas's share price. Why's that?
Sarah: Well, David, you can only transport gas in large quantities if you have a pipeline, so the discovery of a large gas field in the UK won't affect the gas supply in Canada.
D: OK, I see.

Part 2
S: How are Cyberchip shares doing?
D: There's not much change there either, Sarah. Investors are waiting to see if Cyberchip can raise the money to finance the new production plant. If they can, the share price will probably rise significantly, but at the moment they are trading at €120.

Part 3
D: I see the Brazilian coffee producer, Feijão Pretos, is doing very well.
S: Yes, David. A lot of consumers are worried about the reports on Endosulfan and have switched to organic coffee brands. Feijão Pretos share price is up by €10 to €150.

Part 4
D: Genezap's share price is also up €5 on last week.
S: Yes, but there's a lot of speculation there. It's still not clear if the Indian government will pay subsidies on genetically-manipulated seed that is imported or if they will use the money to support local biotech companies. At the moment, Genezap's share price is €110, but it could shoot up if the Indian government announces it will also subsidize imported seed.

Part 5
D: Finally, Sarah, what about Zero Emission Cars' share price?
S: They are doing very well at the moment. They are up €25 on last week at €175. Analysts think the market share for emission-free vehicles in Germany will double in the next 12–18 months. It will take the big car producers at least three to four years to introduce emission-free cars, so shares in companies like ZEC are in great demand at the moment.

8 Going global

8.2 Vocabulary Setting up a franchise

2:34

Dave: So, Maria what made you decide to open a teashop in Lisbon?
Maria: Well, Dave I studied chemistry at Cambridge University for three years, but when I came back to Portugal five years ago, I decided I didn't really want to be an employee at some chemical company. I wanted to be my own boss and run my own business.
D: OK, but why did you choose to run a teashop, Maria? Are teashops popular with the Portuguese?
M: You'd be surprised, Dave! My bank manager was a bit sceptical, but I love spending time in teashops and thought it would be a great idea to open one here in Lisbon.
D: And has it been a success, Maria?
M: Well, yes and no, Dave. It was very hard work at the beginning and finding the right franchise was a lot more difficult than I'd thought it would be.
D: But you found one in the end.
M: Yes, but I had to fly back to the UK five or six times the following year for talks and discussions with various franchisors before I finally found the right one.
D: What other difficulties did you have?
M: Well, raising the franchise fee was OK; it

was only £12,000 which is quite cheap for a franchise, but I also had to attend a two-week training programme in London which cost me another £2,500 which I hadn't budgeted for.
D: You had to pay a course fee?
M: No, but the flight, the hotel and food … and, as you know Dave, London isn't cheap.
D: What about opening and equipping the shop? You opened three years ago, didn't you?
M: Yes, that was the next problem, Dave. The franchisor's European agent wasn't happy with the site I'd chosen. He didn't think it was central enough or in a prestigious enough location.
D: So, the franchisor selects the location of the outlet.
M: No, not really, but the site you select has to meet certain standards before it is approved. It took me almost three months to find a more central site which I could afford to rent, but by then I had spent most of my savings and the biggest expense – equipping and fitting the shop was still to come.
D: And how did you manage to raise the money for that Maria?
M: My bank agreed to lend me €50,000 after they'd seen my business plan and I managed to borrow another €50,000 from the three Fs.
D: The three Fs?
M: Yes, the three Fs, Dave – family, friends and fools.
D: I see and was that enough?
M: Just, Dave, but only just. The franchiser wanted to ship all the equipment and fittings from the UK, but I persuaded them that it would be cheaper to have everything made here. It saved a lot of time and money and I was able to open the shop within six weeks of signing the lease.
D: So who are your customers?
M: The shop has been a real hit amongst the business community here and, of course, we also attract a lot of tourists during the summer months. Our turnover is up 50% over the same period last year.
D: Great! Well done, Maria … and … erm, is there anything you regret about opening a franchise?
M: No, not really. I don't enjoy filling in the paperwork and having to ring the headquarters with a breakdown of sales every month, but who enjoys paperwork?
D: Huh, yes, I know what you mean. Well, thanks very much for taking the time to talk to me.
M: You're welcome, Dave … and good luck with the article.
D: Thanks.

8.4 Speaking Presentations– handling questions

🔊 2:35

Part 1

Good morning, ladies and gentlemen and thank you very much for coming today.

My name is Ingo Anspach and I'm in charge of the press department here. Now, before we begin the tour, I would like to give you some background information about the airport.

The official decision to build a new airport at this location was first made in 1969.

After a lot of protests against the decision and court hearings its construction began in 1980.

The airport was officially opened on the 17th May 1992, 23 years later. It is now the seventh largest airport in Europe and has been named the 'Best Airport in Europe' for the last two years.

Since the mid-90s the airport has become more and more important for transit passengers. Last year we had 30.8 million passengers and there were more than 400,000 take-offs and landings. For those of you who like statistics that means the number of passengers using the airport has increased by 156% and the number of take-offs and landings has gone up by 114% since the airport first opened.

About 30% of the flights are domestic and 70% are international. Broken down amongst business and economy class, we can say that around 5% of passengers fly business class and 95% economy. If we look at the reasons for their flight, we can say that 52% of our passengers say they are flying for private purposes and 48% are flying for business purposes.

Now let's have a look at …

🔊 2:36

Part 2

Ingo: Right then, now if any of you have any questions, I'd be happy to try and answer them.
Questioner 1: Thank you Mr Anspach. That was a very interesting presentation. You said that over 27,400 people work at the airport. What do they all do?
I: That's a very good question. Please don't forget that not everyone who works here checks in luggage or talks to the pilots from the control tower. In many ways the airport is like a small city. Over 550 different companies and organizations work here – that makes the airport the second biggest place of work here in Bavaria.
Questioner 2: What have been the most important developments at the airport since it opened?
I: OK, I'm glad you asked me that. There have obviously been a lot of important technical developments, but in terms of expanding our services and buildings; the Kempinski International hotel was opened in 1994, the Munich Airport Centre which includes a shopping mall was opened in 1999 and a second terminal was added in 2003.
Questioner 3: Do you think the new runway that's planned for 2011 is really necessary?
I: Some people say that it isn't, but if the number of passengers and flights continue to grow as we forecast, we will need to increase the maximum number of take-offs and landings from 90 to 120 an hour and that is only possible with a third runway.
Questioner 4: Are you planning anything else?
I: Yes, of course. As I mentioned in my talk, we are planning to expand our multi-functional service centre. That means more shops, more restaurants, more conference facilities and services such as doctors' and dentists' practices. A new three-star hotel with 250 rooms is also planned for 2009.
Questioner 5: Have a lot of jobs been lost since September 11th, 2001?
I: No, on the contrary. In fact, the airport has created more than 4,000 new jobs in the last two and a half years. That's four new jobs every day.
Questioner 6: What has the airport done to tighten security and make flying safer for passengers?
I: I'm afraid I can't go into the details here, but I expect you know from the newspapers and TV that a lot has been done.
Questioner 7: Is there anything fun that passengers and visitors can do when they come here?
I: I'm glad you asked me that. Yes, we have a visitors' centre with an exhibition hall and famous, old aircraft. We also have a disco called Night-Flight which is big enough for over 3,000 guests and, of course, we have our very own brewery called Airbräu. It produces around 5,000 hectolitres of beer a year. I'm sure some of you might like to try it after your tour. Half a litre only costs €2.10.

8.5 Writing Reports of recommendation

🔊 2:37

David: Well, Ajit, I think this is the best location I've seen since I arrived last week.
Ajit: Yes, David, the land is very cheap. Your company could buy a lot more land here than the locations we looked at in the Mumbai area.
D: Exactly. So we wouldn't have any problems if we wanted to expand later.
A: Yes, but I am a little worried there could be a good reason why this land is so cheap, David.
D: What's that then? What are you worried about?
A: I think we should talk to the locals, David. This area is very flat and there's a large river only a kilometre away.
D: So, you think there's a chance this area could be flooded.
A: Yes, we need to check on that. The other problem here is the high humidity. Materials and parts will have to be kept in special buildings to stop them from rusting.
D: OK, but I think we can live with that, Ajit. Do you see any other problems?
A: Well, the town has good railway connections to Mumbai, but the roads in this area aren't good, especially, during the monsoon period.

D: Yes, but there are plans to build a highway to Mumbai, aren't there?
A: Yes, David, plans, but it could be years before the highway is built.
D: Hmm, what about finding staff?
A: Well, there are a lot of small factories in the area, so finding skilled workers will be easy.
D: Great! That's good.
A: Yes, but you will probably have to invest in some retraining programmes.
D: Yes, that's clear.
A: I've checked to see if there are local suppliers for the parts you need.
D: And what's the score there?
A: That shouldn't be a problem, but I couldn't find a local supplier for the control units you need. You might have to fly them in from the UK at the beginning.
D: OK, we'll have to think about that, Ajit, thanks. So, if we find the area doesn't flood. How long do you think it will take to build the factory here?
A: Well, the construction work and equipping the factory shouldn't take more than six months. There are some very good local construction companies in the area, but first we need to do all the paperwork the authorities need and that could take six months to a year.
D: Six months to a year? Can't you speed that up?
A: I can try, David, but I can't make any promises there.

8.6 Case study Choosing a franchise

2:38–2:40

Finnley's
Lewis: Good morning, ladies and gentlemen. Thank you for coming to my presentation this morning. I'd just like to give you a short overview of Finnley Care and some of the opportunities a franchise with Finnley Care can offer you.
  Finnley Care has been in the care business since 2000. We provide care to help older and disabled people live comfortably and securely in their own homes. The UK care market is worth more than £10 billion a year and this is growing quickly. Home care, ladies and gentlemen, is a high growth market with great potential.
  Our business model clearly works. We now have over 280 franchises in the UK and expanded into Europe three years ago. And we have more than 20 franchises in Spain, Portugal and France caring for British and other foreign residents there.
  You may not have any experience in the care business, but Finnley Care will provide you with all the support and training you need to make your business a success.
  The franchising fee is very reasonable – only £20,000 and includes training and a business package to ensure your business is successful.
  Thank you for listening. Now I'd like to hand you over to …

Toasties
Sarah: … Now I'd like to hand over to my colleague, Tom Darling, who will tell you more about Toasties.
Tom: Thank you, Sarah. OK, so now that Sarah has told us all about the franchising concept, I'd like to give you some background information about Toasties.
  The first Toasties outlet opened in Sydney in 1999. We have expanded rapidly since then and we now have just over 530 outlets in 30 different countries.
  We believe that providing an attractive range of freshly toasted sandwiches in our modern, warm and welcoming outlets is what makes us different from the others in this market.
  Toasties customers are mainly young professionals, office workers and students.
  Our business model has been a great success as you can see from our rapid growth and we make it easy for you to be your own boss and start your very own Toasties franchise. The initial franchise fee costs £7,500 and fitting and equipping a Toasties outlet can cost less than £60,000.
  We want to make Toasties the largest and most successful independent snack retailer in Europe within the next five years.

Classic Cotton Clothes
Laura: So, I'd like to move on now and ask: Why is a franchise with Classic Cotton Clothes different? Well, it's different because we really believe in our products, we believe in our business model and we believe that you can help us make this world greener, cleaner and more sustainable.
  Classic Cotton Clothes has agreements with 25 cotton farms around the world and we have almost 100 franchises.
  The first franchise was opened in 1989, but it was not until the mid-90s when the growth in organic goods began that our concept took off. As you can see from the diagram behind me, sales of organic products in the UK first went above £1 billion in 2003 and they have grown by 25–30% every year since. Organic food sales make up most of these figures but environmentally-friendly clothing is increasing steadily.
  OK, so how does our franchise system work? Well, most of our franchises are in small towns. We encourage franchisees to stay out of the large cities. In smaller places there are fewer department stores and so there is a greater chance of being successful.
  So, what do you need to start a franchise? Well, you need to find suitable premises where you can sell the clothes from, I'll talk a bit more about the delivery side of the franchises later, but the franchising fee costs £18,000 and your total investment could cost between £30,000 and £40,000.

Wordlist

1 Living abroad

1.1 About business:
Working abroad

abroad /əˈbrɔːd/ adverb in or to a foreign country *We try to go abroad at least once a year.*
analyse /ˈænəlaɪz/ verb [transitive] to study or examine something in order to understand it or explain it *the ability to analyse and evaluate information*
application /ˌæplɪˈkeɪʃ(ə)n/ noun [count/uncount] a formal request for permission to do or have something *His application for membership of the club was rejected.*
candidate /ˈkændɪdeɪt/ noun [count] one of the people competing for a job *The candidate must demonstrate good communication skills.*
career /kəˈrɪə(r)/ noun [count] a job or profession that you work at for some time *Rosen had decided on an academic career. He felt like having a career change and went into teaching.*
chameleon /kəˈmiːliən/ noun [count] a type of small lizard with skin that changes colour to match the colours around it
competitive /kəmˈpetɪtɪv/ adjective a competitive activity is one in which companies or teams ar competing against each other *the struggle to survive in a highly competitive marketplace*
cover letter /ˈkʌvə(r) ˌletə(r)/ noun [count] a letter that you send with something, to explain what you are sending or to give extra information
culture /ˈkʌltʃə(r)/ noun [uncount] activities involving music, literature, and other arts *If you're looking for culture, then Paris is the place for you. Britain's literary culture*
CV /ˌsiː ˈviː/ noun [count] BRITISH curriculum vitae: a document giving details of your qualifications and the jobs you have had in the past that you send to someone when you are applying for a job.
drought /draʊt/ noun [count] a long period when there is little or no rain
emergency /ɪˈmɜː(r)dʒ(ə)nsi/ noun [count/uncount] an unexpected situation involving danger in which immediate action is necessary *We always carry a medical kit for emergencies.*
expect /ɪkˈspekt/ verb [transitive] to think that something will happen *We're expecting good weather at the weekend.*
handwrite /ˈhændraɪt/ verb [transitive] to write something with a pen or pencil
homesick /ˈhəʊmˌsɪk/ adjective feeling sad and alone because you are far from home
manufacturer /ˌmænjʊˈfæktʃərə(r)/ noun [count] a person or company that makes a particular type of product, especially in a factory
mirror /ˈmɪrə(r)/ verb [transitive] to match or express the qualities, features, or feelings of someone or something
reference /ˈref(ə)rəns/ noun a statement giving information about you that you ask someone who knows you or has worked with you to provide when you apply for a new job *Her former employer provided a reference for her.*
relevant /ˈreləv(ə)nt/ adjective important and directly connected with what is being discussed or considered *How is that relevant to this discussion?*
relocate /ˌriːləʊˈkeɪt/ verb [intransitive/transitive] to move to a different place, or to make somebody do this.

shortlist /ˈʃɔː(r)tˌlɪst/ verb [transitive] to make a list of people from a larger group to decide who should get a job, prize etc
straightforward /ˌstreɪtˈfɔː(r)wə(r)d/ adjective not complicated or difficult to understand *a straightforward process*
withdraw /wɪðˈdrɔː/ verb [intransitive] to no longer take part in something: *The injury has forced him to withdraw from the competition.*

1.2 Vocabulary:
Living abroad

bulletin board /ˈbʊlətɪn ˌbɔː(r)d/ noun [count] COMPUTING a place on a computer system or on the Internet where you can leave and read messages
contract /ˈkɒntrækt/ noun [count] a written legal agreement between two people or organizations *After six months she was offered a contract of employment.*
deposit /dɪˈpɒzɪt/ noun [count] an amount of money that you pay when you rent something. You get the money back if the thing is not damaged when you return it.
exception /ɪkˈsepʃ(ə)n/ noun [count] someone or something that is different and cannot be included in a general statement *There are some exceptions to every grammatical rule.*
insurance /ɪnˈʃʊərəns/ noun [uncount] an arrangement in which you regularly pay a company an amount of money so that they will give you money if something that you own is damaged, lost, or stolen, or if you die or are ill or injured *Do you have insurance for the house yet?*
landline /ˈlæn(d)ˌlaɪn/ noun [count] a telephone that is not a mobile phone
landlord /ˈlæn(d)ˌlɔː(r)d/ noun [count] a man who owns a house, flat, or room that people can rent
overdraft /ˈəʊvə(r)ˌdrɑːft/ noun [count] an agreement with your bank that allows you to spend money when you have no money left in your account
prepaid /ˌpriːˈpeɪd/ adjective something that is prepaid has already been paid for before you use it *prepaid postage*
register /ˈredʒɪstə(r)/ verb [intransitive/transitive] to put a name or other information on an official list *Births must be registered within 42 days.*
top-up /ˈtɒp ʌp/ noun [count] BRITISH an amount of money added to other money in order to reach the necessary level *Is buying a top-up for this phone easy?*
utility bill /juːˈtɪləti ˌbɪl/ noun [count] a charge for a public service such as gas, water, or electricity that is used by everyone

1.3 Grammar:
Present simple and prepositons of time

attend /əˈtend/ verb [intransitive/transitive] to be present at an event or activity *Most of his colleagues attended the wedding.*
au pair /əʊˈpeə(r)/ noun [count] a young woman who lives with a family in a foreign country and helps to look after their children
budget /ˈbʌdʒɪt/ noun [count] the amount of money a person, organization, or government has to spend, or their plan to spend it *Two-thirds of their budget goes on labour costs.*
canteen /kænˈtiːn/ noun [count] a room in a factory, school, or hospital where meals are served

fireworks /ˈfaɪə(r)wɜː(r)ks/ noun [plural] objects that make loud noises and coloured lights in the sky when they explode

grave /ɡreɪv/ noun [count] the place where a dead body is buried in a deep hole in the ground *He's never even visited his mother's grave.*

kite /kaɪt/ noun [count] a toy that flies in the air while you hold it by a long string

parade /pəˈreɪd/ noun [count] a public celebration in which a large group of people moves through an area, often with decorated vehicles and bands playing music

permanent /ˈpɜːmənənt/ adjective happening or existing for a long time, or for all time in the future *The illness can cause permanent blindness.*

repay /rɪˈpeɪ/ verb [transitive] to give someone back the money that you borrowed from them

shadow /ˈʃædəʊ/ noun [count/uncount] an area of darkness that is created when something blocks light *The dogs are always trying to chase their own shadows.*

vacancy /ˈveɪkənsi/ noun [count] a job that is available *We have several vacancies to fill in the Sales Department.*

winery /ˈwaɪn(ə)ri/ noun [count] a place where wine is made

1.4 Speaking:
Making small talk

conference /ˈkɒnf(ə)rəns/ noun [count] a large meeting where people who are interested in a particular subject discuss ideas *a conference hall/room/centre*

corporate /ˈkɔː(r)p(ə)rət/ adjective relating to a corporation *corporate culture*

divorce /dɪˈvɔː(r)s/ noun [count/uncount] a legal way of ending a marriage *I want a divorce.*

extremely /ɪkˈstriːmli/ adverb very *He knows the area extremely well.*

icebreaker /ˈaɪsˌbreɪkə(r)/ noun [count] something that you say or do to make people feel more relaxed at a party or other social event

have something in common /hæv ˌsʌmθɪŋ ɪn ˈkɒmən/ phrase to have the same interests or opinions as someone else *We've got such a lot in common.*

networking /ˈnetwɜːkɪŋ/ noun [uncount] meeting people in order to make friends who will be useful for your business

technique /tekˈniːk/ noun a method of doing something using a special skill that you have developed *surgical techniques*

unique /juːˈniːk/ adjective very special, unusual, or good *It is her use of colour that makes her work unique.*

1.5 Writing:
Formal and informal emails

agenda /əˈdʒendə/ noun [count] all the things that need to be done or thought about *Cutting the number of workers is not on the agenda.*

attached /əˈtætʃt/ adjective joined or fixed to something

colleague /ˈkɒliːɡ/ noun [count] someone who works in the same organization or department as you *Friends and colleagues will remember him with affection.*

grateful /ˈɡreɪtf(ə)l/ adjective feeling that you want to thank someone because they have given you something or done something for you *I'm very grateful for all your help with the party.*

reservation /ˌrezə(r)ˈveɪʃ(ə)n/ noun an arrangement to have something such as a room in a hotel or a seat in a theatre kept for you to use

1.6 Case study:
Global Recruit

advisor /ədˈvaɪzə(r)/ noun [count] someone whose job is to give advice on subjects that they know a lot about *the Prime Minister's advisors*

boutique /buːˈtiːk/ noun [count] a small fashionable shop, especially one that sells clothes

high-profile /ˈhaɪ ˌprəʊfaɪl/ adjective often seen or mentioned in newspapers or on television *a high-profile campaign/company/politician*

leading /ˈliːdɪŋ/ adjective main, most important, or most successful *He became a leading figure in the London art world.*

location /ləʊˈkeɪʃ(ə)n/ noun [count] the place or position where someone or something is, or where something happens *The talks are taking place at a secret location.*

opportunity /ˌɒpə(r)ˈtjuːnəti/ noun a chance to do something, or a situation in which it is easy for you to do something *The trip sounds like a wonderful opportunity.*

process /ˈprəʊses/ verb [transitive] to put information into a computer in order to organize it *Data is processed as it is received.*

qualification /ˌkwɒlɪfɪˈkeɪʃ(ə)n/ noun [count] BRITISH something such as a degree or a diploma that you get when you successfully finish a course of study *Simon left school with no qualifications.*

requirement /rɪˈkwaɪə(r)mənt/ noun [count] something that is necessary, or that a rule or law says that you must do *a list of safety requirements*

taverna /təˈvɜː(r)nə/ noun [count] a restaurant which serves traditional Greek food

unemployed /ˌʌnɪmˈplɔɪd/ adjective without a job *Have you been unemployed for a year or more?*

Unit 2 Dealing with customers

2.1 About business:
The shopping experience

chain /tʃeɪn/ noun [count] a group of businesses that all belong to the same company *Japan's leading hotel chain*

consultant /kənˈsʌltənt/ noun [count] an expert whose job is to give help and advice on a particular subject

convenience /kənˈviːniəns/ noun [uncount] a condition that helps you to avoid wasting time or effort *Her hair was cut short for convenience rather than fashion.*

department store /dɪˈpɑː(r)tmənt stɔː(r)/ noun [count] a large shop that is divided into separate sections, with each section selling a different type of thing

elegant /ˈelɪɡənt/ adjective beautiful in a graceful and simple way *She always looks so elegant.*

exceptional /ɪkˈsepʃ(ə)nəl/ adjective extremely good or impressive in a way that is unusual *Her scores were quite exceptional.*

facility /fəˈsɪləti/ noun [count] a feature of a machine or system that allows you to do something *the text messaging facility on your phone*

flagship /ˈflæɡʃɪp/ noun [count] the biggest, most important, or best thing in a group

luxury /ˈlʌkʃəri/ adjective very expensive and of the highest quality *a luxury hotel/item/car*
reliable /rɪˈlaɪəb(ə)l/ adjective able to be trusted *a reliable workman/car*
standard /ˈstændə(r)d/ noun [count/uncount] a level of quality or achievement, especially one that most people think is normal or acceptable *What can be done to raise standards in schools?*

2.2 Vocabulary:
Telephoning and customer care

blame /bleɪm/ verb [transitive] to say or think that someone or something is responsible for an accident, problem, or bad situation *If it all goes wrong, don't blame me.*
call centre /ˈkɔːl ˌsentə(r)/ noun [count] a place where a large number of people are employed to deal with customers by telephone
calm /kaːm/ adjective not affected by strong emotions *a calm voice*
confirm /kənˈfɜː(r)m/ verb [intransitive or transitive] to tell someone that something will definitely happen at the time or in the way that has been arranged *You can make an appointment now, and then call nearer the time to confirm.*
dissatisfied /dɪsˈsætɪsˌfaɪd/ adjective annoyed because something is not as good as you expected it to be *a dissatisfied customer*

2.3 Grammar:
Countable & uncountable nouns, requests & offers

busy /ˈbɪzi/ adjective having a lot of things to do *He is an extremely busy man.*
competence /ˈkɒmpɪtəns/ noun [uncount] the ability to do something well *I am not questioning your competence.*
direct number /daɪˌrekt ˈnʌmbə(r)/ noun [count] a telephone number straight to a person and not through a receptionist
extension /ɪkˈstenʃ(ə)n/ noun [count] a telephone line that is one of two or more lines in the same building *I'm on extension 334.*
household /ˈhaʊsˌhəʊld/ noun [count] the people who live in a house or a flat
scale /skeɪl/ noun [singular/uncount] the size, rate, or level of something *Is the Government aware of the scale of the problem (=are they aware of how big it is)?*

2.4 Speaking:
Telephoning – Handling complaints

broken down /ˌbrəʊkən ˈdaʊn/ adjective no longer working, or in very bad condition
distribution centre /dɪstrɪˈbjuːʃ(ə)n ˌsentə(r)/ noun a big building where large amounts of goods are stored
double-book /ˌdʌb(ə)l ˈbʊkt/ verb [intransitive/transitive] [often passive] to promise the same seat, table, or room to two different people at the same time
credit /ˈkredɪt/ verb [transitive] to add an amount of money to an account - opposite DEBIT *The money will be credited to your account.*

urgent /ˈɜː(r)dʒ(ə)nt/ adjective urgent things are things that you need to deal with immediately *He had some urgent business to attend to.*

2.5 Writing:
Dealing with an email of complaint

component /kəmˈpəʊnənt/ noun [count] a part of a machine or piece of equipment
exhibition /ˌeksɪˈbɪʃ(ə)n/ noun [count] a public show where art or other interesting things are put so that people can go and look at them *an exhibition hall/centre/space*
non-refundable /ˌnɒn rɪˈfʌndəb(ə)l/ adjective if the money that you pay for something is non-refundable, you cannot get the money back for any reason *non-refundable tickets*
sincere /sɪnˈsɪə(r)/ adjective showing that you really mean what you say *His apology seemed sincere.*
submit /səbˈmɪt/ verb [transitive] to formally give something to someone so that they can make a decision about it *The plans will be submitted next week.*
unacceptable /ˌʌnəkˈseptəb(ə)l/ adjective too bad to be allowed to continue

2.6 Case study:
The Panorama conference

blanket /ˈblæŋkɪt/ noun [count] a thick cover made of wool or another material that you use to keep warm in bed
check in /ˈtʃek ɪn/ noun [singular/uncount] the place that you go to when you arrive at an airport or hotel, or the process that you go through before you go to your flight or room
thermostat /ˈθɜː(r)məʊˌstæt/ noun [count] a piece of equipment that controls the temperature in a building, machine, or engine

Unit 3 Operations

3.1 About business:
Lean manufacturing

defect /ˈdiːfekt/ noun [count] a fault in someone or something
domestic /dəˈmestɪk/ adjective relating to people's homes and family life *domestic chores domestic appliances*
efficient /ɪˈfɪʃ(ə)nt/ adjective working well and producing good results by using the available time, money, supplies etc in the most effective way *The new machine is far more efficient than the old one.*
eliminate /ɪˈlɪmɪˌneɪt/ verb [transitive] to get rid of something that is not wanted or needed *Many infectious diseases have been virtually eliminated.*
enthusiasm /ɪnˈθjuːziˌæzəm/ noun [uncount] the feeling of being very interested in something or excited by it *His enthusiasm for music has stayed strong.*
flexible /ˈfleksəb(ə)l/ adjective able to make changes or deal with a situation that is changing *A more flexible approach is needed.*
implement /ˈɪmplɪment/ verb [transitive] to make something such as an idea, plan, system, or law start to work and be used
keen /kiːn/ very interested in an activity that you do often because you enjoy it *a keen cyclist/gardener, Luke's keen on swimming.*

Wordlist

premises /ˈpremɪsɪz/ noun [plural] the buildings and land that a business or organization uses

rumour /ˈruːmə(r)/ noun [count or uncount] something that people are saying that may or may not be true *A student had been spreading rumours about the teachers.*

specific /spəˈsɪfɪk/ adjective involving or limited to only one particular thing or purpose *You have to enter the information in a specific order.*

superior /suˈpɪəriə(r)/ adjective of high quality, or better or bigger than something else *The hotel's service is superior.*

systematic /ˌsɪstəˈmætɪk/ adjective done according to a careful plan

turnover /ˈtɜː(r)nˌəʊvə(r)/ noun [count/uncount] the value of the goods and services that a company sells in a particular period of time

warehouse /ˈweə(r)ˌhaʊs/ noun [count] a big building where large amounts of goods are stored

workshop /ˈwɜː(r)kˌʃɒp/ noun [count] an occasion when a group of people meet to learn about a particular subject, especially by taking part in discussions or activities

3.2 Vocabulary:
Trends and planning

aviation /ˌeɪviˈeɪʃ(ə)n/ noun [uncount] the activity of flying or making planes

competitor /kəmˈpetɪtə(r)/ noun [count] a company that sells the same goods or services as another

destination /ˌdestɪˈneɪʃ(ə)n/ noun [count] the place where someone or something is going

hire /ˈhaɪə(r)/ verb [transitive/intransitive] to pay someone to work for you *I hired someone to paint the house.*

leak /liːk/ verb [transitive] if an object or container leaks, liquid or gas comes out of it through a hole.

lifeguard /ˈlaɪfɡɑː(r)d/ noun [count] someone whose job is to save swimmers who are in danger

market leader /ˌmɑː(r)kɪt ˈliːdə(r)/ noun [count] a company that sells more of its products than any other company of its type

pickpocket /ˈpɪkˌpɒkɪt/ noun [count] someone who steals things from people's pockets and bags in crowded places

subsidiary /səbˈsɪdiəri/ noun [count] a company that is owned by a larger company

3.3 Grammar:
Present continuous, adverbs and present simple passive

conventional /kənˈvenʃ(ə)nəl/ adjective using ordinary or traditional methods, not new ideas or new technology *a conventional oven / conventional weapons* (=not nuclear or chemical weapons)

ingredient /ɪnˈɡriːdiənt/ noun [count] one of the foods or liquids that you use in making a particular meal *Mix all the ingredients together carefully.*

laboratory /ləˈbɒrət(ə)ri/ noun [count] a building or large room where people do scientific research *our new research laboratory*

organic /ɔː(r)ˈɡænɪk/ adjective organic food or drink is produced without using artificial chemicals *organic apples/meat*

pesticide /ˈpestɪˌsaɪd/ noun [count] a chemical used for killing insects that damage crops

state /steɪt/ noun [count] a region of a country that has its own government *the state of Michigan*

strict /strɪkt/ adjective strict rules or conditions must be obeyed completely *They operate within strict time limits. Lynn gave us strict instructions to be good.*

3.4 Speaking:
Presentations: signposts and stepping stones

cosmetic /kɒzˈmetɪk/ adjective relating to the improvement of someone's appearance *cosmetic products*

3.5 Writing:
Instructions and procedures for an exhibition stand

annual /ˈænjuəl/ adjective happening once a year *an annual conference/festival/holiday*

attendee /əˌtenˈdiː/ noun [count] someone who is present at an event or activity *There were more than 600 attendees at the conference last month.*

convention /kənˈvenʃ(ə)n/ noun [count] a large meeting of people from a particular profession or organization

costume /ˈkɒstjuːm/ noun [count/uncount] clothes that the actors wear in a play or film

expand /ɪkˈspænd/ verb [transitive/intransitive] if a business or service expands, or if you expand it, it grows by including more people and moving into new areas *We are expanding the programme to provide more student places.*

freebie /ˈfriːbi/ noun [count] something that someone gives you that you do not have to pay for

location /ləʊˈkeɪʃ(ə)n/ noun [count] the place or position where someone or something is, or where something happens *The talks are taking place at a secret location.*

logistics /ləˈdʒɪskɪks/ noun [plural] the practical arrangements that are necessary in order to organize something successfully

seminar /ˈsemɪˌnɑː(r)/ noun [count] a meeting or class in which a small group of people discuss a subject

showcase /ˈʃəʊˌkeɪs/ noun [count] an event that emphasizes the good qualities of someone or something

3.6 Case study:
ScotAir

budget airline /ˌbʌdʒɪt ˈeə(r)laɪn/ noun [count] an air company that has low fares but that doesn't offer many traditional passenger services

carbon footprint /ˌkɑː(r)bən ˈfʌtprɪnt/ noun [count] the total amount of greenhouse gases that a service produces

crew /kruː/ noun [count] the people who work on a ship, aircraft etc: can be followed by a singular or plural verb *All the passengers and crew on board the jet were killed.*

discomfort /dɪsˈkʌmfə(r)t/ noun [count] something that makes you feel slightly ill or uncomfortable *the discomforts of life in the desert*

emision /ɪˈmɪʃ(ə)n/ noun [count] a substance, especially a gas, that goes into the air *New laws are aimed at reducing vehicle emissions.*

route /ruːt/ noun [count] the roads or paths that you use when you go from one place to another *The tunnel is the route taken by most drivers.*

second hand /ˌsekənd ˈhænd/ adjective owned or used by someone else before you *second-hand books/clothing*

short-haul /ˈʃɔː(r)t ˌhɔːl/ adjective travelling a short distance, especially by air

uniform /ˈjuːnɪˌfɔː(r)m/ noun [count] a set of clothes that you wear to show that you are part of a particular organization or school *He was still wearing his school uniform.*

Unit 4: Success stories

4.1 About business:
Business leaders and success stories

ambition /æmˈbɪʃ(ə)n/ noun [uncount] determination to become successful, rich, or famous

contact /ˈkɒntækt/ noun [count or uncount] communication between people, countries, or organizations *Do you and Jo still keep in contact?*

dedication /ˌdedɪˈkeɪʃ(ə)n/ noun [uncount] the belief that something is good or right that makes you spend a lot of time and effort doing or supporting it *his dedication to the fight against AIDS*

financial /faɪˈnænʃ(ə)l/ adjective involving money *banks and other financial institutions*

icon /ˈaɪkɒn/ noun [count] someone who is very famous and who people think represents a particular idea

immigrant /ˈɪmɪgrənt/ noun [count] someone who comes to live in a country from another country

lipstick /ˈlɪpˌstɪk/ noun [count or uncount] a coloured substance in the form of a small stick that women put on their lips, or a stick of this

luck /lʌk/ noun [uncount] success that you have by chance *We'd all like to wish you luck in your new job.*

motto /ˈmɒtəʊ/ noun [count] a short statement that expresses a principle or aim

original /əˈrɪdʒ(ə)nəl/ adjective new, interesting, and different from anything else *a highly original design, a very original songwriter*

secrecy /ˈsiːkrəsi/ noun [uncount] a situation in which you keep something secret

sophisticated /səˈfɪstɪˌkeɪtɪd/ adjective knowing and understanding a lot about a subject *Consumers are getting more sophisticated.*

tip /tɪp/ noun [count] a useful suggestion or piece of information that someone gives you *The booklet gives some good tips on getting the most out of your software.*

waft /wɒft/ verb [intransitive] if a smell or a noise wafts, it floats through the air

4.2 Vocabulary:
Describing yourself and being successful

cope /kəʊp/ verb [intransitive] to deal successfully with a difficult situation *Considering how bad her injuries are, she's coping very well. The safety system is designed to cope with engine failure.*

file /faɪl/ noun [count] a set of documents or records that you keep because they contain information *medical files*

habit /ˈhæbɪt/ noun [count or uncount] something that you do often *healthy eating habits*

risk /rɪsk/ noun [count or uncount] the possibility that something unpleasant or dangerous might happen *The risks to consumers are being analysed.*

role model /ˈrəʊl ˌmɒd(ə)l/ noun [count] someone whose behaviour is a good example for other people to copy

stand out from the crowd /ˌstænd aʊt frɒm ðə ˈkraʊd/ phrase to be different and easy to notice *He's the kind of man who stands out from the crowd*

well-informed /ˌwel ɪnˈfɔː(r)md/ adjective knowing a lot about a subject or a situation

4.3 Grammar:
Past simple, past continuous and *used to*

basket /ˈbɑːskɪt/ noun [count] a container for carrying or keeping things in, made from thin pieces of plastic, wire, or wood woven together *a laundry basket*

collateral /kəˈlæt(ə)rəl/ noun [uncount] property that you agree to give to a bank if you fail to pay back money that you have borrowed

entrepreneur /ˌɒntrəprəˈnɜː(r)/ noun [count] someone who uses money to start businesses and make business deals

found /faʊnd/ verb [transitive] to start an organization or institution *The newspaper was founded in 1909.*

launch /lɔːntʃ/ verb [transitive] to make a new product available for the public to buy for the first time *The company will launch a new version of the software in July.*

poverty /ˈpɒvə(r)ti/ noun [uncount] a situation in which someone does not have enough money to pay for their basic needs *Half the world's population is living in poverty.*

reality show /riˈæləti ˌʃəʊ/ noun [count] television programmes that do not use professional actors but show real events and situations involving ordinary people

rural /ˈrʊərəl/ adjective relating to the countryside, or in the countryside *rural areas/roads/schools*

vicious circle /ˌvɪʃəs ˈsɜː(r)k(ə)l/ noun [singular] a process in which the existence of a problem causes other problems, and this makes the original problem worse

4.4 Speaking: Appraisals

element /ˈelɪmənt/ noun [count] an important basic part of something, for example a system or plan *Fieldwork is a key element of this course. Advertising is not the only element in the marketing process.*

flexitime /ˈfleksɪˌtaɪm/ noun [uncount] BUSINESS BRITISH a system in which workers choose the hours each day that they work, as long as the hours add up to the same fixed number of hours every week or month

intern /ˈɪntɜː(r)n/ noun [count] a student who works in a job in order to get experience

pressure /ˈpreʃə(r)/ noun [count or uncount] attempts to persuade or force someone to do something *Pressure for political change increased in the 1990s.*

self-assessment /ˌself əˈsesmənt/ noun [uncount] the process of forming your own opinion about something that you have done

4.5 Writing: Profiles of business leaders

charity /ˈtʃærəti/ noun [count or uncount] an organization that gives money and help to people who need it

campaign /kæmˈpeɪn/ noun [count] a series of actions that are intended to achieve something such as a social or political change: *an election/advertising campaign*

float /fləʊt/ verb [transitive] BUSINESS to start to sell a company's shares

limited edition /ˌlɪmɪtɪd ɪˈdɪʃ(ə)n/ noun [count] a book, picture, etc that has been produced in very small numbers

merchandise /ˈmɜː(r)tʃ(ə)nˌdaɪz/ noun [uncount] FORMAL goods that people buy and sell

polio /ˈpəʊliəʊ/ noun [uncount] a serious infectious disease that mostly affects children and destroys muscles

shortage /ˈʃɔː(r)tɪdʒ/ noun [count/uncount] a lack of something that you need or want *Refugees are facing serious food and fuel shortages.*

trademark /ˈtreɪdmɑː(r)k/ noun [count] a name or design that belongs to a particular company and is used on its products

wheelchair /ˈwiːlˌtʃeə(r)/ noun [count] a chair with large wheels that someone who cannot walk uses for moving around

4.6 Case study: The English Academy

industrial estate /ɪnˌdʌstriəl ɪˈsteɪt/ noun [count] BRITISH an area where there are a lot of factories

magnate /ˈmæɡneɪt/ noun [count] a successful and powerful person in a particular industry – compare TYCOON *an oil magnate*

orphanage /ˈɔː(r)f(ə)nɪdʒ/ noun [count] a building where orphans live and are looked after

outskirts /ˈaʊtˌskɜː(r)ts/ noun [plural] the areas of a town or city that are furthest from the centre *a park on the outskirts of Edinburgh*

prestigious /preˈstɪdʒəs/ adjective admired and respected by a lot of people

quality /ˈkwɒləti/ noun [count or uncount] the quality of something is how good or how bad it is *This cut in funding will affect the quality of education in our schools. The food is of the highest quality.*

refugee /ˌrefjʊˈdʒiː/ noun [count] someone who leaves their country because of a war or other threatening event

steel /stiːl/ noun [uncount] a strong metal made from a mixture of iron and carbon

tanker /ˈtæŋkə(r)/ noun [count] a large ship, truck or plane that carries petrol or oil

tailor /ˈteɪlə(r)/ noun [count] someone who makes clothes for men

untimely /ʌnˈtaɪmli/ adjective happening earlier than you expected

whaler /ˈweɪlə(r)/ noun [count] a large boat used for hunting whales

Unit 5 Selling

5.1 About business: Advertising

billboard /ˈbɪlˌbɔː(r)d/ noun [count] a large board for advertisements

branded /ˈbrændɪd/ adjective branded goods are made by well-known companies, and have the company name on them

desire /dɪˈzaɪə(r)/ noun [count or uncount] a strong feeling of wanting to have or do something *a desire for peace*

differentiate /ˌdɪfəˈrenʃieɪt/ verb [intransitive or transitive] to see or show a difference between things *Neil is colour-blind and cannot differentiate between red and green.*

forehead /ˈfɔː(r)hed/ noun [count] the upper part of your face, between your eyes and your hair

hype /haɪp/ noun [uncount] INFORMAL the use of a lot of advertisements and information to interest people

lease /liːs/ verb [transitive] to have a legal agreement in which someone pays you to use your building, land, or equipment

logo /ˈləʊɡəʊ/ noun [count] a symbol that represents an organization or company

potential /pəˈtenʃ(ə)l/ adjective possible or likely in the future *a potential disaster The disease is a potential killer.*

proposition /ˌprɒpəˈzɪʃ(ə)n/ noun [count] a statement that people can examine in order to decide whether it is true

run /rʌn/ verb [intransitive] if a piece of clothing or a colour runs, the colour spreads when it becomes wet

tasteful /ˈteɪstf(ə)l/ adjective showing good judgment about what is attractive or suitable

taboo /təˈbuː/ noun [count] something that people do not do or talk about because it is offensive or shocking

word of mouth /ˌwɜː(r)d əv ˈmaʊθ/ noun informal conversations between people *Most of our customers hear about us by word of mouth.*

5.2 Vocabulary: Buying and selling

characteristics /ˌkærɪktəˈrɪstɪks/ noun [count] a typical quality or feature *the main characteristics of 20th-century culture*

complicated /ˈkɒmplɪkeɪtɪd/ adjective difficult to do, deal with, or understand

potential /pəˈtenʃ(ə)l/ adjective possible or likely in the future *a potential disaster*

pricey /ˈpraɪsi/ adjective INFORMAL expensive

rival /ˈraɪv(ə)l/ noun [count] a person, team, or business that competes with another *She scored twice as many points as her rival.*

5.3 Grammar: Comparatives, superlatives and asking questions

assure /əˈʃɔː(r)/ verb [transitive] FORMAL to tell someone that something is definitely true or will definitely happen *There's no mistake, I can assure you.*
breakdown /ˈbreɪkˌdaʊn/ noun [count] a situation in which a machine or vehicle stops working
detection /dɪˈtekʃ(ə)n/ noun [uncount] the process of telling someone where something is *aircraft capable of avoiding detection*
downloadable /daʊnˈləʊdəb(ə)l/ adjective COMPUTING if information is downloadable it can be moved to your computer from a computer system or from the Internet
exotic /ɪɡˈzɒtɪk/ adjective interesting or exciting because of being unusual or not familiar
helmet /ˈhelmɪt/ noun [count] a hard hat that you wear to protect your head
integrate /ˈɪntɪˌɡreɪt/ verb [intransitive or transitive] to become a full member of a society or group and be involved completely in its activities, or to help someone to do this
portable /ˈpɔː(r)təb(ə)l/ adjective easy to carry or move *a portable television/heater*
satellite /ˈsætəlaɪt/ noun [count] an object that is sent into space to travel round the Earth in order to receive and send information *a spy/communications/weather satellite*
state-of-the-art /ˌsteɪt əv ðɪ ˈɑː(r)t/ adjective very new and modern
steering wheel /ˈstɪərɪŋ wiːl/ noun [count] the wheel that you hold and turn in order to control the direction that a vehicle travels in
trolley /ˈtrɒli/ noun [count] BRITISH a large container with wheels that you push and use for carrying things in a supermarket or at an airport
waterproof /ˈwɔːtə(r)ˌpruːf/ adjective waterproof clothes or materials do not let water pass through them

5.4 Speaking: Negotiating

agenda /əˈdʒendə/ noun [count] a list of things that people will discuss at a meeting
ballet /ˈbæleɪ/ noun [uncount] a type of complicated dancing that is used for telling a story and is performed in a theatre
compromise /ˈkɒmprəmaɪz/ noun [count/uncount] a way of solving a disagreement in which both people accept that they cannot have everything that they want *Neither of them is willing to make compromises.*
subsidize /ˈsʌbsɪˌdaɪz/ verb [transitive] to pay some of the cost of goods or services so that they can be sold to people at a lower price
sum up /ˌsʌm ˈʌp/ verb to give a summary of something
trekking /ˈtrekɪŋ/ noun a long and difficult journey on foot. Some people go on holiday to do this *He had trekked across South Africa. She's going trekking in New Zealand.*

5.5 Writing: Negotiating by email

etiquette /ˈetɪket/ noun [uncount] a set of rules for behaving correctly in social situations
inclusive /ɪnˈkluːsɪv/ adjective including all costs
prompt /prɒmpt/ adjective immediate or quick *Prompt action is required.*

5.6 Case study: Coolhunters

brochure /ˈbrəʊʃə(r)/ noun [count] a small magazine containing details of goods or services that you can buy
disposable income /dɪˈspəʊzəb(ə)l ˌɪnkʌm/ noun [uncount] money that you have left to spend after you have paid your bills
innovative /ˈɪnəvətɪv/ adjective new and advanced
pamper /ˈpæmpə(r)/ verb [transitive] to look after someone very well, especially by making them feel very comfortable
relatively /ˈrelətɪvli/ adverb in comparison with someone or something similar *a relatively small flat*
status symbol /ˈsteɪtəs ˌsɪmb(ə)l/ noun [count] a possession that is a symbol of someone's money or power
track down /ˌtræk ˈdaʊn/ phrasal verb to find someone or something after a long search *I finally managed to track him down in Manchester.*
trendspotter /ˈtrendˌspɒtə(r)/ noun [count] a person whose job it is to identify things that will be popular in the future

Unit 6: The organization

6.1 About business: Entrepreneurs

debt /det/ noun [count] an amount of money that you owe *By this time we had debts of over £15,000.*
expand /ɪkˈspænd/ verb [transitive/intransitive] to become larger, or to make something larger *The population is expanding rapidly.*
festivities /feˈstɪvətiz/ noun [plural] lively and enjoyable activities in which people celebrate something
headquarters /ˌhedˈkwɔː(r)tə(r)z/ noun [plural] the place where a company, organization, or military unit has its main offices or its main centre of control
liability /ˌlaɪəˈbɪləti/ noun [uncount] legal responsibility for causing damage or injury, or for paying something
paperwork /ˈpeɪpə(r)ˌwɜː(r)k/ noun [uncount] the part of a job that involves producing reports, keeping records, and writing letters

6.2 Vocabulary: Types of companies

bankrupt /ˈbæŋkrʌpt/ adjective a person or business that is bankrupt has officially admitted that they have no money and cannot pay what they owe
diversify /daɪˈvɜː(r)sɪˌfaɪ/ verb [transitive/intransitive] BUSINESS to develop additional products or activities
global warming /ˌɡləʊb(ə)l ˈwɔː(r)mɪŋ/ noun [uncount] the increase in the temperature of the Earth that is caused partly by increasing amounts of carbon dioxide in the atmosphere

monopoly /məˈnɒpəli/ noun [count or uncount] complete control over something by one organization or person

pollute /pəˈluːt/ verb [transitive] to make air, water, or land dirty and dangerous *The oil spillage has polluted the harbour.*

6.3 Grammar:
Reported speech

cognac /ˈkɒnˌjæk/ noun [uncount] a type of French brandy

face to face /ˈfeɪs tə feɪs/ adjective involving two people who are together in the same place *a face to face meeting*

interrupt /ˌɪntəˈrʌpt/ verb [intransitive or transitive] to say or do something that stops someone when they are speaking or concentrating on something *Please don't interrupt her while she's working.*

6.4 Speaking:
Interrupting in meetings

absenteeism /ˌæbsənˈtiːˌɪz(ə)m/ noun [uncount] the habit of not being at school or work when you should be

clarification /ˌklærəfɪˈkeɪʃ(ə)n/ noun [uncount] FORMAL an explanation that makes something easier to understand

counterproductive /ˌkaʊntə(r)prəˈdʌktɪv/ adjective having the opposite result to the one that you intended

frown /fraʊn/ verb [intransitive] to move your eyebrows down and closer together because you are annoyed, worried, or thinking hard

lose the thread /ˌluːz ðə ˈθred/ phrase to stop concentrating so that you do not understand what someone is saying *More than once she lost the thread and had to ask them to speak more slowly.*

6.5 Writing:
Agendas and action minutes

atmosphere /ˈætməsˌfɪə(r)/ noun [singular] the mood that exists in a place and affects the people there *There is an atmosphere of tension in the city today.*

demotivated /diːˈməʊtɪveɪtɪd/ adjective someone who is demotivated has lost their interest in something

hot desking /ˌhɒt ˈdeskɪŋ/ noun [uncount] BUSINESS a way of working in an office where people don't have their own desk but use any desk that is available

newsletter /ˈnjuːzˌletə(r)/ noun [count] a short simple magazine with information for members of an organization

quarterly /ˈkwɔː(r)tə(r)li/ adjective, adverb done or produced four times a year

quotation /kwəʊˈteɪʃ(ə)n/ noun [count] the price that someone says that they will charge you for doing a job

structure /ˈstrʌktʃə(r)/ noun [count or uncount] the way in which the parts of something are organized or arranged into a whole *the structure of DNA, the changing structure of agriculture in this country*

summary /ˈsʌməri/ noun [count] a short account of something that gives only the most important information *The text provides summaries of the plots of Shakespeare's plays.*

temporary /ˈtemp(ə)rəri/ adjective existing, done, or used for only a limited period of time *These measures are only temporary.*

6.6 Case study
Soup kitchen vs Gourmet to go

be located /bi ləʊˈkeɪtɪd/ phrase to exist in a particular place *The centre is conveniently located close to many historical sites.*

biodegradable /ˌbaɪəʊdɪˈgreɪdəb(ə)l/ adjective decaying naturally in a way that is not harmful to the environment

cater /ˈkeɪtə(r)/ verb [intransitive or transitive] to provide food and drinks at an event such as a party or meeting

healthy /ˈhelθi/ adjective making you strong and not ill - opposite UNHEALTHY *healthy food/a healthy diet/ lifestyle*

pot /pɒt/ noun [count] a deep round container that you cook or serve food in *a set of pots and pans*

utensil /juːˈtens(ə)l/ noun [count] something that you use for cooking or eating with

wholesome /ˈhəʊls(ə)m/ adjective wholesome food is good for you

Unit 7 The stock markets
7.1 About business:
Keep it in the family

buyback /ˈbaɪbæk/ noun [count] an arrangement in which someone agrees to buy back shares or goods that they previously sold to someone *a share buy-back*

consolidated /kənˈsɒlɪdeɪtɪd/ adjective several small things that have been put together into one large unit

dividend /ˈdɪvɪˌdend/ noun [count] a part of the profits of a company that is paid to the people who own shares in the company

secure /sɪˈkjʊə(r)/ [transitive] FORMAL to get or achieve something important *The team secured their second victory of the season.*

stock exchange /ˈstɒk ɪksˌtʃeɪndʒ/ noun [count] a place where people buy and sell shares in companies

7.2 Vocabulary:
Dealing with figures

annually /ˈænjuəli/ adverb calculated over a period of one year *an annual salary*

lifespan /ˈlaɪfˌspæn/ noun [count] the length of time that someone lives for, or the length of time that something exists

overtake /ˌəʊvə(r)ˈteɪk/ verb [transitive] to become better, bigger, or faster than someone or something else *The women students seem to be overtaking the men.*

phishing /ˈfɪʃɪŋ/ noun [uncount] trying to trick someone into giving their secret bank information by sending them an email that looks as if it comes from their bank and that asks them to give their account number or password

productivity /ˌprɒdʌkˈtɪvəti/ noun [uncount] the rate at which goods are produced, especially in relation to the time, money, and workers that are needed to produce them

surplus /ˈsɜː(r)pləs/ noun [count/uncount] more of something than is necessary *a surplus of oil*

unemployment /ˌʌnɪmˈplɔɪmənt/ noun [uncount] a situation in which people do not have jobs, or the fact that someone does not have a job *Unemployment rose last month to its highest level in five years.*

vehicle /ˈviːɪk(ə)l/ noun [count] a way of expressing ideas or of making something happen *He launched the newspaper as a vehicle for his campaign.*

virus /ˈvaɪrəs/ noun [count] COMPUTING a program that enters your computer and damages or destroys information that you have stored *Most viruses are spread over the Internet.*

7.3 Grammar:
will and won't, be going to, first conditional

curry /ˈkʌri/ noun [count/uncount] an Indian food consisting of meat, fish, or vegetables cooked in a sauce with a hot flavour

dozen /ˈdʌz(ə)n/ determiner a set of 12 things or people *a dozen red roses*

nuclear /ˈnjuːklɪə(r)/ adjective relating to energy that is produced by changing the structure of the central part of an atom *nuclear power/energy*

pensioner /ˈpenʃ(ə)nə(r)/ noun [count] someone who receives a pension

power plant /ˈpaʊə(r) ˌplɑːnt/ noun [count] a large building that with machines which produce power, especially electricity

risky /ˈrɪski/ adjective involving the possibility of danger, harm, or failure

solar panel /ˈsəʊlə(r) ˌpæn(ə)l/ noun [count] a piece of equipment that uses energy from the Sun in order to create power

terrorist /ˈterərɪst/ noun [count] someone who uses violence in order to achieve political aims *a suspected/convicted terrorist*

villa /ˈvɪlə/ noun [count] a large house, especially one used for holidays

7.4 Speaking:
Negotiations: making offers and agreeing deadlines

catalogue /ˈkætəˌlɒg/ noun [count] a book that contains pictures of things that you can buy *a mail order catalogue*

guarantee /ˌgærənˈtiː/ verb [transitive] to make it certain that something will happen or will exist *The government provides help for small businesses, but it cannot guarantee their success.*

maintenance /ˈmeɪntənəns/ noun [uncount] work that is done to keep something in good condition *aircraft maintenance*

turnover /ˈtɜː(r)nˌəʊvə(r)/ noun [count or uncount] the value of the goods and services that a company sells in a particular period of time

7.5 Writing:
Describing figures

resignation /ˌrezɪgˈneɪʃ(ə)n/ noun [count or uncount] the act of leaving a job permanently *Rebel groups have demanded the resignation of the government.*

run out /ˌrʌn ˈaʊt/ phrasal verb to use all of something and not have any left *Many hospitals are running out of money.*

short-lived /ˌʃɔː(r)t ˈlɪvd/ adjective lasting for a short period of time

takeover /ˈteɪkˌəʊvə(r)/ noun [count] a situation in which one company or country takes control of another company or country

turbulent /ˈtɜː(r)bjʊlənt/ adjective a turbulent situation, place, or time is one in which there is a lot of uncontrolled change *the country's turbulent history*

7.6 Case study: Trading stocks

barrel /ˈbærəl/ noun [count] a large round container with a flat top and bottom, used for storing liquids

chip /tʃɪp/ noun [count] a very small piece of silicon that is marked with electronic connections. It is used in computers and other machines

fabricate /ˈfæbrɪkeɪt/ verb [transitive] BUSINESS to make something such as a machine from different parts

field /fiːld/ noun an area where gas, coal, oil, or other useful substances are found

frost /frɒst/ noun [uncount] a thin white layer of ice that looks like powder and that forms on things outside when the weather is very cold *bushes covered with frost*

genetically-modified /dʒəˌnetɪkli ˈmɒdɪfaɪd/ adjective used for describing crops whose genes have been changed, or for describing foods made from these crops

pipeline /ˈpaɪpˌlaɪn/ noun [count] a long underground pipe that carries water, gas etc from one place to another *a 500-kilometre oil pipeline*

plant /plɑːnt/ noun [count] a large factory *a nuclear/chemical plant*

processed /ˈprəʊsest/ adjective treated with chemicals or machines *processed meat/cheese*

profitability /ˌprɒfɪtəˈbɪləti/ noun [uncount] the degree to which something makes a profit

refinery /rɪˈfaɪnəri/ noun [count] a factory where things are removed from a natural substance to make it pure

speculation /ˌspekjʊˈleɪʃ(ə)n/ noun [count or uncount] guesses about why something has happened or what might happen

triple /ˈtrɪp(ə)l/ adjective involving three things of the same kind *a triple killing*

Unit 8: Going global
8.1 About business:
Franchising

corporate identity /ˌkɔː(r)p(ə)rət aɪˈdentɪti/ noun [count] the public image of a company *We need to think of a new corporate identity for the Asian market.*

establish /ɪˈstæblɪʃ/ verb [transitive] to start an organization or company *The company was established in 1860.*

fulfil /fʊlˈfɪl/ verb [transitive] to reach a particular standard or have the qualities that are necessary for something *Do you fulfil the entry requirements for the course?*

global player /ˈɡləʊb(ə)l ˌpleɪə(r)/ noun [count] a large and influential multinational company

globe /ɡləʊb/ noun [count] the world

legislation /ˌledʒɪˈsleɪʃ(ə)n/ noun [uncount] a law, or a set of laws *a complex piece of legislation*

outlet /ˈaʊtˌlet/ noun [count] a shop or place where a particular product is sold

overseas /ˌəʊvə(r)ˈsiːz/ adjective existing in, or coming from, a country that is across the sea from your country *overseas visitors/students/markets*

relocate /ˌriːləʊˈkeɪt/ verb [intransitive/transitive] to move to a different place, or to make someone do this

reputation /ˌrepjʊˈteɪʃ(ə)n/ noun [count/uncount] the opinion people have about how good or bad someone or something is *The town has a bad reputation.*

tried and tested /traɪd ən ˈtestɪd/ adjective known to be good or effective

8.2 Vocabulary:
Setting up a franchise

appeal /əˈpiːl/ noun [count] an urgent request for people to do something or give something *There have been several appeals for an end to the fighting.*

contact /ˈkɒntækt/ verb [transitive] to communicate with someone by phone, email, letter etc *Please contact us if you have any information.*

market research /ˌmɑː(r)kɪt rɪˈsɜː(r)tʃ/ noun [uncount] the process of collecting information about what products people like to buy, or what people like or dislike about a particular product

persuade /pə(r)ˈsweɪd/ verb [transitive] to make someone agree to do something by giving them reasons why they should *He did finally come with us, although it took a long time to persuade him.*

prestigious /preˈstɪdʒəs/ adjective admired and respected by a lot of people

realistic /rɪəˈlɪstɪk/ adjective based on facts and situations as they really are - opposite UNREALISTIC *Changing your job is the only realistic solution. I don't think it's very realistic to expect her to help us.*

sceptical /ˈskeptɪk(ə)l/ adjective having doubts about something that other people think is true or right *I'm very sceptical about the results of the survey.*

8.3 Grammar:
Past simple and past perfect

appliance /əˈplaɪəns/ noun [count] a piece of electrical equipment that you have in your home *appliances such as washing machines and refrigerators*

asset /ˈæset/ noun [count] something such as money or property that a company owns

diamond /ˈdaɪəmənd/ noun [count or uncount] a very hard clear colourless stone that is used in expensive jewellery *a diamond ring/necklace/bracelet*

household /ˈhaʊsˌhəʊld/ adjective used in homes, or relating to homes *household appliances, household goods*

joint venture /ˌdʒɔɪnt ˈventʃə(r)/ noun [count] BUSINESS an agreement between two companies to work together on a particular job

light bulb /ˈlaɪt bʌlb/ noun [count] a glass object that you put in an electric light to produce light

misunderstanding /ˌmɪsʌndə(r)ˈstændɪŋ/ noun [count or uncount] a failure to understand someone or something correctly *There's been a misunderstanding: Mr Jones isn't expecting you until tomorrow.*

radical /ˈrædɪk(ə)l/ adjective a radical change or way of doing something is new and very different from the usual way *a radical solution to the problem of juvenile crime*

restructure /riːˈstrʌktʃə(r)/ verb [transitive] to change the way that a company is organized

silicon /ˈsɪlɪkən/ noun [uncount] a chemical element, used especially for making computer chips

8.4 Speaking:
Presentations: handling questions

control tower /kənˈtrəʊl ˌtaʊə(r)/ noun [count] a tall building at an airport from which planes are given permission to take off and land

domestic /dəˈmestɪk/ adjective relating to a particular country *domestic politics*

fog /fɒɡ/ noun [uncount] thick clouds that form close to the ground and are difficult to see through

groundwater /ˈɡraʊndˌwɔːtə(r)/ noun [uncount] SCIENCE water that collects under the ground

impact /ˈɪmpækt/ noun [count] an effect or influence *Internet shopping has begun to have a serious impact on traditional bookshops.*

runway /ˈrʌnweɪ/ noun [count] a long road that is used by planes when they land and TAKE OFF

statistics /stəˈtɪstɪks/ noun [plural] a group of numbers that represent facts or describe a situation

terminal /ˈtɜː(r)mɪn(ə)l/ noun [count] a part of an airport where passengers arrive and leave

transit /ˈtrænsɪt/ noun [uncount] the movement of people or things from one place to another *Our suitcases were damaged in transit.*

8.5 Writing:
Reports of recommendation

availability /əˌveɪləˈbɪləti/ noun [uncount] the state of being able to be used *Parents are concerned about the availability of drugs in the school.*

component /kəmˈpəʊnənt/ noun [count] a part of a machine or piece of equipment

criteria /kraɪˈtɪəriə/ noun [pural] standards that are used for judging something or for making a decision about something *Everyone whose qualifications meet our criteria will be considered.*

dependent /dɪˈpendənt/ adjective if one thing is dependent on another, it is affected by the other thing and changes if the other thing changes *Your pay is dependent on your work experience.*

disruption /dɪsˈrʌpʃ(ə)n/ noun [count/uncount] a problem or action that interrupts something and prevents it from continuing

drawback /ˈdrɔːˌbæk/ noun [count] a feature of something that makes it less useful than it could be *The main drawback of the plan is its expense.*

The **Business** 157

flood /flʌd/ noun [count or uncount] a large amount of water that covers an area that was dry before *The southwest of England has been badly hit by floods.*

forecast /ˈfɔː(r)kɑːst/ verb [transitive] to make a statement about what is likely to happen, usually relating to the weather, business, or the economy

humidity /hjuːˈmɪdətɪ/ noun [uncount] the amount of water that is in the air

infrastructure /ˈɪnfrəˌstrʌktʃə(r)/ noun [count] the set of systems in a country or organization that affect how well it operates, for example telephone and transport systems

monsoon /mɒnˈsuːn/ noun [count] a period of heavy rain in India and Southeast Asia

rust /rʌst/ noun [uncount] the red substance that damages the surface of metal

8.6 Case study: Choosing a franchise

bonus /ˈbəʊnəs/ noun [count] extra money that you are paid in addition to your usual salary *a Christmas bonus*

cotton /ˈkɒt(ə)n/ noun [uncount] cloth made from the white fibres of a plant called a cotton plant *a cotton dress*

disabled /dɪsˈeɪb(ə)ld/ adjective unable to use part of your body or brain normally

overtime /ˈəʊvə(r)ˌtaɪm/ noun [uncount] extra hours that someone works at their job, or money that is paid for working extra hours

retire /rɪˈtaɪə(r)/ verb [intransitive] to stop working permanently, especially when you are old *He retired from the army last month.*

sustainable /səˈsteɪnəb(ə)l/ adjective using methods that do not harm the environment

List of irregular verb forms

Infinitive	Past simple	Past participle	Infinitive	Past simple	Past participle
be	was/ were	been	lay	laid	laid
beat	beat	beaten	lead	led	led
become	became	become	learnt	learnt /learned	learnt / learned
begin	began	begun	leave	left	left
bend	bent	bent	lend	lent	lent
bite	bit	bitten	let	let	let
blow	blew	blown	lose	lost	lost
break	broke	broken	make	made	made
bring	brought	brought	meet	met	met
build	built	built	pay	paid	paid
burn	burned / burnt	burned / burnt	put	put	put
burst	burst	burst	read	read	read
buy	bought	bought	ride	rode	ridden
catch	caught	caught	ring	rang	rung
choose	chose	chosen	rise	rose	risen
come	came	come	run	ran	run
cost	cost	cost	say	said	said
cut	cut	cut	see	saw	seen
deal	dealt	dealt	sell	sold	sold
dig	dug	dug	send	sent	sent
do	did	done	shake	shook	shaken
draw	drew	drawn	shine	shone	shone
drink	drank	drunk	shoot	shot	shot
drive	drove	driven	sing	sang	sung
eat	ate	eaten	sink	sank	sunk
fall	fell	fallen	sit	sat	sat
feed	fed	fed	sleep	slept	slept
feel	felt	felt	speak	spoke	spoken
fight	fought	fought	spend	spent	spent
find	found	found	stand	stood	stood
fly	flew	flown	steal	stole	stolen
forgive	forgave	forgiven	stick	stuck	stuck
freeze	froze	frozen	swim	swam	swum
get	got	got	take	took	taken
give	gave	given	teach	taught	taught
go	went	gone	tear	tore	torn
grow	grew	grown	tell	told	told
hang	hung	hung	think	thought	thought
hear	heard	heard	throw	threw	thrown
hide	hid	hidden	understand	understood	understood
hit	hit	hit	wake	woke	woken
hold	held	held	wear	wore	worn
hurt	hurt	hurt	win	won	won
keep	kept	kept	write	wrote	written
know	knew	known			

Macmillan Education
Between Towns Road, Oxford OX4 3PP
A division of Macmillan Publishers Limited
Companies and representatives throughout the world

ISBN 978-0-230-02154-9

Text © Karen Richardson, Marie Kavanagh and John Sydes 2008
Design and illustration © Macmillan Publishers Limited 2008
First published 2008

All rights reserved; no part of this publication may be reproduced, stored in a retrieval system, transmitted in any form, or by any means, electronic, mechanical, photocopying, recording, or otherwise, without the prior written permission of the publishers.

Designed by Keith Shaw, Threefold Design Ltd
Illustrated by Coburn, Mark Duffin, Peter Ellis and Peter Harper
Cover design by Keith Shaw, Threefold Design Ltd
Cover photograph by Getty; ImageSource

Authors' acknowledgements
Karen Richardson
Many people have had a hand in shaping this book and of course, in an ideal world I'd thank them all individually. In particular, though, I would like to thank Helga Falk-Zarse from the Human Resources department at E. Breuninger GmbH & Co. in Stuttgart for granting me an interview, Steffi Layer for her wine expertise, and the ladies at Wala in Eckwälden who offer the garden tours and Dr Hauschka cosmetic demonstrations. Thanks should also go to Christian Schmidt for rescuing me when my computer crashed, and to all my students who answered my questions no matter how strange they may have seemed at the time. And last but not least, thanks to my husband, Werner, and daughter, Zoë, for not getting too impatient when I didn't listen to what they were saying as I "just have to finish what I'm writing".

Marie Kavanagh
I would like to say thank you to all my participants at the Audi Akademie on whom I piloted the units and who gave me useful feedback. I would also like to mention my children and thank them for their understanding for all my evenings spent over the laptop. I have a special mention for my daughter Patty at University for allowing me to try out some of the material.

John Sydes
I would like to thank Günter Wörl, senior partner of AWT-Horwath, Ingo Anspach, press officer of München Flughafen GmbH, München Flughafen GmbH for the photos they provided, my students at MTU Aero Engines GmbH and EADS Deutschland GmbH for their help in piloting the units and all my colleagues at Target GmbH for their support.

The publishers would like to thank the following people for piloting and commenting on material for this coursebook: Jacqueline Cruz, Target Inglês Instrumental, Brazil; Terry Bland, Università Carlo Cattaneo, Castellanza, Italy; Stephan Cooper, Economics University, Turin, Italy; Nicole Ioakimidis, Commercial School, Geneva, Switzerland; Dr Soe Than, Assumption University, Bangkok, Thailand.

The authors and publishers would like to thank the following for permission to reproduce their photographs:
AFP pp16(m), 37(mbr), 55(t), 55(b), 95(m); Alamy/Roy Hsu p24(l), Alamy/mediacolors' p42(b), Alamy/Lindsey Stock p45, Alamy/Nicholas Pitt p49, Tim Cuff p64(bm), Alamy/Dagmar Schwelle p64(br), Alamy/B.A.E. Inc p91(t), Alamy/Photo Central p91(b), Alamy/Dee Fish p91(mt), Alamy/Jon Arnold p98, Alamy/Mary-Ella Keith p102; Bilderlounge p24(ml); Corbis/Jim Craigmyle p6(t), Corbis/Hugh Sutton 6(mt), Corbis/Artiga Photo p6(mb), Corbis/Michael Prince p6(b), Corbis/Bernd Vogel p9(mt), Corbis/ML Sinibaldi p28, Corbis/Jose Fuste Raga p35, Corbis/Chuck Haney p36, Corbis/Peter Dench p40, Corbis/Bettmann p42(top), Corbis/John Van Hasselt p48, Corbis/Elena Segatini p93(b); EmpicsPA/AP Photo Kin Cheung p53; Getty Images/ Andreas Rentz p19, Getty/Jade Lee p97; Hola Images pp23, 43(6); Hulton Archive pp55(mt), 85; Iconica pp69(b), 69(c), 106(t); National Geographic p59; Nordic Photos pp16(b); Photonica pp 9(t), 17(mb), 64(bl); Photographer's Choice pp9(b), 17(t), 20, 37(t), 50, 95(tm); Photolibrary.com pp24(mr), 24 (r), 37(bl), 37(mbl), 46, 76, 95(bm), 105, 106(m); Photonica pp37(br); Reuters p75; Rex Features/ Action Press pp52,53; Riser pp9(mb), 17(b), 16(t), 43(4); Stone pp14(m), 29, 43(l), 43(3), 64(tl), 64(tr), 69(d), 71, 91(mb), 95(t), 100,106(b); Taxi pp7, 8, 17(mt), 43(2), 64(a); The Image Bank pp13, 74, 80; Time & Life Pictures p44, 55(mb); Upper Cut Images p95(b).

The authors and publishers are grateful for permission to reprint the following copyright material: Definitions from Macmillan Essential Dictionary (Macmillan Publishers Limited, 2003), text © Bloomsbury Publishing Plc 2003, reprinted by permission of the publisher; Englishclub.com for an extract from www.englishclub.com; Women's Foreign Language Publications of China for an extract about Zhang Yin adapted from www.womenofchina.cn; Global Investor Bookshop for an extract adapted from the Incademy.com Director's Dealings course copyright © www.global-investor.com; The Wikipedia Foundation for extracts concerning Munich International Airport.

These materials may contain links for third party websites. We have no control over, and are not responsible for, the contents of such third party websites. Please use care when accessing them.

Although we have tried to trace and contact copyright holders before publication, in some cases this has not been possible. If contacted we will be pleased to rectify any errors or omissions at the earliest opportunity.

Printed and bound in Hong Kong

2012 2011 2010 2009
10 9 8 7 6 5 4 3 2